The European Tour
Yearbook 1997

O F F I C I A L      P U B L I C A T I O N

Lennard
Queen Anne Press

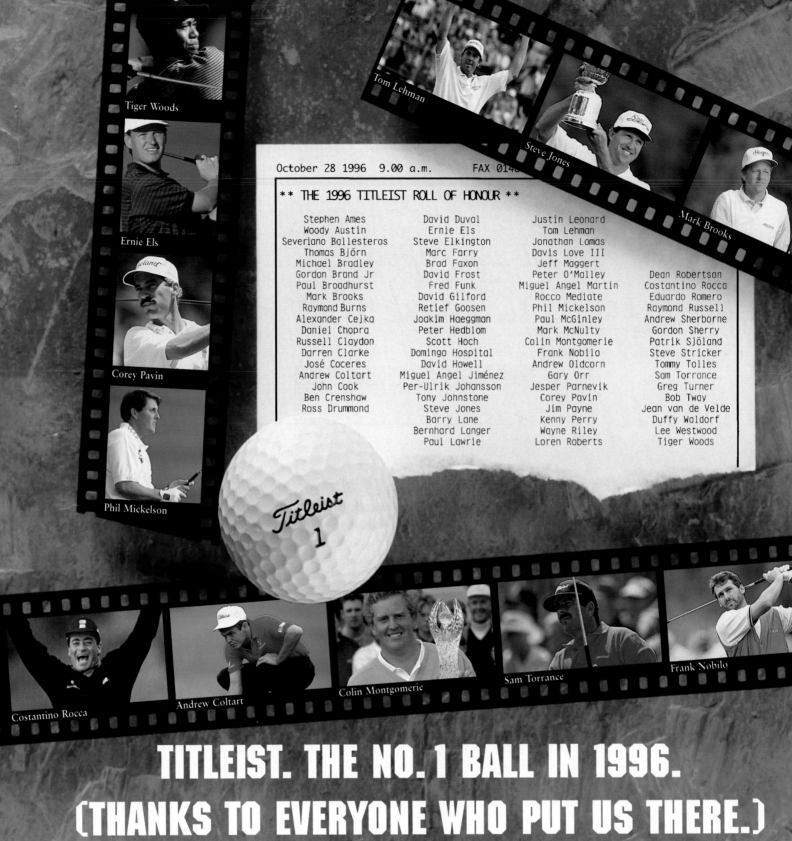

** THE 1996 TITLEIST ROLL OF HONOUR **

October 28 1996 9.00 a.m.   FAX 014...

Stephen Ames	David Duval	Justin Leonard	
Woody Austin	Ernie Els	Tom Lehman	
Severiano Ballesteros	Steve Elkington	Jonathan Lomas	
Thomas Björn	Marc Farry	Davis Love III	
Michael Bradley	Brad Faxon	Jeff Maggert	
Gordon Brand Jr	David Frost	Peter O'Malley	Dean Robertson
Paul Broadhurst	Fred Funk	Miguel Angel Martin	Costantino Rocca
Mark Brooks	David Gilford	Rocco Mediate	Eduardo Romero
Raymond Burns	Retief Goosen	Phil Mickelson	Raymond Russell
Alexander Cejka	Joakim Haeggman	Paul McGinley	Andrew Sherborne
Daniel Chopra	Peter Hedblom	Mark McNulty	Gordon Sherry
Russell Claydon	Scott Hoch	Colin Montgomerie	Patrik Sjöland
Darren Clarke	Domingo Hospital	Frank Nobilo	Steve Stricker
José Coceres	David Howell	Andrew Oldcorn	Tommy Tolles
Andrew Coltart	Miguel Angel Jiménez	Gary Orr	Sam Torrance
John Cook	Per-Ulrik Johansson	Jesper Parnevik	Greg Turner
Ben Crenshaw	Tony Johnstone	Corey Pavin	Bob Tway
Ross Drummond	Steve Jones	Jim Payne	Jean van de Velde
	Barry Lane	Kenny Perry	Duffy Waldorf
	Bernhard Langer	Wayne Riley	Lee Westwood
	Paul Lawrie	Loren Roberts	Tiger Woods

Tiger Woods

Ernie Els

Corey Pavin

Phil Mickelson

Tom Lehman

Steve Jones

Mark Brooks

Costantino Rocca

Andrew Coltart

Colin Montgomerie

Sam Torrance

Frank Nobilo

TITLEIST. THE NO. 1 BALL IN 1996.
(THANKS TO EVERYONE WHO PUT US THERE.)

As 1996 comes to a close, we salute all those players who've made our 17th consecutive season as the No.1 ball in golf one of Titleist's finest years ever, with a record ball count on the European Tour of an astonishing 83%*.

Even sweeter were the victories for Steve Jones at the US Open, Tom Lehman at The Open and Mark Brooks at the US PGA Championship. To say nothing of over 80 other wins on the world's Tours and the thousands of other successful Titleist players too numerous to mention here by name.

1996 SEASON		
PGA European Tour		
	Wins	Ball Count
Titleist	27	83%
Next Ball	8	9%
US PGA Tour		
	Wins	Ball Count
Titleist	32	71%
Next Ball	5	16%

Overwhelmingly, Titleist remains the choice the Tour Pro who wants consistent performan round after round.

This year's results have been achieved with th Titleist balls earning their keep in the professional are Titleist Tour Balata, Titleist Professional and Titleist H Tour, in its debut year, performed to perfection in PGA Tours on both sides of the Atlantic.

So, once again, a big thank you to every player who chose Titleist in '96. Without your dedication, hard work and commitment, we wouldn't be where we are today.

Titleist
Nº1 ball in golf.

Titleist, St. Ives, Cambs PE17

Visit our Web site at http://www.titleis

* Sports Marketing Surveys Ltd. / Darrell Surveys.

Introduction from the PGA European Tour

Executive Editor
Mitchell Platts

Editor
Chris Plumridge

Consultant Editor
Mark Wilson

Photographic Editor
David Cannon

Art Director
Rob Kelland

Production Controller
Denise Thurling

The European Tour Yearbook 1997
is published by
PGA European Tour Enterprises Ltd,
Wentworth Drive, Virginia Water,
Surrey GU25 4LX.

Distributed through Lennard Queen Anne Press.

Colour reproduction and printing by
The Manson Group.

© PGA European Tour Enterprises Ltd.

ISBN 1 85291 575 7

Colin Montgomerie's superb accomplishment in leading the Volvo Ranking for a record-equalling fourth time was one of three particularly invigorating moments for European golf to savour during the 25th Anniversary season in 1996. The others were, of course, Nick Faldo's third US Masters triumph and Costantino Rocca's victory in the Volvo PGA Championship.

Colin enjoyed another season-long encounter for number one honours, and he finally moved clear of Ian Woosnam – winner of four 1996 titles – with record earnings of £875,146 when the curtain came down with the ninth Volvo Masters, won at Valderrama by Mark McNulty. Once again, Colin demonstrated his astonishing consistency by not only winning the Dubai Desert Classic, Murphy's Irish Open and Canon European Masters, but also by finishing runner-up no fewer than three times. His achievement in matching the four successive number one performances by Peter Oosterhuis (1971-74) provided further evidence of his unique ability to maintain a level of play which will inspire others to raise their own standards and many more to play this great game. Incidentally, Colin was eight years old when Peter launched his own term of domination in 1971, in which year John Jacobs became the first Tournament Director General.

The 25th Anniversary season was highlighted by another outstanding illustration of Nick Faldo's ability to produce golf of the highest calibre in the major championships. His third success at Augusta National, coupled with his three Open Championship wins, means that only ten players in the history of the game have won more majors.

To reach the top in professional sport requires dedication, determination and patience, and Costantino Rocca's win in the Volvo PGA Championship at the Wentworth Club, perhaps more than any other performance in 1996, exemplified the rewards that exist on the European Tour. His rise from the European Challenge Tour in 1989 to become the first Italian to play in the Ryder Cup by Johnnie Walker provided ample evidence of his prowess, and his victory in the European Tour's flagship event was as deserved as it was emotional.

Costantino's path from the Challenge Tour has now been followed by many others and two, Thomas Bjorn (Loch Lomond World Invitational) and Diego Borrego (Turespaña Masters Open Comunitat Valenciana Paradores de Turismo), were among 13 first-time winners on the 1996 European Tour.

The saddest aspect of the 1996 Tour season was the continued absence through illness of José Maria Olazábal, whose return to sufficient health for him to again compete will be the hope of all.

Now, with the increasing co-operation between the five major Tours and the formation of the PGA Tours International Federation, we start the next 25 years in Europe buoyed by the knowledge that we share the principle that any increase in international competition must be beneficial to the game of golf, and positively impact the image of the sport and its players.

This Yearbook vividly illustrates the breadth of competition in Europe and I hope you enjoy the content in addition to witnessing at first hand Tour competition at all our superb locations.

KENNETH D SCHOFIELD CBE
Executive Director • PGA European Tour

Contents

A *very healthy balance sheet*

The 1996 European Tour produced

an unprecedented number of new winners

in company with a classic array of old skills

A new age of European golf has dawned bringing with it a legion of fresh young heroes who will carry the game well into the next century to even greater heights of achievement. It is the long-awaited moment in the great renaissance of the sport that began with Tony Jacklin more than 25 years ago and was enhanced by the famous five – Severiano Ballesteros, Nick Faldo, Bernhard Langer, Sandy Lyle and Ian Woosnam – then later given additional point by Jose Maria Olazábal and Colin Montgomerie until it has now found new compelling momentum.

In a year when Montgomerie himself came desperately close to topping the world rankings and made personal history by winning the Volvo Ranking for the fourth successive season against opposition of the highest international quality, the ultimate judgement on 1996 may well reflect a wider and more collective significance.

No fewer than 13 first-time winners made their mark in 37 events during a global pilgrimage that encompassed 18 countries on four continents to underline forcefully once again the traditional strengths of the European game that can adapt and play supremely well in whatever circumstances occur. It is an inherited ability that has its origins in the globe-trotting exploits of previous champions, and now manifests itself in profusion among the new generation and marks a milestone in the development of the European game as this fresh young breed waits in readiness to take over from their famous predecessors who showed the way and set the standards.

All in good time of course. The great figures of the European game are not yet ready to step meekly aside. Indeed, the main narrative from the very start of the year involved Ian Woosnam, back in vintage form, and his thrilling duel with Colin Montgomerie for the Volvo Ranking honours. By the end of the sea-

son the Welshman had established a formidable collection of titles that included the Johnnie Walker Classic in Singapore, the Heineken Classic from Australia plus the Scottish Open at Carnoustie and the Volvo German Open at Nippenburg. But the achievement was not quite enough to pass Montgomerie who won the Dubai

Colin Montgomerie and Ian Woosnam were the high-flyers on the Volvo Ranking.

Desert Classic, as well as the Murphy's Irish Open at The Druid's Glen and the Canon European Masters in Crans-sur-Sierre and put together a crucially more consistent record to finish the season with £875,146 while Woosnam took second place with £650,423.

There was more to their rivalry than simply the balance sheet and basic statistics because they provided a drama that not only ran and ran but gave added point

to every event in which they played. Montgomerie was still on winter leave when Woosnam won his first two events in the Far East and Australia and collected £211,005 prize-money. The big Scot trained for much of the early season before winning the Dubai Desert Classic at the Emirates Golf Club. But by the end of the Alamo English Open at the Forest of Arden in June, Montgomerie was no longer visible in Woosnam's rear-view mirror and had overtaken him on the money list. The Welsh professional hit back with a win in the Volvo German Open and resumed his place at the top until Montgomerie toppled him once again by winning the Canon European Masters two weeks later and thereafter held on to the pole position.

While this engrossing confrontation between two of the world's most accomplished performers captured much attention, a new and immensely important scenario began to unfold. A cast of new characters pushed their way through to the front rank with titles and prize-money to remind everybody that there is a vast

Exercising on the green were Rolf Muntz (left) Costantino Rocca (centre) and Miguel Angel Jiménez (right). Nick Faldo makes a meal of a missed putt (below).

wealth of talented young players who are good enough to win and just awaiting their chance to prove it.

Such a healthy state was not brought about by mere chance or good fortune but is the result of a structured, competitive Tour that is not only lucrative enough to attract the very best young players from around the world, including the United States, but also provides sufficient depth through the Challenge Tour to reach down and give emerging professionals their chance to learn the craft of the game. It is therefore not surprising that most of

the new winners graduated through the system in various ways to reach their present eminence which not only underlines the importance of this particular learning process but sets a path of progress for others to follow so that the supply of fresh and eager talent remains constant and assures the long-term future of the game.

The first sign of the new success came at the Alfred Dunhill South African PGA Championship at the Houghton Club in Johannesburg when the young German professional Sven Strüver put together an exhilarating 63 that included ten birdies and was simply too good for Ernie Els and the rest of his rivals to match in the rain-shortened event.

When the Tour returned to the European zone, another first-time winner took centre stage as Scotland's Paul Lawrie captured the Open Catalonia at Bonmont, Tarragona, and his victory once again highlighted the fine line between success and failure because only a year earlier Paul's form had dipped so seriously he almost lost his player's card.

8

By the time Sweden's Peter Hedblom had won the Moroccan Open at Royal Golf Rabat a week later, there was sufficient evidence to suggest that the new young force was a reality and beginning to make its presence felt, particularly when Scotland's Raymond Russell, who had attended Apollo Week for young professionals, finished with two birdies to win the Air France Cannes Open at Royal Mougins in only his tenth event.

The list of new champions increased as Diego Borrego won the Turespaña Masters Open Comunitat Valenciana Paradores de Turismo at El Saler and Irishman Padraig Harrington, a professional for only six months, captured the Peugeot Open de España at Club de Campo in Madrid. South African professional Retief Goosen took the Slaley Hall Northumberland Challenge at Hexham, and the winning mood seemed so infectious that even those campaigners who had waited patiently for their chance joined in, and French professional Marc Farry was rewarded after 17 years with his breakthrough in the BMW International Open which had been reduced to 36 holes because of the poor weather in Munich.

There was more good news as Lee Westwood confirmed the predictions that had been made for him by winning the Volvo Scandinavian Masters at Forsgarden, Goteborg, and a week later Irishman Paul McGinley captured the Hohe Brücke Open at Litschau in

Whatever the weather, the sun never sets on the European Tour and there's still time for Barry Lane (below) to go fishing at The K Club.

Austria with a last round 62. Within a week another new winner had emerged when Jonathan Lomas, the 1994 Sir Henry Cotton Rookie of the Year, took the Chemapol Trophy Czech Open at Mariánské Laznè. Nor was this extraordinary winning streak yet over because Denmark's Thomas Bjorn took on a high calibre international field to win the inaugural Loch Lomond World Invitational along the shores of that magnificent stretch of water.

In strict terms, there was yet another first-time winner on the European Tour in 1996 because American Tom Lehman, while not a Tour regular, made his winning debut on this side of the Atlantic by capturing the Open Championship at Royal Lytham & St Annes after a classic duel with Nick Faldo who had earlier in the year brought honour to himself and the Tour by winning his third US Masters to put his place in history in both American and European golf beyond question.

Such a saga of success might give the impression that the young bloods rampaged through the European Tour during the season, brushing aside the established regime and taking no prisoners in the process. Nothing could be further from the truth because most of the seasoned campaigners on the Tour could reflect on

Robert Allenby (top left), Seve Ballesteros (right) and Colin Montgomerie (left) demonstrate different ways of keeping fit.

another satisfactory year.

Mark McNulty from Zimbabwe added three more titles – the Dimension Data Pro-Am in Sun City, the Sun Dutch Open at Hilversum and the Volvo Masters at Valderrama – to his extensive collection while Wayne Westner took the FNB Players Championship in Durban and Australian Wayne Riley captured the Portuguese Open in Lisbon. Jim Payne made a welcome return after a serious

back condition had threatened his future but showed no signs of weakness as he took the Conte of Florence Italian Open.

Sam Torrance earned the promise of greater riches when he won the Andersen Consulting European Regional Championship at The Oxfordshire for a place in the world final just after Stephen Ames from Trinidad and Tobago had thwarted the efforts of the entire 1995 Ryder Cup squad to win the Benson and Hedges

International Open.

The Swedish presence was immensely impressive as Per-Ulrik Johansson won the Smurfit European Open at The K Club, near Dublin, after Jesper Parnevik had taken the Trophée Lancôme at St Nom la Bretèche near Paris and Jarmo Sandelin had opened the honours earlier in the year by winning the Madeira Island Open.

Frank Nobilo from New Zealand confirmed his growing

Dusk falls on Jarmo Sandelin (left). Winning display from Tom Lehman at the Open Championship.

world-class reputation in the major events and also took the Deutsche Bank Open-TPC of Europe at Hamburg while Darren Clarke moved a step closer to his full potential by winning the Linde German Masters at the Berliner Golf and Country Club.

The excellence of Robert Allenby's play is already beyond dispute, but he too confirmed the best is yet to come when he picked up three titles throughout the season that spanned the Alamo English Open at the Forest of Arden, the One 2 One British Masters at Collingtree Park and the Peugeot Open de France at the National Golf Club in Paris.

The most joyful win of the year – certainly by the size of the smile on his face – came from the genial Italian Costantino Rocca when he captured the Volvo PGA Championship at Wentworth against the best European field imaginable. It was proof, if needed, that this courtly man had all the attributes of a true champion.

The European balance sheet looks very healthy because the very best performers are still setting standards and showing the way, but equally important, the new generation is responding eagerly to that challenge and determined to move on. It is more than enough to carry the game into the next century. And in the shorter term, Severiano Ballesteros must ponder on the exact nature of the Ryder Cup by Johnnie Walker team he will lead against the Americans at Valderrama. New faces, most certainly. Old skills, of course.

Michael McDonnell

'Team Montgomerie' paves the way to success

Colin Montgomerie's fourth consecutive
Volvo Ranking title is the product
of a dedicated team

There are enough of them to make a hand of bridge and have a few left over. They do not wear uniforms, nor do they have an anthem or a motto, unless it is to make sure that their man does well.

They are the people who smooth the way for Colin Montgomerie, assessing his fitness, arranging his flights, drawing up his deals, carrying his bags, sharpening his mental processes. They allow him to play golf successfully. They revolve around him, not he around them. They are 'Team Monty'.

They are doing their jobs as well as he is doing his. Montgomerie won the Volvo Ranking for a fourth successive time. In Europe, where he won three titles, he recorded the lowest round of the year, the lowest 72-hole total and set one course record. He is ranked number six in the world.

'Having good people around me is crucial.' Montgomerie said. 'It has taken time, but now I've got the people I want. I've got my manager, my personal fitness trainer, my caddie, Julie Dulton, in the office, deals with my travel arrangements.

I've got some team, I can tell you. That is why I win.'

Guy Kinnings, 33, Montgomerie's manager, is a trained lawyer, who is rarely seen without a briefcase and who could cut a deal with the crease in his trousers. At the International Management Group, he has been handling Montgomerie's affairs for two years and is Montgomerie's first point of reference on most issues. 'Guy's the same age as me with similar

interests.' Montgomerie said. 'He's intelligent. We get on well together.'

Frank Williams, Greg Norman's manager, once described his man as 'an absolute stark raving perfectionist'. Kinnings shudders when asked to make a similar assessment of the man to whom he talks each day and works for many hours each day. 'Colin applies the highest standards to his work off the course,' he said. 'Anyone who works around him and for him has got to be able to hit those standards. The nature of his business is demanding and complicated. You have got to get it right and everybody who works with him has to get it right, whatever capacity they're in.'

Montgomerie is one of Britain's richest sportsmen, with an estimated annual income exceeding £2 million. Is he obsessive, like Norman, reading his e-mail on his own portable computer each day, checking every piece of mail into and out of his office? 'All major discussions on the schedule and on a merchandising basis go through with his input,' Kinnings said. 'He has an office at home and everything that he needs to have.

'Golf is the main focus, but away from it he has many interests. He keeps himself up to speed on current affairs. When you are with Colin you don't talk just about golf. His interests are cars, travel, films, theatre and books. The latest book he read was probably a John Grisham. He likes Grisham.'

Montgomerie is highly complimentary about the contributions to his success made by Eimear, his wife — though he often cracks jokes about her ability to spend money — and clearly he dotes on his elder daughter, Olivia, and Venetia,

the younger daughter, who was born in January. Less public are his remarks about Hugh Mantle, a senior lecturer in psychology at Liverpool John Moores University, with whom Montgomerie first made contact four years ago.

'My job as a psychologist is to bring the team together in a way that is effective as well as having to deal with the golfer,' Mantle, 51, twice voted UK coach of the year in the past four years, said. 'In short, I am there to create an environment where excellence is inevitable, and I genuinely feel we are getting there with golfers like Colin.

'One of the biggest driving factors in sport is a fear of inadequacy. That effects your confidence. If you are able to write down golf goals that can be achieved then you can make yourself a winner even if you come last. Colin and all the others in the top 30 must be doing something right. They can all improve, however,'

No one is closer to Montgomerie while he is on a golf course than Alastair McLean, 40, who has worked for him for five years. The Scots must be one of the few player-caddie partnerships who both attended university. Montgomerie has a BA in business management and law and

COLIN MONTGOMERIE 1996 TOURNAMENT RECORD

Tournament	Posn	R1	R2	R3	R4	Agg	Par	Winnings £	Cumulative £
Dubai Desert Classic	1	67	68	67	68	270	-18	108330	108330
Peugeot Open de España	146 T	74				74	2	—	108330
Benson and Hedges Int	9 T	72	68	67	84	291	3	14163	122493
Volvo PGA Championship	7 T	73	68	69	69	279	-9	25766	148260
Deutche Bank Open TPC	2	71	65	69	66	271	-17	80550	228810
Alamo English Open	2 T	75	68	68	68	279	-9	56450	285260
Peugeot Open de France	70 T	73	69			142	-2	—	285260
Murphy's Irish Open	1	69	69	73	68	279	-5	127551	412811
The Scottish Open	16 T	70	77	71	81	299	11	5383	418194
125th Open Golf Ch'ship	105 T	73	74			147	5	650	418844
Volvo Scand Masters	12 T	69	76	72	70	287	-1	10605	429449
One 2 One British Masters	9 T	68	76	77	69	290	2	12751	442201
Canon European Masters	1	65	71	61	63	260	-24	127950	570151
Trophée Lancôme	2	66	70	66	71	273	-7	72210	642361
Loch Lomond World Invit.	4 T	72	70	70	70	282	-2	34635	676996
Smurfit European Open	24 T	73	74	70	68	285	-3	7650	684646
Linde German Masters	4	70	67	65	65	267	-21	32500	717146
Volvo Masters	19 T	71	75	71	75	292	8	8000	725146
Volvo Bonus Pool	1							1500000	875146

Rounds: 61 − Strokes: 4275 − Stroke Average: 70.08 − total Par: -87

ROLL OF HONOUR

	1993	1994	1995	1996
Volvo Ranking Position	1	1	1	1
Volvo Ranking Money	£613,682	£762,719	£835,051	£875,146
Tournaments	24	21	20	18
Wins	2	3	2	3
Top Tens	9	13	14	8
To Par	-65	-160	-146	-87
Stroke Average	70.81	69.60	69.70	70.26
Total Money	£798,145	£920,647	£1,038,708	£1,034,752

McLean an MA (Hons) in modern history. 'Alastair knows what's right and what's wrong,' Montgomerie said. 'He is an intelligent lad. I look after him and he looks after me. I would not dream of employing anyone else.'

McLean grinned. 'We look after each other,' he said. 'He tries hard all the time and he expects me to try hard all the time, and in that respect we both just get on with it. I think I've got the best job on Tour. He's always up there when it counts and he is always making a lot of money for me. It's much more fun knowing you're always going to do well.'

Montgomerie said: 'I need people, good people, around me to help me, support me. I can't do ten jobs at once, I can only do one. So I have to trust people. I pay them good and for that I deserve good back.'

John Hopkins

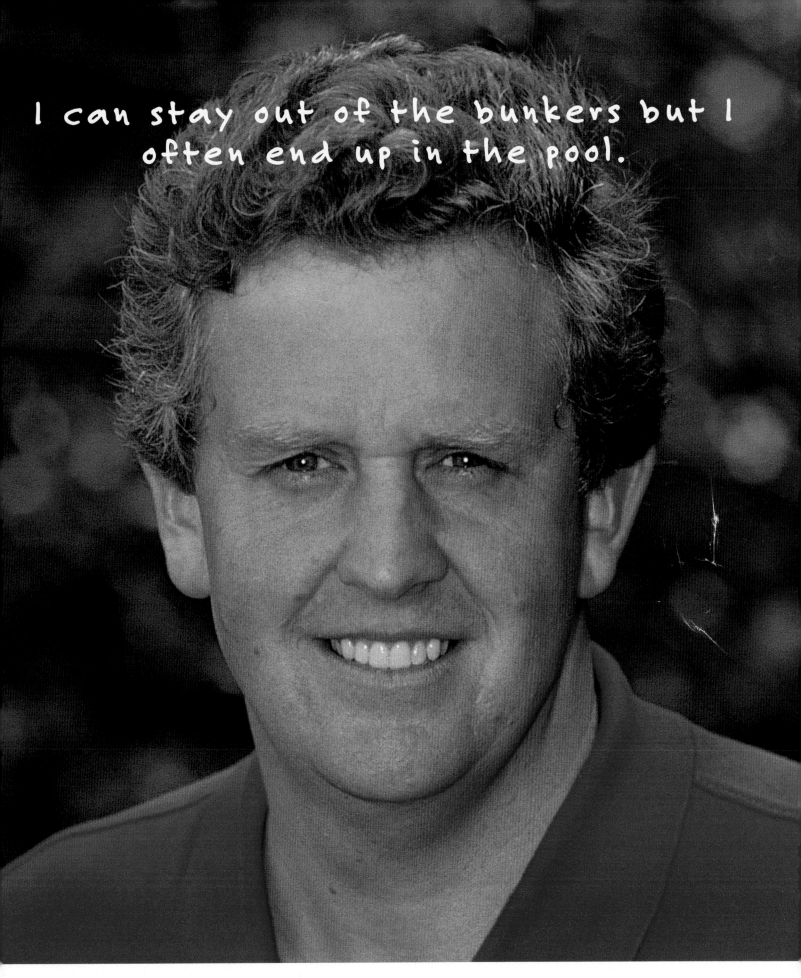

I can stay out of the bunkers but I often end up in the pool.

A Vintage Crop

The 1996 Apollo Week once again demonstrated its
value to the emerging talent on the European Tour

Steve Webster had been struggling with a stiff neck for some time. Not for much longer. Not after fitness and martial arts expert Ted Pollard got hold of him. There was a loud click. 'I thought I was out for the season,' said Webster.

'Ted really helped me with my flexibility. Before this week I could not touch my toes.' Webster, 5ft 8ins and aged just 21, was back at the San Roque club in southern Spain where he won the Qualifying School in 1995.

For him, and 23 other graduates of the Qualifying School and the Challenge Tour, the Apollo Week is their finishing class. Pollard is just one of the specialists brought in to advise each new year's group of rookies as they start on the European Tour.

The players form an eclectic bunch, some with reputations, others only local heroes, but all knowing that they will be judged on what happens from now on. Webster, from Atherstone in the West Midlands, won the silver medal at the Open at St Andrews in 1995.

He was not picked for the Walker Cup, but Stephen Gallacher, Bernard's nephew and a former Scottish and European Amateur champion, enjoyed the

Steve Webster, Padraig Harrington, Michael Welch
and Stephen Gallacher on line for the new season.

victory at Royal Porthcawl.

As did Ireland's Padraig Harrington, who had played in each of the last three matches and had worked as an accountant while his countryman, Francis Howley, still had a year to go on his assistant pro training when he won his card. Denmark's Thomas Bjorn won the European Challenge Tour Order of Merit with four victories; Bristol's Simon Hurley earned his card by the same route after trying the Qualifying School every year since 1986.

Robert Coles, from Essex, wants to put the memories of getting up at 4.30am on freezing winter mornings to set up his father's market stall behind him.

What will make the difference? 'The players that earn the right to come here have all got talent. That is self-evident,' said Andy Taylor, managing director of sponsors Apollo. 'We aim to make them fit to compete. That means eliminating all the interferences that in the big, real world of high competition are going to impact on your performance.'

Knowing how to deal with these interferences is the province of sports psychologist Alan Fine. Even the other coaches pinpoint the mental side of the game as the key area that will separate future champions. 'I have often said that if I had the chance to come again, I'd be looking for help on the mental game,' says the major domo of golf gurus, John Jacobs, 'We didn't even know it existed.'

Adds Tommy Horton, whose prototype training school of the 1970s was a far cry from the modern version: 'Because the standard of teaching is so much better these days, these guys are technically so good. So the next step is the psychological part. We knew how to teach players

Padraig Harrington (above) is watched by Tommy Horton and John Jacobs. Steve Gregg juggles his dietary needs (right).

John Paramor rules coaching session (above). Ted Pollard gives George Ryall the neck treatment (left).

how to swing a club. We didn't know how to teach them to win, we just knew how we did it.'

Fine had studied the performance of athletes under pressure. He has worked with David Feherty and thinks the Irishman won't be long away from the game. Historically, young, inexperienced amateur golfers, except those from an enlightened country such as Sweden, have rarely been appreciative of what Fine can do for them. But that has changed. 'One indicator,' he reports, 'is that everyone showed up to my sessions this year and most people came with something to talk about.

'Really what it is about is helping people produce their best golf. In golf there is much more stroke-play than match-play. So it is how you get the best out of yourself. You are not trying to vanquish anyone else. Everybody's different. There are some generalisations about what makes for excellence and there is a lot of individuality. What I am aiming to do is help people understand their pattern of high-performance. If they understand, then they can repeat it more often.

'There is a model of what makes performance – passion, vision and action. The most common problem I see is that

they don't take action on what they already know. Some of them learned some new things this week from everybody, and some were just reminded of stuff they weren't doing.

'I asked, 'how many of you think nutrition is important?' So we had a show of most hands. 'So how many of you have talked to a nutritionist?' Two hands went up.

'We did that on all the parts of the game and there was always a gap. It is a week to say 'look, you are very good now, but imagine what you could be if you attend to these details.'

The details for the week are provided by Jacobs on the range and Frank Nobilo's coach Denis Pugh with video analysis – preferred by the continentals than most home players.

Horton looked after the short game,

Harold Swash putting, John O'Leary course management, and chief referee John Paramor reviewed the rules.

The players also met the media, though a competition at nearby Valderrama was washed out. How many will be at the Volvo Masters in October? Or at the Ryder Cup in 1997? 'Our target is still to get six of our graduates to the next Ryder Cup,' says Taylor. David Gilford and Paul Broadhurst have already made it.

The last three Rookies of the Year – Gary Orr, Jonathan Lomas and Jarmo Sandelin – were all improved by Apollo Week, but the story is not all good. Only nine of last year's 24 retained their card. The overall success rate is 40 per cent.

Paramor says: 'There is now more competition to get on to Apollo Week, whereas in the early days we had to entice them. Now the guys want to come and they want to hear from the experience that is around.' This year's innovation was the first time appearance of putting specialist Swash. Sums up Horton: 'If they take notes, they can refer back to this week for years. These are not tips we are giving them, this is common sense stuff that can last a lifetime.'

Andrew Farrell

17

Woosnam back in the groove

Ian Woosnam ended his
victory drought in the season's
opener in Singapore

There was something missing from the 1995 PGA European Tour season, something which had lit up each of the preceding nine. But nobody had to wait long to see it again in 1996.

It was the sight, the wonderful sight, of Ian Woosnam in full flow, with that rhythmical swing of his firing on all cylinders and that jauntiness in his stride as he sensed victory.

There are always questions needing answers at the start of a new year, and one of the most burning as the star-studded field for the Johnnie Walker Classic gathered at Singapore's Tanah Merah club concerned the 37-year old Welshman. People had written him off before, but now he was genuinely worried himself. It was bad enough that after 13 years among Europe's top 12 he had fallen to 65th in the 1995 Volvo Ranking and, for the first time since they were introduced, was outside the leading 50 in the Sony Ranking. But worse than both of those facts were his fears about his back. It was killing him. 'I wondered if it was going to be like that for the rest of my life. If it was I didn't want to play,' he admitted. 'I was hitting the ball so short. I was 30 yards behind guys that I knew I could hit it 20 yards past. That was the most frustrating part.'

Rest and relaxation, he was advised by a specialist, was the best cure. So rest and relaxation he took. Ten weeks of it. But still he could not be sure what lay ahead as he set off in the first round of the season's opening event. For a start Woosnam

does not relish the sort of heat that was promised ('I don't so much sweat as leak') and for another his back had bothered him again in practice. The omens were not good. Nor was this a gentle opener. Apart from the strong European, Australian and Asian Tour contingents, also present were Open champion John

Daly, defending champion Fred Couples, newly crowned South African Open champion Ernie Els and Greg Norman. The Queenslander, though, was struck down by a chest infection just before the event and was never to be a factor. The biggest impression the Great White Shark made was to arrive for the third and

Greg Norman was an easy rider.

only two off the pace and Woosnam tucked in just behind him with a 69 that did his confidence the world of good.

He felt even better after improving on that by a shot the following day, but Els returned a second successive 67, taking over top spot in stunning fashion. At the 194-yard eighth – his 17th – a towering six iron over the lake landed and stopped only two feet from the flag and on the 558-yard ninth a perfect drive and perfect three iron almost led to an albatross, the ball rolling towards the hole, but stopping 18 inches short.

The third day brought another change at the head of the leaderboard. Els, after 38 holes without a bogey, suddenly had three in a row and allowed Lancashire's Paul Eales and Australian Wayne Riley to slip past. With a round to go they stood 12 under and Woosnam,

fourth rounds as a Great White Biker – an offer to try out a Harley Davidson was too good to miss.

Fastest off the line in the tournament were Sweden's Olle Karlsson and Norman's fellow countryman, Bradley

Hughes. Karlsson actually reached eight under par after 16 holes, but two bogeys in the last three left him in a tie for the lead on 66, one in front of Els, Daly, Ulster's Darren Clarke and another Australian, Anthony Painter. Couples was

THE COURSE

The 7,001-yard Garden Course at Tanah Mereh (it means 'Red Earth' in Malay) could not be better named. A truly beautiful setting for the opening event of the 1996 European Tour season – even allowing for the noise of planes landing at and taking off from nearby Changi International Airport. A different type of tree is planted at every hole and water comes into play at 11 of them.

again building more self-belief with a 69, was ten under along with Couples, Els and Painter.

Nobody could argue with Couples and Els being made the joint favourites, but golf makes a habit of ignoring scripts. At one point as the £100,000 first prize came closer into view on day four, nine players were separated by a single shot, but then Scot Andrew Coltart burst through with a spectacular run of seven birdies in nine holes, the last of them from inches away after he nearly aced the 180-yard 14th. The 25-year old parred in from there for a course record-equalling 65 and 16 under par target of 272. His first solo European Tour victory looked on the cards as, one by one, the pursuers failed to make up ground. Woosnam, though, refused to give up hope.

Needing two birdies in the last

A plane puts the strain on Paul Afleck (above). Runner-up Andrew Coltart (left).

four holes to tie he pitched to four feet on the long 15th and made it. He could not birdie the 16th or 17th, but at the 448-yard last his putt from 25 feet never looked like going anywhere but in the cup. It all added up to a 66.

It was dramatic, it was tough on Coltart – and it was to be repeated. At the third play-off hole, the 18th again, Woosnam conjured up a magical recovery after hooking his drive, found himself in the exact same spot and made the putt again.

Just to be back in contention had felt good. Just to be swinging freely again had felt great. To win again was fantastic – for Woosnam, for the Tour and for golf.

Mark Garrod   21

SHOT OF THE WEEK

When Ernie Els hit a three iron to within 18 inches of the ninth hole for an eagle three on day two it was hard to imagine anything topping it. But then along came Ian Woosnam with the shot that decided the championship. In trouble off the tee at the third play-off hole with Andrew Coltart, Woosnam not only drilled a five iron through a tiny gap in the trees, but also hooked it 15 yards onto the green. The birdie putt that followed was the icing on the cake.

Tanah Merah, Singapore, January 25-28, 1996 · Yardage 7001 · Par 72

Pos	Name	Country	Rnd 1	Rnd 2	Rnd 3	Rnd 4	Total	Prize Money £		Name	Country	Rnd 1	Rnd 2	Rnd 3	Rnd 4	Total	Prize Money
										Sam TORRANCE	(Scot)	68	72	70	73	283	4960
										Raymond BURNS	(N.Ire)	73	69	68	73	283	4960
1	Ian WOOSNAM	(Wal)	69	68	69	66	272	100000		Isao AOKI	(Jap)	70	68	71	74	283	4960
2	Andrew COLTART	(Scot)	69	68	70	65	272	66660		David MCKENZIE	(Aus)	68	70	71	74	283	4960
3	Olle KARLSSON	(Swe)	66	69	74	66	275	30986	38	Gary ORR	(Scot)	71	72	69	72	284	4140
	Paul CURRY	(Eng)	68	70	69	68	275	30986		Bernhard LANGER	(Ger)	68	74	71	71	284	4140
	Wayne RILEY	(Aus)	70	67	67	71	275	30986		Peter SENIOR	(Aus)	69	71	73	71	284	4140
6	Nam-Sin PARK	(Kor)	72	67	72	65	276	15076		Jack O'KEEFE	(USA)	70	72	74	68	284	4140
	Bradley HUGHES	(Aus)	66	72	70	68	276	15076	42	Terry PRICE	(Aus)	69	72	72	72	285	3540
	Craig PARRY	(Aus)	72	68	67	69	276	15076		Periasamy GUNASAGARAN	(Mal)	71	70	72	72	285	3540
	Ernie ELS	(SA)	67	67	72	70	276	15076		Perry MOSS	(USA)	69	71	73	72	285	3540
	Anthony PAINTER	(Aus)	67	70	69	70	276	15076		Mike HARWOOD	(Aus)	71	70	73	71	285	3540
	Fred COUPLES	(USA)	68	69	69	70	276	15076		Gary NICKLAUS	(USA)	71	72	74	68	285	3540
12	Adam HUNTER	(Scot)	69	71	68	69	277	9970		Jay TOWNSEND	(USA)	68	74	69	74	285	3540
	Paul EALES	(Eng)	69	67	68	73	277	9970	48	Sang Ho CHOI	(Kor)	70	69	73	74	286	2880
14	Darren CLARKE	(N.Ire)	67	70	73	68	278	9000		Guan-Soon CHUA	(Sing)	75	67	71	73	286	2880
	Paul MCGINLEY	(Ire)	71	68	69	70	278	9000		Jim PAYNE	(Eng)	73	68	73	72	286	2880
16	Doug DUNAKEY	(USA)	71	68	70	70	279	8280		Greg NORMAN	(Aus)	71	72	73	70	286	2880
	Richard BOXALL	(Eng)	73	70	65	71	279	8280		Fredrik LINDGREN	(Swe)	71	71	70	74	286	2880
18	Don FARDON	(Aus)	69	70	71	70	280	7350	53	Zaw MOE	(Myr)	68	70	74	75	287	2340
	Christian CEVAER	(Fr)	72	70	68	70	280	7350		David BRANSDON	(Aus)	70	71	72	74	287	2340
	John DALY	(USA)	67	73	69	71	280	7350		Stewart GINN	(Aus)	70	73	72	72	287	2340
	Sven STRÜVER	(Ger)	71	70	68	71	280	7350		Robert ALLENBY	(Aus)	74	68	76	69	287	2340
22	Katsuyoshi TOMORI	(Jap)	70	73	70	68	281	6570	57	Peter FOWLER	(Aus)	71	72	71	74	288	1980
	Anthony GILLIGAN	(Aus)	73	69	69	70	281	6570		Peter MCWHINNEY	(Aus)	72	70	75	71	288	1980
	Howard CLARK	(Eng)	70	68	71	72	281	6570	59	Peter O'MALLEY	(Aus)	72	70	71	76	289	1800
	Jean VAN DE VELDE	(Fr)	69	71	69	72	281	6570		Lee WESTWOOD	(Eng)	73	70	74	72	289	1800
	Chawalit PLAPHOL (AM)	(Thai)	72	69	70	70	281			Mark LITTON	(Wal)	68	75	76	70	289	1800
26	Shigenori MORI	(Jap)	74	68	72	68	282	5940	62	Jong-Duk KIM	(Kor)	72	70	71	77	290	1650
	Russell CLAYDON	(Eng)	73	67	70	72	282	5940		Paul AFFLECK	(Wal)	69	74	75	72	290	1650
	Jeff SENIOR	(Aus)	71	71	68	72	282	5940	64	Michael JONZON	(Swe)	71	72	76	73	292	1530
29	Jeev Milkha SINGH	(Ind)	69	73	71	70	283	4960		Darren COLE	(Aus)	69	73	78	72	292	1530
	Mark MOULAND	(Wal)	73	70	71	69	283	4960	66	Stephen AMES	(T&T)	68	70	78	77	293	900
	Richard GREEN	(Aus)	73	69	70	71	283	4960	67	Chin-Sheng HSIEH	(Tai)	69	73	74	79	295	897
	Andrew SHERBORNE	(Eng)	68	74	70	71	283	4960		Dean ROBERTSON	(Scot)	71	72	75	77	295	897
	Robert WILLIS	(Aus)	73	65	72	73	283	4960									

• The Johnnie Walker World of Golf •

Golf and whisky are surely Scotland's two greatest gifts to the world. They are made for each other: it would be a poor 19th hole that didn't stock the drink whose name is Gaelic for 'water of life'. It was therefore almost inevitable that Johnnie Walker, the world's best selling Scotch whisky and a symbol of whisky excellence world-wide should become a driving force behind the game. Indeed, if a further reason were needed, Johnnie Walker is based in Kilmarnock, the Ayrshire town on whose neighbouring links golf first began.

Now, the distinctive Johnnie Walker logo goes striding across the globe: from the Classic, Asia's Premier Golfing Event, to the wonderful courses of Portugal's Algarve, where the Johnnie Walker Amateur Euro Classic takes place every May - the company supports golf at every level.

1995 Johnnie Walker
Player of the year
Colin Montgomery

Johnnie Walker's links with the game of golf go back a long way. It all began in 1910, when the debonaire 'striding figure' logo appeared in a golfing scene for advertising. In 1926 came the launch of an international promotion that still holds the interest of thousands of golfers everywhere - the Hole-in-One Award. When the first Ryder Cup matches were staged in the USA in 1927, Johnnie Walker gave support to the British team. In the 1970's the company's involvement entered the international professional arena, supporting such all-time masters as Bernhard Langer and Seve Ballesteros.

The Ryder Cup
Johnnie Walker's support a vital
factor in raising world awareness

One of Johnnie Walker's greatest moments in golf came with the sponsorship of the European Ryder Cup Team in 1987. As the team headed west, captain Tony Jacklin said that the company's support would make all the difference to their game. And indeed it did, as the United States suffered their first home defeat. Johnnie Walker's continued support for the Ryder Cup has been a vital factor in raising world awareness of the event which is recognised as a glorious example of true sportsmanship and international goodwill. The biannual contest has since produced a tie in 1989 (Europe retained the Cup) and two close wins for the US in 1991 and 1993. In 1995, during what can only be described as one of the most exciting events ever staged in the history of the matches, captain Bernard Gallacher led the European Team to an impressive win of 14.5 points to the USA's 13.5 points. Europe's second only win on US soil. As the 1997 event returns to home ground for the European team in Valderrama, Spain, Johnnie Walker will once again be Event Sponsor.

In Europe, Johnnie Walker sponsors the PGA Cup matches between the UK's top club professionals and those of the US. On the PGA European Tour, the Johnnie Walker Tour Course Record Award of £3,000 every week has encouraged 71 players from 20 countries to establish or share new records.

Johnnie Walker's sponsorship programme now stretches through 100 countries around the world. The Hole-

in-One Award has been adopted at China's Chung Shan Hot Spring Club. The long running success of the Hong Kong Open encouraged the company to launch the Johnnie Walker Classic in Asia. Within 5 years the event has grown into Asia's premier golfing tournament. In 1996 Ian Woosnam took the laurels in Singapore.

The Johnnie Walker World Championship held for the last 5 years in Jamaica, fulfilled its five year contractual life span in December 1995. This last event under Johnnie Walker's sponsorship was won by Fred Couples,

Ian Woosnam - the 1996
Johnnie Walker Classic champion

after a three way tie at the end of 72 holes caused a play off between himself, Vijay Singh and Loren Roberts. Couples' win was a fitting end to a sponsorship that he also won in its inaugural year, 1991. The 1992 event was won by Nick Faldo, 1993 by Larry Mize and 1994 by Ernie Els. The sponsorship was extremely successful for Johnnie Walker, providing TV coverage in 140 countries worldwide.

Wherever the game of golf is played, the name of Johnnie Walker is invariably near at hand. It is not just the most natural of associations, but - as great champions like Fred Couples, Seve Ballesteros, Bernhard Langer, Greg Norman and Nick Faldo have found - a winning partnership.

VALDERRAMA SOTOGRANDE ANDALUCIA SPAIN
SEPTEMBER 26-28

Woosnam records a refreshing double

Successive wins put Ian Woosnam firmly on top of the Volvo Ranking

Joe Bugner came to Perth, and won his fight, but on the same weekend in Western Australia pugnacious Ian Woosnam, who as a teenager traded a few winning punches in a Holiday Camp bout, was surely sports' ringmaster. He completed what in boxing parlance is known as the old one-two following his success in Singapore the previous week with another in the Heineken Classic.

'It's not a dream come true,' Woosnam said. 'You see I've done it before.' True, the Welshman had, because in 1990 he put together back-to-back wins in the Monte Carlo and Scottish Opens. Yet even Woosnam admitted that victory was sweeter this time around on two counts. It confirmed that his self-imposed winter break, during which he relaxed rather than worked out, had revitalised his game, and that the decision to keep his swing simple – in his old-fashioned way – was the key behind his emergence from the wilderness of 16 months without a win.

Woosnam had, following his win in Singapore, spoken of his winter of content. In Perth he credited teacher Bill Ferguson for his revival. Back in the summer of 1995, Woosnam had talked about quitting the game that has made him a multi-millionaire. He was in constant pain with his back. He disliked the way he was swinging his club to protect the back. And he disliked the exercise programme designed to put him back on course. 'Everything had backfired on me,' he recalled. 'Then I saw this specialist, and he told me that the best thing for the back was not to lift anything, not to exercise, not to jog. It was perfect – music to my ears. I relaxed, and actually thought to myself that if I didn't play well again then it wouldn't matter.'

Then came the impromptu golf lesson in an hotel car park from Ferguson at the US Open. Ferguson had been following both his protégé, Colin Montgomerie, and Woosnam during a practice round. Woosnam, frustrated, had walked in after nine holes. Later, Ferguson convinced Woosnam that the ball was too far forward in his stance which meant he could not take the club back properly. The result was loss of power and accuracy. Woosnam listened, and invited Ferguson over to his Jersey home for more lessons.

'If it wasn't for Bill I wouldn't have

got back to winning in Singapore and Perth.' Woosnam explained. 'I like the way he talks about the swing. He doesn't complicate things; it's all about rhythm. I'm a natural swinger. I just get up there and swing the club. The more I think about it the more it complicates it. The last time I was in Perth I was going through a full swing change, and it's fairly obvious by the results that it didn't work.'

Indeed, the 1994 Heineken Classic was a case in point. Woosnam shot 81-78 to comfortably miss the halfway cut. Coincidentally, John Daly had suffered a similar embarrassment at the 1995 edition – he shot rounds of 80 and 76. Now the two protagonists had returned to mark the first occasion of a tournament, co-sanctioned by the European Tour and the PGA Tour of Australasia, being played on Australian soil, and they more than redeemed themselves.

Last round scuppered John Daly (opposite).

No home victory for Greg Norman.

Three rounds of outstanding golf from both players contrived to bring them together, sharing the lead, as the final day began under another cloudless Perth sky. The temperature had climbed as high as 44 C during the first three days when initially Wayne Smith, of Australia and Greg Turner, of New Zealand, led after opening 66s. Smith, runner-up at The Vines in both 1994 and 1995, scored a second round of 68 to lead on 134 by three strokes from Scotland's Dean Robertson

and Ireland's Paul McGinley. Smith carried with him the support of all West Australia into the third round, but his ability to keep the ball in play deserted him. 'I hit some dreadful iron shots,' he admitted.

Woosnam, however, was in control. He packed eight birdies into a course record 65. Daly's course management also remained exemplary, as for the third successive round he refused to reach for his driver, and with his second straight 67 he joined Woosnam on 205 – one ahead of

THE COURSE

Located in the picturesque Swan Valley, 30 minutes drive north-east of Perth. The Vines Resort Championship Course places a premium on accuracy, emphasised by John Daley's decision to keep his driver in the bag. Course architects Graham Marsh and Ross Watson created a challenging examination, carving holes out of the natural woodland and strategically positioning grassy hollows and bunkers to ensure the golfer must stay focused at all times. The condition of the course was outstanding, and the links-like quality of the sand in the bunkers was praised by all. The 18th is a wonderful closing hole with water down the left and a lake guarding the front of the green. It can be reached in two, but...

**Paul McGinley
came close again.**

Jean Van de Velde, of France, and McGinley with England's David Carter, following a superb 66, one shot further back.

For much of the final round Woosnam and Daly duelled, until the American missed the 12th green and ran up a double-bogey six, but ahead of them McGinley and Van de Velde refused to be overshadowed. McGinley's game from the tee to green was the best, but his putter remained cold in the soaring heat., and when he failed to get up and down from a bunker at the long 18th he virtually knew his fate. Van de Velde did make his birdie from the same bunker, to tie McGinley on 278, but a cursory glance at the leaderboard told both that Woosnam, now standing in the middle of the fairway, required a birdie to win. Moments later, Woosnam struck a peerless five iron over the bunker which had caught both McGinley and Van de Velde to ten feet from the hole. Two putts, and the title was his. Peter Thomson, five times Open champion, watched, and reflected: 'I've never been around when Ian Woosnam has played well, and I've had my doubts about him. He erased all those doubts.'

Who said champions don't come back. In Perth Joe Bugner, the former British, Commonwealth and European champion did, and so did Ian Woosnam.

Mitchell Platts

The Vines Resort, Perth, February 1-4, 1996 • Yardage 7112 • Par 72

Pos	Name	Country	Rnd 1	Rnd 2	Rnd 3	Rnd 4	Total	Prize Money £
1	Ian WOOSNAM	(Wal)	69	71	65	72	277	93338
2	Paul MCGINLEY	(Ire)	69	68	69	72	278	43947
	Jean VAN DE VELDE	(Fr)	72	67	67	72	278	43947
4	Stewart GINN	(Aus)	72	72	66	70	280	24890
5	John DALY	(USA)	71	67	67	76	281	18667
	Anthony PAINTER	(Aus)	70	73	72	66	281	18667
	Richard GREEN	(Aus)	70	74	70	67	281	18667
8	Wayne SMITH	(Aus)	66	68	75	73	282	12756
	Bradley HUGHES	(Aus)	69	70	74	69	282	12756
	Don FARDON	(Aus)	69	72	69	72	282	12756
	Dean ROBERTSON	(Scot)	70	67	76	69	282	12756
	Martyn ROBERTS	(Wal)	70	72	69	71	282	12756
13	Andrew SHERBORNE	(Eng)	70	72	70	71	283	8478
	Rick GIBSON	(Can)	67	73	69	74	283	8478
	Rodney PAMPLING	(Aus)	69	69	72	73	283	8478
	Craig PARRY	(Aus)	72	69	74	68	283	8478
17	Scott LAYCOCK	(Aus)	69	73	73	69	284	5655
	Darren CLARKE	(N.Ire)	73	71	69	71	284	5655
	Matthew GOGGIN	(Aus)	70	71	72	71	284	5655
	Grant DODD	(Aus)	74	68	69	73	284	5655
	Steven RICHARDSON	(Eng)	70	69	75	70	284	5655
	Greg NORMAN	(Aus)	73	68	75	68	284	5655
	Greg TURNER	(NZ)	66	74	74	70	284	5655
	Richard BOXALL	(Eng)	70	73	67	74	284	5655
25	Paul DEVENPORT	(NZ)	75	66	73	71	285	3933
	David SMAIL	(NZ)	70	74	72	69	285	3933
	Anthony GILLIGAN	(Aus)	75	69	71	70	285	3933
	Eiji MIZUGUCHI	(Jap)	69	72	71	73	285	3933
	Adam HUNTER	(Scot)	68	72	73	72	285	3933
	Roger CHAPMAN	(Eng)	72	71	69	73	285	3933
	Roger WESSELS	(SA)	73	66	70	76	285	3933
32	Gary EVANS	(Eng)	68	72	74	72	286	3007
	Mike HARWOOD	(Aus)	70	73	76	67	286	3007
	Darren COLE	(Aus)	71	69	72	74	286	3007
	Fredrik LINDGREN	(Swe)	72	71	68	75	286	3007
	Robert STEPHENS	(Aus)	69	72	74	71	286	3007
37	Mark DAVIS	(Eng)	68	75	73	71	287	2385
	Andre STOLZ	(Aus)	71	73	73	70	287	2385
	David CARTER	(Eng)	73	69	66	79	287	2385
	Brett OGLE	(Aus)	70	74	70	73	287	2385
	Frank NOBILO	(NZ)	69	72	73	73	287	2385
	Per HAUGSRUD	(Nor)	71	72	73	71	287	2385
	Steven PORCH	(Aus)	71	72	72	72	287	2385
44	Robert ALLENBY	(Aus)	74	70	67	77	288	1814
	Richard BACKWELL	(Aus)	72	72	67	77	288	1814
	Leith WASTLE	(Aus)	70	69	73	76	288	1814
	Stephen LEANEY	(Aus)	71	72	73	72	288	1814
48	Stephen SCAHILL	(NZ)	74	70	70	75	289	1451
	Mike CLAYTON	(Aus)	73	70	73	73	289	1451
	Mats LANNER	(Swe)	69	72	72	76	289	1451
51	Niclas FASTH	(Swe)	72	71	76	71	290	1199
	Michael LONG	(NZ)	72	72	71	75	290	1199
	Simon OWEN	(NZ)	70	74	73	73	290	1199
	Phillip PRICE	(Wal)	71	72	70	77	290	1199
55	Stuart CAGE	(Eng)	74	69	73	75	291	1109
	Jonathan LOMAS	(Eng)	69	72	76	74	291	1109
	Robert WILLIS	(Aus)	71	73	70	77	291	1109
	Rob WHITLOCK	(Aus)	75	69	70	77	291	1109
	Malcolm BAKER	(Aus)	73	71	69	78	291	1109
60	Shane TAIT	(Aus)	70	72	76	74	292	1068
	Glenn JOYNER	(Aus)	73	71	73	75	292	1068
	Paul EALES	(Eng)	72	70	76	74	292	1068
63	David HILL	(Aus)	69	75	75	75	294	1047
64	Greg CHALMERS	(Aus)	73	70	75	77	295	1031
	David BRANSDON	(Aus)	71	73	72	79	295	1031
66	Craig JONES	(Aus)	69	72	81	74	296	739
67	Michael JONZON	(Swe)	70	73	76	81	300	737

SHOT OF THE WEEK

John Daly faced a dilemma at the 15th (445-yards) in the third round when he pushed his tee shot into a bunker. 'I had 199 yards to go and knew I needed a six iron,' he said. 'But I had to get the ball up quickly to clear the bunker lip and the trees ahead so I ripped a seven iron. I hit the ball about as far as I could to make the green.' Daly two-putted to save par and continue a flawless inward half of 31 which enabled him to tie Ian Woosnam with one round left.

McNulty magic still working

Mark McNulty ended a 17-month wait for victory in the first of the co-sanctioned South African events

Fittingly, there was a neat coincidence as the PGA European Tour arrived in South Africa for the first of three co-sanctioned events with the FNB Tour. Ian Woosnam had won his last two events, in Singapore and Perth, and Wayne Westner had achieved the same feat on his home circuit.

But in a week that was all about doubling-up and going-halves, a hat-trick was not on the agenda at the Dimension Data Pro-am. Instead, Sun City saw Mark McNulty win his 23rd title on his home Tour, and the 13th of his European Tour career. In a tournament that featured 320 players, half amateurs, half professionals, two golf courses for the first two days (the Lost City layout giving way to the Gary Player Country club on the weekend) and two rounds played in brilliant sunshine and two in miserable rain, McNulty was four shots better than Nick Price, young South African Brenden Pappas, and England's Ricky Willison.

A chip-in from off the 15th green finally put too much daylight between the Zimbabwean and his chasers. He had opened up the four-shot lead after 36 holes with a 69 at Lost City and then a 67 on the Player course. The latter is a course McNulty agreed was designed to be played with the sun on your back and when the weather turned it was a matter of switching into defensive mode. Though matching weekend rounds of 73 may not look so pretty in the scorebook, he got the job done with his usual style and elegance.

'I can't remember a tougher round than today,' he said after his victory, which added to those of the 1986 Barclays Classic and the 1987 Million Dollar Challenge at Sun City. 'It was a matter of hanging on. It was such hard work that you almost forgot there was a tournament to win. I enjoyed it because it became par golf and not birdie golf.'

At 7,484 yards, even at altitude, the Player Course was playing every inch of its monster length and the kikuyu rough was thick enough to prevent a player being

After missing the fairway at the par four 15th on Sunday, McNulty came up ten yards short of the green with his second. He then chipped in to seal his four-shot win. 'I was helped by one of my amateur partners who had a similar chip just before me. He hit a good shot and I could judge the pace of the green. I knew I had hit a good chip and turned away so I only knew it had gone in when I heard the cheer. Obviously, that was the shot that won me the tournament, that and my 67 in the second round.'

able to stop the ball on the hard and firm greens. Straight driving was McNulty's best ally, plus his long iron approach play, and the touch of his renowned short game. 'I have been working on a better address position and getting a better spine angle at impact,' said McNulty, who had recovered from a serious knee injury that curtailed his 1995 season. 'That is the key to why Nick Price is such a good striker of the ball and I feel I am striking it more crisply already. I know I can still become better.' And added the 42-year old after his 39th career win: 'If I can catch up my age with my career victories, I know I'll

Nick Price on home soil.

33

have had a good year.'

Price was happy enough with his first outing of the year and, certainly, with the format whereby play was in fourballs (two pros, two amateurs) for all four rounds. 'The format is popular with the sponsors because where else can people get to play with professionals under tournament conditions. We knew we were in for five-hour rounds when we got here. The amateurs will have had a great time this week and if any of the pros start complaining, they should call their bank managers.'

Woosnam's bid for three wins in a row came unstuck with a first round 74, but he did battle away to finish 14th. Westner started with a 72 but later in the day, began to hit balls on the tenth tee of the Gary Player course, which at past tournaments was always allocated as a practice area. Not this time and Tournament Director Andy McFee had the unfortunate job of disqualifying the South African for practising on the course.

Brothers Deane (above) and Brenden Pappas (below) with Johnnie Walker Tour Course Record Award.

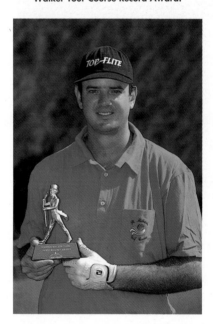

Brenden Pappas, who had previously been runner-up to Price in the Zimbabwe Open and to Ernie Els in the South

African Open, established a Johnnie Walker Tour record 64 on the Player layout on Saturday. In the process the 25-year old, one of four golfing brothers, set a new mark for nine holes when he played the front nine (after starting at the tenth) in 28. That included just nine putts and a hole-in-one, with a four iron, at the 206-yard seventh. 'I just cannot express what I feel or how it happened,' Pappas said.

On Sunday, the best round of the day came from Ricky Willison, the former Walker Cup man who had earned his place back on Tour from the 1995 Challenge Tour. His 68 was fashioned in weather more appropriate to his home club of Ealing and his top ten finish earned him a spot in the following week's Alfred Dunhill South African PGA. The same went for Wales' Marcus Wills, and England's Gary Evans, who after going to the turn in 43, bravely holed a birdie putt from 35 feet on the last.

Andrew Farrell

34

SUN CITY, SOUTH AFRICA, FEBRUARY 8-11, 1996 • YARDAGE 7504 • PAR 72

Pos	Name	Country	Rnd 1	Rnd 2	Rnd 3	Rnd 4	Total	Prize Money £
1	Mark MCNULTY	(Zim)	69	67	73	73	282	62491
2	Brenden PAPPAS	(SA)	69	77	64	76	286	30771
	Ricky WILLISON	(Eng)	73	73	72	68	286	30771
	Nick PRICE	(Zim)	68	72	74	72	286	30771
5	André CRUSE	(SA)	73	67	73	74	287	16353
6	Mike CHRISTIE	(USA)	71	73	72	72	288	14023
7	Trevor DODDS	(Nam)	74	72	72	71	289	10007
	Marco GORTANA	(It)	71	73	69	76	289	10007
	Patrick MOORE	(USA)	72	73	71	73	289	10007
10	Des SMYTH	(Ire)	73	73	73	71	290	6942
	Marcus WILLS	(Wal)	77	67	73	73	290	6942
	Gary EVANS	(Eng)	72	72	69	77	290	6942
	John MCHENRY	(Ire)	72	71	73	74	290	6942
14	Eamonn DARCY	(Ire)	73	73	72	73	291	5139
	Ian WOOSNAM	(Wal)	74	72	74	71	291	5139
	Bobby LINCOLN	(SA)	75	72	73	71	291	5139
	Steve VAN VUUREN	(SA)	76	70	75	70	291	5139
	Thomas BJORN	(Den)	72	73	69	77	291	5139
	Pat HORGAN	(USA)	72	73	75	71	291	5139
	Paolo QUIRICI	(Swi)	73	70	75	73	291	5139
	Mats HALLBERG	(Swe)	71	72	77	71	291	5139
	Deane PAPPAS	(SA)	72	69	78	72	291	5139
23	Michael DU TOIT	(SA)	74	71	73	74	292	4100
	Raymond BURNS	(N.Ire)	75	69	74	74	292	4100
	Greg TURNER	(NZ)	72	72	75	73	292	4100
	Sven STRÜVER	(Ger)	68	75	74	75	292	4100
	Thomas GÖGELE	(Ger)	72	70	75	75	292	4100
28	Ian HUTCHINGS	(Eng)	73	73	72	75	293	3539
	Chris DAVISON	(Eng)	71	74	76	72	293	3539
	Desmond TERBLANCHE	(SA)	71	74	71	77	293	3539
	David J RUSSELL	(Eng)	73	71	76	73	293	3539
	Justin HOBDAY	(SA)	74	69	72	78	293	3539
33	Ian PALMER	(SA)	72	75	73	74	294	3278
34	Domingo HOSPITAL	(Sp)	77	70	75	73	295	3120
	Alexander CEJKA	(Ger)	71	76	74	74	295	3120
	Pierre FULKE	(Swe)	73	72	76	74	295	3120
37	Steven BOTTOMLEY	(Eng)	78	69	72	77	296	2844
	Paul CURRY	(Eng)	74	73	78	71	296	2844
	Warren SCHUTTE	(SA)	72	72	75	77	296	2844
	Christian CEVAER	(Fr)	74	68	77	77	296	2844
41	Bruce VAUGHAN	(USA)	77	68	80	72	297	2607
	Retief GOOSEN	(SA)	72	72	78	75	297	2607
43	Steve WOODS	(USA)	74	69	79	76	298	2449
	Mike BOARD	(USA)	73	69	75	81	298	2449
45	David HOWELL	(Eng)	74	72	73	80	299	2172
	Dean VAN STODEN	(SA)	74	72	77	76	299	2172
	Gavin LEVENSON	(SA)	73	72	76	78	299	2172
	Pedro LINHART	(Sp)	73	71	80	75	299	2172
	Rodney BUTCHER	(USA)	71	73	77	78	299	2172
50	Mathias GRÖNBERG	(Swe)	72	75	80	73	300	1817
	Francis QUINN	(USA)	74	72	77	77	300	1817
	Dean ROBERTSON	(Scot)	74	71	81	74	300	1817
	Nic HENNING	(SA)	72	71	80	77	300	1817
54	Derek JAMES	(SA)	75	72	77	77	301	1619
55	Iain PYMAN	(Eng)	73	73	81	75	302	1461
	Peter HEDBLOM	(Swe)	74	72	78	78	302	1461
	Wayne BRADLEY	(SA)	73	72	75	82	302	1461
58	Frank NOBILO	(NZ)	73	74	80	76	303	1264
	Richard KAPLAN	(SA)	69	77	81	76	303	1264
	Michael GREEN	(SA)	75	69	81	78	303	1264
61	Mark LITTON	(Wal)	74	73	78	80	305	1185
62	Gerry COETZEE	(SA)	76	70	76	84	306	1145
63	Schalk VAN DER MERWE	(SA)	70	75	77	85	307	1106
64	Vanslow PHILLIPS	(Eng)	72	75	83	81	311	1066
65	Phillip PRICE	(Wal)	71	70	W/D			1030

THE COURSE

The Gary Player Country Club at Sun City, among the rugged Pilanesberg Mountains, is a monster challenge in anyone's yardage book at 7,484 yards. It has been the host of the annual Million Dollar Challenge since 1979, but, with the conditions, has rarely played longer or tougher. 'It is a course you want to play with the sun on your back.' said McNulty. Gary Player also designed the Lost City course which opened in 1993 and which features among its many water hazards a pool at the par three 13th.

Strüver storms to maiden victory

A stunning final round of 63
gave Sven Strüver his first
European Tour title

As thunder and lightning rumbled away near the Houghton course in Johannesburg, Sven Strüver may just have considered the safest option, and the quickest way back to the clubhouse, was to take as few shots as possible.

Strüver's inspired effort – a third and final round of nine under par 63 – merely gave the 28- year old a sleepless night before discovering whether he would win his maiden Tour title. With 42 players still to compete 54 holes of a tournament ravaged by the weather, Strüver thought about missing the fairway at the last, and his recovery that ensured a par and 202 total.

Would it be enough? 'I thought the worst that could happen was that I would be in a play-off, but then someone said what if it rains again all day Monday and it all had to be washed out? I was praying it wouldn't rain,' admitted the son of a Hamburg professional.

Overnight Strüver, at 14 under par, led by three from Ernie Els. The South African had been in front until Strüver came rushing past on Sunday afternoon. When he bogeyed his first two holes on the resumption, he needed to birdie the last five to tie. He did so at the par five 14th, and then holed from 15 feet at the next. At the 16th, he put it to four feet, but missed the chance. 'I hit a terrible putt

and that was the end of it,' said Els. 'It was a tough thing to do, getting five birdies in a row. It would have been the finish of the century.'

Instead, Strüver, watching on television, could at last start to celebrate. 'I have been nervous out on the course, but this was different,' he said after becoming his country's third Tour winner after Bernhard Langer and Alex Cejka. 'It is great that there are more German players looking to win tournaments.'

That he was given the chance to produce his remarkable effort, was only due to an equally Herculean one by the officials and groundstaff to thwart a week of record rainfall in Johannesburg. The course was closed on Monday afternoon, the Canon Shoot-Out was cancelled on Tuesday, as was the pro-am on Wednesday. A helicopter was brought in by sponsors Alfred Dunhill to fan away the water and 40 minutes before Thursday's scheduled 6.45am start, the

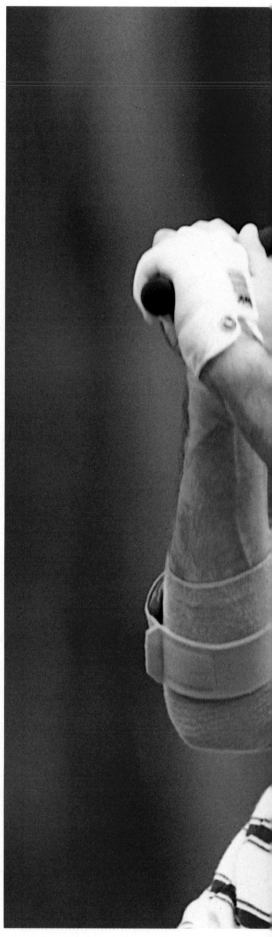

Drying time after the rain (above), David Feherty (right) made a welcome return.

course was ready for play. Then 24mm of rain fell in a 25-minute cloudburst and a start could not be made until Friday.

Strüver, without a practice round, or having walked the course, went to the turn in six under and his 66 put him two behind Els. Els had won the South African Open at Houghton in 1992 and, wearing contact lenses in competition for the first time, was immediately in command. After beginning his second round late on Saturday, three more birdies would have put him well clear but for David Feherty

grabbing three birdies in a row, including a chip-in in the 11th as darkness called a halt.

Feherty was in his second tournament since his return to the European Tour after losing his US Tour card in 1995. A long-term tennis elbow injury was being treated with regular physiotherapy and guarded by wearing a three-layer bandage. Two shots behind on Saturday night, that was still the position going into the final round. But neither the South African nor the Irishman was still playing as well as a

Ernie Els was signed in by President Mandela but then found trouble (above). Frank Nobilo (below) was in the top ten.

SHOT OF THE WEEK

On the 218-yard sixth on Sunday, Sven Strüver hit a three iron to a foot and tapped in for the first of six birdies in a row during his final round 63. 'I had missed three putts in the first three holes,' he said, 'but then it all started to happen. When I got on that run of birdies, I didn't want it to end.'

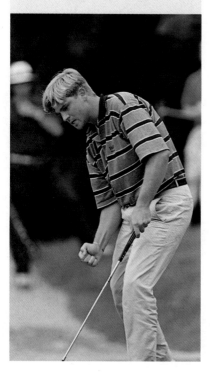

week of interruptions took its toll. Els was introduced to President Nelson Mandela on the first tee. The President signed his cap: 'To Ernie, with compliments, Nelson Mandela, 18.2.96.' Els promptly missed the fairway and took a double bogey six.

That was all the encouragement Strüver needed. Starting seven shots behind, he birdied the fourth and then had six in a row from the sixth. After missing out at the 12th, he continued at the 13th and 14th. Three putts at the 15th from ten feet led to a bogey, which was recovered at the next. He had had just 26 putts. 'I did not play well in the four holes of the second round I had to finish off in the morning, but I went to the practice range and my rhythm came back,' he said. Strüver had previously finished fourth three times since making his card from invitations in 1992.

'The record books show that to be a visiting player here, you have to play very well to beat the best of their best,' said Ken Schofield, Executive Director of the PGA European Tour. 'You saw that in the days of Bobby Locke, and today with Ernie Els. I wasn't certain that a young German player could come down here and beat, in their own PGA Championship, such a field.'

Andrew Farrell

HOUGHTON GOLF CLUB, JOHANNESBURG, SOUTH AFRICA, FEBRUARY 15-18, 1996 • YARDAGE 7035 • PAR 72

Pos	Name	Country	Rnd 1	Rnd 2	Rnd 3	Total	Prize Money £
1	Sven STRÜVER	(Ger)	66	73	63	202	47459
2	David FEHERTY	(N.Ire)	65	69	71	205	27675
	Ernie ELS	(SA)	64	68	73	205	27675
4	Richard BOXALL	(Eng)	69	68	69	206	13589
	Iain PYMAN	(Eng)	69	67	70	206	13589
6	Carl MASON	(Eng)	70	67	70	207	9765
	Brett LIDDLE	(SA)	70	66	71	207	9765
8	Tony JOHNSTONE	(Zim)	70	71	67	208	5329
	Paul BROADHURST	(Eng)	68	74	66	208	5329
	Ian PALMER	(SA)	71	69	68	208	5329
	Costantino ROCCA	(It)	68	72	68	208	5329
	Trevor DODDS	(Nam)	70	69	69	208	5329
	Frank NOBILO	(NZ)	72	66	70	208	5329
	David HOWELL	(Eng)	66	71	71	208	5329
	Bruce VAUGHAN	(USA)	67	70	71	208	5329
	Andrew COLTART	(Scot)	69	67	72	208	5329
17	Chris DAVISON	(Eng)	67	74	68	209	3530
	Adilson DA SILVA	(Bra)	70	71	68	209	3530
	Greg TURNER	(NZ)	69	71	69	209	3530
	Wayne WESTNER	(SA)	70	70	69	209	3530
	David FROST	(SA)	70	68	71	209	3530
	Des SMYTH	(Ire)	72	66	71	209	3530
	Allan MCLEAN	(Eng)	71	67	71	209	3530
	Michael SCHOLZ	(SA)	65	71	73	209	3530
	Gary ORR	(Scot)	72	64	73	209	3530
26	Silvio GRAPPASONNI	(It)	70	71	69	210	2703
	Bobby LINCOLN	(SA)	73	69	68	210	2703
	Ronan RAFFERTY	(N.Ire)	74	69	67	210	2703
	Rolf MUNTZ	(Hol)	71	68	71	210	2703
	Mike CHRISTIE	(USA)	71	68	71	210	2703
	Oyvind ROJAHN	(Nor)	69	70	71	210	2703
	Mark MOULAND	(Wal)	69	70	71	210	2703
	Cameron BECKMAN	(USA)	69	69	72	210	2703
	Eamonn DARCY	(Ire)	70	67	73	210	2703
35	José COCERES	(Arg)	73	68	70	211	2159
	Miguel Angel JIMÉNEZ	(Sp)	73	68	70	211	2159
	Olle KARLSSON	(Swe)	71	71	69	211	2159
	Paul MCGINLEY	(Ire)	71	71	69	211	2159
	Gavin LEVENSON	(SA)	71	71	69	211	2159
	Francis QUINN	(USA)	71	71	69	211	2159
	Marco GORTANA	(It)	70	71	70	211	2159
	Warrick DRUIAN	(SA)	66	73	72	211	2159
43	Gordon BRAND JNR.	(Scot)	69	72	71	212	1680
	Brenden PAPPAS	(SA)	66	75	71	212	1680
	Adam HUNTER	(Scot)	71	71	70	212	1680
	Philip JONAS	(SA)	73	70	69	212	1680
	Ricky WILLISON	(Eng)	73	70	69	212	1680
	Peter HEDBLOM	(Swe)	69	71	72	212	1680
	Ignacio GARRIDO	(Sp)	69	71	72	212	1680
	Mathias GRÖNBERG	(Swe)	70	69	73	212	1680
51	Pedro LINHART	(Sp)	72	69	72	213	1350
	Warren SCHUTTE	(SA)	69	71	73	213	1350
	Paul CURRY	(Eng)	75	65	73	213	1350
54	Ray FREEMAN	()	67	75	72	214	1169
	Jean VAN DE VELDE	(Fr)	73	70	71	214	1169
	Stephen AMES	(T&T)	70	70	74	214	1169
57	Stuart CAGE	(Eng)	72	70	73	215	950
	Richard KAPLAN	(SA)	68	74	73	215	950
	Dean VAN STADEN	(SA)	73	70	72	215	950
	Ian HUTCHINGS	(Eng)	72	71	72	215	950
	Dean ROBERTSON	(Scot)	70	73	72	215	950
	Michael JONZON	(Swe)	71	70	74	215	950
63	Kevin STONE	(SA)	71	71	74	216	720
	Steven RICHARDSON	(Eng)	69	73	74	216	720
	Deane PAPPAS	(SA)	70	73	73	216	720
	Greg PETERSON	(USA)	72	68	76	216	720
67	Sammy DANIELS	(SA)	70	71	76	217	444
	Miguel Angel MARTIN	(Sp)	69	74	74	217	444
	Per-Ulrik JOHANSSON	(Swe)	73	70	74	217	444
	De Wet BASSON	(SA)	73	70	74	217	444
	Jannie LE GRANGE	(SA)	70	67	80	217	444
72	Justin HOBDAY	(SA)	72	71	76	219	438
73	Paul EALES	(Eng)	71	72	77	220	436

THE COURSE

Originally laid out in 1923 by the club's first professional, Houghton is an attractive parkland course and is a sanctuary to a variety of birdlife. Measuring 7,035 yards, there are nine par fours over 400 yards and there is heavy rough just off the fairway. A number of tees were redesigned and the seventh and eighth had bunkers added in work done specially for the event.

Westner is happy at home

Victory in Durban left Wayne Westner happy to have won in his own backyard

Wayne Westner's third victory in four weeks on home soil in the FNB Players Championship at Durban Country Club was a case of form horses for courses.

Having won the South African Opens of 1988 and 1991 on this jewel of a seaside course, and achieved back-to-back victories a couple of weeks earlier in the South African Masters and the Wild Coast Classic in the self-same province of Kwazulu, Natal, he was the man to put your shirt on in this last of the 1996 co-sanctioned events in South Africa. And the Johannesburg professional, who lists his hobbies as 'fishing, flying and the bush', did not let his supporters down.

On the face of it the big-hitting South African – he was European Tour Statistics leader in driving distance in 1992 (286.8 yards) and 1993 (284.7 yards) – ought not to be best suited to a windblown layout with small greens and rolling fairways severely narrowed by trees and dense shrubbery. But Westner's strategy of bringing the course to heel by leaving his driver in his bag proved the key to a third success at the Indian Ocean venue.

Westner, a thinking man's golfer and a committed Christian who likes to relax by 'communing with nature' in his country's wide open spaces, had to settle for a share of the lead with eventual runner-up José Coceres of Argentina and Trinidad and Tobago's Stephen Ames after an opening 66. Five of his seven birdies in a second round 67 in cooler, windier weather came at successive holes from the tenth, the most spectacular being a 30-yard chip-in at the par five 14th. He was unlucky not to record the third ace of his professional career with a six iron at the 187-yard 15th. The ball pitched two feet past the pin but instead of spinning back into the cup it plugged in a green still soggy after overnight thunderstorms.

Westner was four clear of Coceres, who fired a second round 71, at the halfway stage, with Lancashire's Paul Eales, two strokes further back after a 69, 70 opening, poised to make his presence felt. From the outset of the season, Eales, winner of Spain's Extremadura Open in

43

SHOT OF THE WEEK

Winner Wayne Westner twice went within inches of a hole-in-one at the 187-yard 15th, but Frenchman Tim Planchin's drive at the 273-yard 18th on day one was surely the week's most memorable shot – the ball pitched short and skipped up on to the putting surface, struck the flag and stopped dead for a tap-in eagle two.

Wayne Westner (right) stooped and conquered.

1994, had his sights firmly set on July's Open Championship at Royal Lytham & St Annes. He explained: 'It's not every year a professional has the chance to win the Open at his home club and making sure I qualify to play is my target.'

Victory in Durban, after he had faltered when taking an early lead in the final round in the Johnnie Walker Classic in Singapore would have given his official prizewinnings a £61,486 boost, and a record seven-birdie third round 65 hoisted him into second place – four behind Westner, who carded another 67, and two ahead of Coceres. 'I used my third different putting stroke of the week – I just concentrated on getting more comfortable at address and it worked,' explained Eales.

With ante-post favourite Ernie Els seven strokes adrift with Welshman Mark Mouland, Las Palmas-born Englishman Carl Suneson and in-form Scot Andrew Coltart, Westner looked set for a comfortable passage to his second

European Tour title following his 1993 Dubai Desert Classic victory. It did not turn out so.

He went five ahead with a birdie at the third but admitted he was 'panicking a bit' after reaching the turn in 38 with

dropped shots at the fifth, eighth and ninth to be only one ahead, and declared: 'I had to go out and win the tournament all over again.'

After another two at the short 15th, this time from 18 inches, he was three clear of Coceres, but the little Argentinian, who comes from a family of 11 and has five brothers who are also professionals, was in hot pursuit. He was out in 34 and five under par for his round after 14 and when Westner bogeyed the 16th Coceres struck instantly with a six iron to a foot to narrow the gap to a single stroke again. He kept the pressure firmly on by getting up and down from a bunker for a birdie at the 18th and a record-equalling 65, but Westner showed his steel by chipping to

Paul Eales (above), José Coceres (left) and Andrew Coltart (right) all featured strongly.

five feet to match his three for a 70 and 270 tally that matched the winning score the year before of American Ron Whittaker, nephew of US Ryder Cup Captain Lanny Wadkins, and a one stroke win, with Eales bravely birdieing the last from 20 feet to edge out David Feherty, Costantino Rocca and Ross McFarlane for third place on 274.

Westner declared: 'It's great to win again and earn another three-year exemption on the European Tour, where the standard is so high. It's a wonderful thing that Ken Schofield has done in bringing the Tour here. It's nice to play in your own backyard after playing in everyone else's backyard.'

Gordon Richardson

DURBAN C.C., SOUTH AFRICA, FEBRUARY 22-25, 1996 • YARDAGE 6642 • PAR 72

Pos	Name	Country	Rnd 1	Rnd 2	Rnd 3	Rnd 4	Total	Prize Money £
1	Wayne WESTNER	(SA)	66	67	67	70	270	61486
2	José COCERES	(Arg)	66	71	69	65	271	44774
3	Paul EALES	(Eng)	69	70	65	70	274	26934
4	Ross MCFARLANE	(Eng)	67	74	67	67	275	16336
	Costantino ROCCA	(It)	69	69	71	66	275	16336
	David FEHERTY	(N.Ire)	69	70	69	67	275	16336
7	David FROST	(SA)	72	67	69	68	276	11504
8	Andrew COLTART	(Scot)	71	69	67	70	277	9017
	Mark MCNULTY	(Zim)	72	69	69	67	277	9017
10	Andrew SHERBORNE	(Eng)	70	70	68	70	278	6445
	Tony JOHNSTONE	(Zim)	70	69	70	69	278	6445
	Ernie ELS	(SA)	69	71	67	71	278	6445
	Deane PAPPAS	(SA)	72	68	71	67	278	6445
	Carl SUNESON	(Eng)	68	72	67	71	278	6445
	Ignacio GARRIDO	(Sp)	69	72	69	68	278	6445
16	Steve WOODS	(USA)	71	70	68	70	279	5441
17	Bruce VAUGHAN	(USA)	68	75	71	66	280	4955
	Jay TOWNSEND	(USA)	71	69	68	72	280	4955
	Stuart HENDLEY	(USA)	73	69	69	69	280	4955
	Ronan RAFFERTY	(N.Ire)	72	72	68	68	280	4955
21	Mark MOULAND	(Wal)	70	68	69	74	281	4391
	Paul MCGINLEY	(Ire)	69	74	68	70	281	4391
	Steven RICHARDSON	(Eng)	72	67	70	72	281	4391
24	Gavin LEVENSON	(SA)	71	71	71	69	282	3860
	Christian CEVAER	(Fr)	72	71	70	69	282	3860
	Paul BROADHURST	(Eng)	70	75	69	68	282	3860
	Mike MCLEAN	(Eng)	69	69	74	70	282	3860
	Desmond TERBLANCHE	(SA)	69	71	71	71	282	3860
	Marco GORTANA	(It)	71	72	71	68	282	3860
30	Gary ORR	(Scot)	67	78	70	68	283	3420
	Warren SCHUTTE	(SA)	67	73	73	70	283	3420
32	Dean VAN STADEN	(SA)	68	76	71	69	284	3031
	Pierre FULKE	(Swe)	76	69	69	70	284	3031
	Desvonde BOTES	(SA)	71	71	72	70	284	3031
	Per-Ulrik JOHANSSON	(Swe)	68	75	70	71	284	3031
	Pedro LINHART	(Sp)	71	73	71	69	284	3031
	Jonathan LOMAS	(Eng)	73	72	69	70	284	3031
	Eamonn DARCY	(Ire)	72	73	70	69	284	3031
	Stephen AMES	(T&T)	66	75	75	68	284	3031
40	Brenden PAPPAS	(SA)	73	71	66	75	285	2487
	Lee WESTWOOD	(Eng)	75	70	70	70	285	2487
	Sven STRÜVER	(Ger)	70	74	71	70	285	2487
	Sammy DANIELS	(SA)	72	71	71	71	285	2487
	Jean VAN DE VELDE	(Fr)	71	72	68	74	285	2487
	André CRUSE	(SA)	73	72	68	72	285	2487
46	Paul FRIEDLANDER	(Swa)	67	72	75	72	286	2137
	Bobby LINCOLN	(SA)	70	74	72	70	286	2137
	Jean Charles CAMBON	(Fr)	71	71	72	72	286	2137
49	Ricky WILLISON	(Eng)	73	72	72	70	287	1865
	Des SMYTH	(Ire)	71	71	70	75	287	1865
	Miguel Angel MARTIN	(Sp)	71	73	73	70	287	1865
	Padraig HARRINGTON	(Ire)	72	71	73	71	287	1865
53	Olle KARLSSON	(Swe)	70	72	74	72	288	1632
	Mark MURLESS	(SA)	71	71	72	74	288	1632
55	Trevor DODDS	(Nam)	69	74	71	75	289	1399
	Richard KAPLAN	(SA)	71	74	75	69	289	1399
	Steven BOTTOMLEY	(Eng)	68	75	69	77	289	1399
	André BOSSERT	(Swi)	72	71	71	75	289	1399
59	Ray FREEMAN	(USA)	73	72	72	73	290	1185
	Ashley ROESTOFF	(SA)	69	74	74	73	290	1185
	John MCHENRY	(Ire)	72	73	74	71	290	1185
	Malcolm MACKENZIE	(Eng)	72	72	72	74	290	1185
63	Michael ARCHER	(Eng)	69	75	71	76	291	1049
	Adam MEDNICK	(Swe)	75	70	73	73	291	1049
	Derek JAMES	(SA)	70	74	73	74	291	1049
66	Hugh INGGS	(SA)	71	74	75	72	292	583
67	Niclas FASTH	(Swe)	72	73	76	75	296	581

THE COURSE

Monkeys are a common sight on the 6,642-yard par 72 course, whose finish, with a potentially blind second at the roller coaster 387-yard 17th and the 18th eminently reachable at 273 yards, might lack a little, but the narrow opening five holes along the sandhills flanking the ocean rank among the most challenging in the game.

Lawrie reigns in Spain

Paul Lawrie secured his first European Tour

title in the gales at Bonmont.

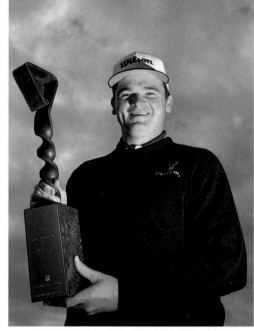

When somebody takes part in a four-lap race and is declared the winner after only two have been completed, it makes him something of a lucky winner, right? Wrong, and Paul Lawrie would be the first to stand up and say so.

Lawrie took the Open Catalonia title after a gale-swept four days and, in the event, won on the last day without striking a ball with a total of 135, nine under par. But that does not mean that he did not endure death by a thousand cuts on the final day of a tournament reduced to matchwood by gales that invaded the Bonmont course like avenging angels throughout the tournament.

The wind that sweeps over this area of Catalonia is a feature of the micro-climate that surrounds the Bonmont lay-out.

Not even in these parts, though are the elements usually as mischievous as they were on the second and third days of the tournament.

The first round was completed, just, the second round was abandoned completely when David Garland, the Tournament Director, watched as balls placed on the back of certain greens blew clean across the putting surface and 60 yards back down the fairway.

Garland's worthy intention as he announced that play had been scrapped on the Friday of the tournament was to finish the second round on the Saturday and play 36 holes on Sunday. As intentions go and laudable as it was, it was too optimistic.

By the middle of Saturday it was obvious that nothing of the sort was going to be possible, and short of pushing the tournament into a fifth day, which would itself have been something of a gamble, given the remorseless wind, the best that could be hoped for was to play the tournament over 36 holes.

That was duly completed, and Lawrie was declared the victor on the scheduled final day of the tournament and picked up the full winning cheque of £50,000. His uncomplaining endurance of agony on that abbreviated Sunday as he waited, and watched, and waited, his second and final round completed the thick end of 24 hours before, made it worth every penny.

As the remainder of the field trailed out onto the course, David Howell, who had been a shot behind Lawrie in the dim

**Domingo Hospital
plays under azure skies.**

and distant past of Thursday, seemed to be the best placed. He was six under par after nine and needed three more birdies to come home in 33 and force a play-off. Ultimately, the young former Walker Cup player's inexperience was his undoing as he took 38 for the back nine to finish with a 74 to leave himself five strokes shy.

Lawrie settled himself in front of the television and tried to look relaxed, and signally failed to do so. A surge from nowhere by the chunky Italian, Emanuele Bolognesi, brought Lawrie's rear end inch-

ing towards the edge of his seat, and for a while the Italian gave the 27-year old Scot a serious run for his money. Bolognesi, who started at the tenth, had five birdies and only one bogey in a front nine completed in 32, then picked up another shot on the second. He needed three more birdies over the last seven holes to tie, and he was on a roll.

Lawrie is a stoical character who does not allow himself wild excesses of public emotion, but he could not prevent the odd flicker of concern to cross features

that are as craggy as the buildings of his native Aberdeen. He did not permit himself a small smile of triumph until Bolognesi put his ball in a bunker on the short fifth, his 14th, and dropped a shot. The Italian was now four behind with only four to play; the tournament was won and lost. Fernando Roca, a Qualifying School graduate, finished second, a shot behind Lawrie, with Domingo Hospital a further stroke astern.

On the first day of the tournament Howell, whose 66 put him a shot behind Lawrie, showed the confidence born of a fruitful amateur career, the highlight of which had been membership of the victorious Walker Cup team the previous year. Still only 20 at the time of the tournament, he had put himself under the grizzled wing of Andrew Chandler, the former Tour player, who had already negotiated two commercial sponsorships for his young charge. Unusual ones, too – one of his backers makes butcher's aprons and the other manufactures plastic bags

THE COURSE

Attention was diverted, a little unfairly, from the Bonmont course by talk about the gales that howled all round it for days. This Robert Trent Jones creation, carved out of rugged terrain in the Catalonian country-side a few miles away from Tarragona, is a demanding lay-out that even without the wind would have been a test for the best.

Anders Forsbrand, 17th hole, second round. Forsbrand was going nowhere in particular in the tournament when he came to the long penultimate hole, played downwind. The ball was 210 yards from the hole, and Forsbrand pulled out his five-iron, drew a bead and hit. The ball pitched on the green 15 yards to the left of the pin, swiftly drew to a halt and trickled slowly down the slope for an albatross two, the first of the 1996 European Tour season.

good one. Even with his cricket team of a score, he still managed to break 80 – just. He was not the only one; Steve Webster, leading amateur in the Open Championship in 1995 and winner of the Qualifying School, had a similar score.

Paul Lawrie had no such traumas to overcome, and three days later he was celebrating the first victory of his European career. Like so many others at Bonmont that week, he suffered; unlike nearly all of them, he proved that suffering a nasty attack of the wind can sometimes be positively healthy.

Mel Webb

for Marks and Spencer.

While all this was going on Russell Claydon, the burly young chap from Cambridgeshire, was putting himself in all sorts of highly entertaining bother on the long 17th, clocking up an 11 with a brief surge of blood to the head. Three increasingly desperate times he went into a barranco, a deep, wide and very nasty dried-up water course, and having escaped, avoided a 12 only by sinking a putt of six feet. As 11s go, it was a pretty

BONMONT, TARRAGONA, SPAIN, FEBRUARY 29-MARCH 3, 1996 · YARDAGE 7050 · PAR 72

Pos	Name	Country	Rnd 1	Rnd 2	Rnd 3	Rnd 4	Total	Prize Money £		Name	Country	Rnd 1	Rnd 2	Rnd 3	Rnd 4	Total	Prize Money
										Ross DRUMMOND	(Scot)	73	71			144	2313
										Francisco VALERA	(Sp)	72	72			144	2313
1	Paul LAWRIE	(Scot)	65	70			135	50000		Andrew COLLISON	(Eng)	72	72			144	2313
2	Fernando ROCA	(Sp)	66	70			136	33330		Padraig HARRINGTON	(Ire)	75	69			144	2313
3	Domingo HOSPITAL	(Sp)	66	71			137	18780		Anders SORENSEN	(Den)	71	73			144	2313
4	Emanuele BOLOGNESI	(It)	71	67			138	13850		Per NYMAN	(Swe)	71	73			144	2313
	Andrew SHERBORNE	(Eng)	67	71			138	13850		Diego BORREGO	(Sp)	73	71			144	2313
6	Juan Carlos PIÑERO	(Sp)	68	71			139	9750		Fredrik LINDGREN	(Swe)	72	72			144	2313
	José COCERES	(Arg)	67	72			139	9750	41	José Manuel CARRILES	(Sp)	74	71			145	1620
8	David HOWELL	(Eng)	66	74			140	7095		John BICKERTON	(Eng)	72	73			145	1620
	Carl SUNESON	(Eng)	74	66			140	7095		Michel BESANCENEY	(Fr)	72	73			145	1620
10	Stephen MCALLISTER	(Scot)	72	69			141	5220		David WILLIAMS	(Eng)	70	75			145	1620
	José RIVERO	(Sp)	69	72			141	5220		Peter MITCHELL	(Eng)	74	71			145	1620
	Eduardo ROMERO	(Arg)	71	70			141	5220		Max ANGLERT	(Swe)	75	70			145	1620
	Miguel Angel MARTIN	(Sp)	71	70			141	5220		John MELLOR	(Eng)	76	69			145	1620
	Richard GREEN	(Aus)	73	68			141	5220		Emanuele CANONICA	(It)	71	74			145	1620
15	Rolf MUNTZ	(Hol)	72	70			142	3851		Stuart CAGE	(Eng)	73	72			145	1620
	David A RUSSELL	(Eng)	72	70			142	3851		Raphael JACQUELIN	(Fr)	74	71			145	1620
	Eric GIRAUD	(Fr)	72	70			142	3851		Andrew OLDCORN	(Scot)	71	74			145	1620
	Peter BAKER	(Eng)	70	72			142	3851		Jose ROZADILLA	(Sp)	72	73			145	1620
	Paul MCGINLEY	(Ire)	72	70			142	3851		Simon HURLEY	(Eng)	70	75			145	1620
	Anders FORSBRAND	(Swe)	74	68			142	3851	54	Oyvind ROJAHN	(Nor)	72	74			146	940
	Pedro LINHART	(Sp)	72	70			142	3851		Miles TUNNICLIFF	(Eng)	72	74			146	940
	Manuel PIÑERO	(Sp)	71	71			142	3851		Paul WAY	(Eng)	73	73			146	940
23	Marcus WILLS	(Wal)	69	74			143	3015		Juan QUIROS	(Sp)	71	75			146	940
	Neal BRIGGS	(Eng)	72	71			143	3015		Glenn RALPH	(Eng)	72	74			146	940
	Mats HALLBERG	(Swe)	70	73			143	3015		David GILFORD	(Eng)	70	76			146	940
	Santiago LUNA	(Sp)	74	69			143	3015		Scott WATSON	(Eng)	69	77			146	940
	Mark PLUMMER	(Eng)	73	70			143	3015		Derrick COOPER	(Eng)	74	72			146	940
	Richard DINSDALE	(Wal)	70	73			143	3015		Richard BOXALL	(Eng)	76	70			146	940
	Patrik SJÖLAND	(Swe)	72	71			143	3015		Mike MCLEAN	(Eng)	73	73			146	940
	Manuel MORENO	(Sp)	74	69			143	3015		Philip WALTON	(Ire)	75	71			146	940
31	Stephen FIELD	(Eng)	70	74			144	2313		Ignacio FELIU	(Sp)	73	73			146	940
	Gary EMERSON	(Eng)	70	74			144	2313									

Attack Life.

GREG NORMAN

Hedblom goes the distance

Recovered from a birthday boxing prank,

Peter Hedblom was the winner

over four rounds in Rabat

Sweden's Peter Hedblom is always game for a laugh but he was deadly serious after finding himself in the lead after the first round of the Moroccan Open championship at the Royal Dar-es-Salam course in Rabat. It was the first time he had led a tournament on the European Tour and he enjoyed the experience so much that he never relinquished the lead and held on grimly for a nerve-tingling one stroke victory, his first win outside Sweden since turning professional in 1988.

Hedblom, 26, delighted a larger-than-usual Press turn-out – Severiano Ballesteros was making his tournament comeback after a five-month sabbatical – with his carefree attitude to golf and to life in general. His leisure activities include the dangerous sports of boxing and ice-hockey and he explained how he was laid low for several weeks at the beginning at the 1995 season with bruised ribs and pneumonia following a bout with the Swedish 60 kilos champion.

'It was my 25th birthday and my friends blindfolded me and took me for a night out,' he said. 'When they took off the blindfold I was in the boxing ring with this Swedish champion. I weighed 85 kilos and was much stronger than him but

he was quick and kept hammering me in the ribs. I knocked him down in the third round, but I think he did it on purpose. The bruised ribs meant I couldn't breathe properly and that led to pneumonia, which put me out of golf for a few weeks.'

Hedblom's road to Morocco included pre-season practice in the indoor nets in his home town of Gavle, where he is coached by his father, because there was

two feet of snow on the ground. 'I came to Rabat not expecting too much and now I've won my first tournament,' said the delighted Swede after collecting the £58,330 first prize.

'This is what I've been practising for since I was a kid, to win on the European Tour. This means everything to me because I've been playing golf since I was six years old and I've spent my whole life dreaming about this moment.'

The Moroccan Open was due to be played at the Royal Golf Links in Agadir but following months of heavy rain was switched at short notice to the 7,362-yard Royal Dar-es-Salam course, which played to its full length and suited Hedblom's powerful hitting.

After an opening 68 to edge one shot clear, and a second round of 67, the strapping Swede led by four shots from Welshman Phillip Price and 1995 Volvo Masters champion Alexander Cejka, and he was still four ahead of the field despite a third round 74.

An outward 35 in the final round which included three birdies and two bogeys kept Hedblom in the driving seat, but with experienced hands Eduardo Romero, Wayne Westner, Santiago Luna,

Ian Woosnam and Tony Johnstone, all tournament winners, breathing down his neck, the nerves were bound to set in. Hedblom dropped a shot at the 206-yard 14th but he showed his mettle on the next two holes when he drove into trees at the 15th and into a fairway bunker at the 16th. Each time, though, he saved par with excellent chipping and putting and demonstrated he has the bottle for the big

occasion. He held on to win by a shot from Romero and declared: 'I played the last round under pressure and I think I handled it pretty well. A place in the Ryder Cup team is now a definite target.'

Ballesteros, the Johnnie Walker Ryder Cup captain, would have been greatly impressed by the manner in which Hedblom secured his maiden European Tour win. Alas, the charismatic Spaniard

had departed Rabat after two rounds, much to the disappointment of Moroccan golf fans and the international Press, after missing the halfway cut.

The sixth Moroccan Open saw the cream rise to the top and the seven players immediately behind Hedblom had amassed between them 88 tournament victories world-wide, which made the Swede's achievement even more reward-

53

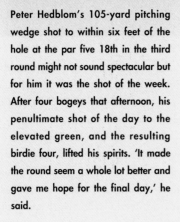

Seve Ballesteros (top) in trouble, while Angel Cabrera (above) makes a splash.

Peter Hedblom's 105-yard pitching wedge shot to within six feet of the hole at the par five 18th in the third round might not sound spectacular but for him it was the shot of the week. After four bogeys that afternoon, his penultimate shot of the day to the elevated green, and the resulting birdie four, lifted his spirits. 'It made the round seem a whole lot better and gave me hope for the final day,' he said.

ing. Six of those seven were in contention at some stage during the final two rounds.

But while the champions were picking up the big cheques, several new European Tour cardholders were making their presence felt. Ten graduates of either the 1995 Challenge Tour or the final Qualifying School, some of them making their first appearances of the season, finished in the top 30. And of those ten, seven had benefited from the pre-season Apollo Week

training school at San Roque, in Spain.

The best of them in joint ninth place were Frenchman Tim Planchin, second to Thomas Bjorn in the 1995 Challenge Tour ranking, and Qualifying School card winners Miles Tunnicliff and former Walker Cup international Raymond Russell. They each won £6,582 and qualified automatically for places in the following week's Dubai Desert Classic.

Richard Dodd

ROYAL GOLF RABAT, DAR-ES-SALAM, MARCH 7-10, 1996 • YARDAGE 7362 • PAR 72

Pos	Name	Country	Rnd 1	Rnd 2	Rnd 3	Rnd 4	Total	Prize Money £
1	Peter HEDBLOM	(Swe)	68	67	74	72	281	58330
2	Eduardo ROMERO	(Arg)	72	74	67	69	282	38880
3	Wayne WESTNER	(SA)	71	72	72	68	283	19705
	Santiago LUNA	(Sp)	73	69	72	69	283	19705
5	Costantino ROCCA	(It)	70	75	69	72	286	12526
	Ian WOOSNAM	(Wal)	72	73	71	70	286	12526
	Tony JOHNSTONE	(Zim)	70	73	70	73	286	12526
8	Mathias GRÖNBERG	(Swe)	75	70	72	71	288	8750
9	Stephen AMES	(T&T)	75	70	75	69	289	6582
	Miles TUNNICLIFF	(Eng)	71	72	74	72	289	6582
	Tim PLANCHIN	(Fr)	74	69	72	74	289	6582
	Peter MITCHELL	(Eng)	71	72	71	75	289	6582
	Raymond RUSSELL	(Scot)	69	74	70	76	289	6582
14	David A RUSSELL	(Eng)	74	71	70	75	290	4742
	Andrew COLLISON	(Eng)	72	72	74	72	290	4742
	John MCHENRY	(Ire)	70	73	72	75	290	4742
	Retief GOOSEN	(SA)	71	72	74	73	290	4742
	José Maria CAÑIZARES	(Sp)	75	73	69	73	290	4742
	Francis HOWLEY	(Ire)	72	74	74	70	290	4742
	Per NYMAN	(Swe)	73	73	72	72	290	4742
21	Jamie SPENCE	(Eng)	75	73	72	71	291	4042
	Russell CLAYDON	(Eng)	72	74	74	71	291	4042
23	Mark MOULAND	(Wal)	71	73	76	72	292	3465
	Rolf MUNTZ	(Hol)	74	74	71	73	292	3465
	Angel CABRERA	(Arg)	77	72	70	73	292	3465
	Alexander CEJKA	(Ger)	70	71	78	73	292	3465
	Silvio GRAPPASONNI	(It)	72	73	70	77	292	3465
	Anders HANSEN	(Den)	76	72	70	74	292	3465
	Padraig HARRINGTON	(Ire)	72	71	73	76	292	3465
	Niclas FASTH	(Swe)	74	74	75	69	292	3465
	Ian PALMER	(SA)	75	74	71	72	292	3465
32	Gordon BRAND JNR.	(Scot)	74	75	72	72	293	2800
	Steven RICHARDSON	(Eng)	73	76	70	74	293	2800
	Paul AFFLECK	(Wal)	75	69	75	74	293	2800
	Juan Carlos PIÑERO	(Sp)	75	72	72	74	293	2800
	Darren CLARKE	(N.Ire)	72	73	73	75	293	2800
37	Olle KARLSSON	(Swe)	75	74	71	74	294	2380
	Mark JAMES	(Eng)	75	72	76	71	294	2380
	Bob MAY	(USA)	73	74	73	74	294	2380
	Heinz P THÜL	(Ger)	75	70	75	74	294	2380
	Diego BORREGO	(Sp)	77	70	70	77	294	2380
	Thomas GÖGELE	(Ger)	74	75	73	72	294	2380
	Michel BESANCENEY	(Fr)	72	71	75	76	294	2380
44	Michael ARCHER	(Eng)	75	74	74	72	295	2100
45	Sam TORRANCE	(Scot)	73	73	74	76	296	1925
	José COCERES	(Arg)	70	77	75	74	296	1925
	Alberto BINAGHI	(It)	76	70	80	70	296	1925
	Liam WHITE	(Eng)	74	74	77	71	296	1925
49	Greg CHALMERS	(Aus)	74	74	74	75	297	1540
	Nicolas VANHOOTEGEM	(Bel)	75	72	74	76	297	1540
	Anders FORSBRAND	(Swe)	71	74	74	78	297	1540
	Philip WALTON	(Ire)	73	74	75	75	297	1540
	David J RUSSELL	(Eng)	72	74	73	78	297	1540
	John MELLOR	(Eng)	74	73	71	79	297	1540
	Steven BOTTOMLEY	(Eng)	72	72	75	78	297	1540
56	Scott WATSON	(Eng)	74	73	77	74	298	1141
	Brenden PAPPAS	(SA)	73	74	74	77	298	1141
	Paul R SIMPSON	(Eng)	72	75	76	75	298	1141
	Phillip PRICE	(Wal)	71	68	76	83	298	1141
	Eric GIRAUD	(Fr)	73	74	79	72	298	1141
61	Per HAUGSRUD	(Nor)	73	76	78	72	299	980
	Mohamed MAKROUNE	(Mor)	75	73	76	75	299	980
	Neal BRIGGS	(Eng)	73	75	79	72	299	980
64	Thomas BJORN	(Den)	76	71	73	80	300	645
	Marcus WILLS	(Wal)	74	75	74	77	300	645
	Gavin LEVENSON	(SA)	73	76	76	75	300	645
	Robert COLES	(Eng)	70	76	78	76	300	645
	Joakim GRÖNHAGEN	(Swe)	69	78	75	78	300	645
	Stephen GALLACHER	(Scot)	74	75	74	77	300	645
70	Marc FARRY	(Fr)	69	75	79	78	301	517
71	Brian MARCHBANK	(Scot)	74	75	79	74	302	515
72	Gordon J BRAND	(Eng)	73	73	75	83	304	513

THE COURSE

Dar-es-Salam means 'House of Peace' and this 45-hole complex on the outskirts of the Moroccan capital of Rabat is as beautiful as it is peaceful. Designed by Robert Trent Jones and opened for play in 1971, the 7,362 – yard Red Course abounds with the colours of exotic trees and flowers – silver cork oaks, cypress, palm, eucalyptus, mimosa, roses, hyacinths, water lilies and narcissus. The competing professionals agreed it was one of the finest venues of the 1996 European Tour season.

Montgomerie returns in style

After a prolonged winter break,
Colin Montgomerie started his season
in the best possible way

He had not played a tournament round for three months, but it was as if he had never been away.

Colin Montgomerie began his 1996 campaign as he had ended the last three, dominating his rivals with familiar authority to win Dubai's Desert Classic at the Emirates Club. Although four rounds under 70 showed that the quality of his strokeplay had in no way diminished, it was a much leaner Montgomerie who emerged from his winter break, looking a picture of health.

Lighter by some 30lb (13 kilos) and with a waistline reduced from 40 to 36 inches the new-look European number one revealed he had not been idle during his holiday from golf and had set out to reduce his weight while awaiting the birth of his second daughter. The Scot had turned the garage of his Surrey home into a gymnasium stocked with state-of-the-art fitness aids, and after taking professional advice on the appropriate exercises and diet, had set out to add true fitness to his talent. 'I wasn't happy with my image but now I feel much more comfortable with myself and confident about my appearance,' he said. It was mostly leg work but the streamlining of his upper body bulk had an immediate benefit in that he found he was able to get the club a little higher on the backswing, and consequently improve his iron shots.

Montgomerie clearly had designs on that long-awaited first major success, and the initial results were highly encouraging as he produced a triumphant 18 under par total of 270 to beat off the determined challenge of Miguel Angel Jiménez and secure his tenth Tour victory. But the Malaga professional has a special liking for the Gulf's premier golf oasis, and gave Montgomerie a good run before the Scot secured the most money with a memorable shot at the 72nd hole.

Jiménez began with a career-best 63 to take command of a field that included

dence once he had dispelled his apprehension with a birdie at his first hole. He followed with a 68 that featured a hat-trick of birdies from the third, and as on the first day his only bogey was the result of three putts. 'I have exceeded my expectations in getting into contention so quickly, so I might as well go for the win,' he declared.

Meanwhile South African Roger Wessels had already removed one jackpot by aceing the 178-yard seventh to win a cash prize of 100,000 dirhams (£18,000). There was no such luck for Argentinian José Coceres who had a hole-in-one at the fourth in the first round, or Sweden's Peter Hedblom, the new Moroccan Open champion, who aced the 15th on the second day. Despite their marksmanship both were victims of the cut that fell at one under par.

Jiménez still led after 54 holes but his advantage over Montgomerie had been whittled down to one because of the Spaniard's double-bogey seven at the

nine of Europe's victorious Ryder Cup by Johnnie Walker team as well as American Fred Couples, the defending champion. The Spaniard had nine birdies and took his total to 16 in 36 holes by adding a 68 the next day for a four-shot advantage over Montgomerie and American Jay Townsend, who had celebrated his 34th birthday with a 64.

Montgomerie had begun with a 67 that oozed confi-

First round leader Miguel Angel Jiménez (above). Steve Webster (right) in sylvan setting.

Three aces ensured there was no shortage of candidates, but the master stroke was played by Colin Montgomerie at the 18th in the last round. Faced with a carry into the wind of 215 yards over water, he used his driver to send his ball soaring over the hazard and close out rival Miguel Angel Jimenez. It was a title-winner from the moment the ball left the clubface.

Per-Ulrik Johansson (top) focuses and Ian Woosnam (above) hedges his bets.

13th where he blocked his three wood second shot into the greenside pond, and put his next into a bunker. His pursuer took advantage with five more birdies in his second 67. 'Situation rosy' remarked Montgomerie despite the threat of Volvo Ranking leader Ian Woosnam who sank a bunker shot for an eagle and had five birdies in a 65 to be on his heels. Ireland's Raymond Burns also had 65 to share third place with a round to go.

Jiménez had held off the formidable Nick Faldo to win his first title in Belgium, but resisting a lean and hungry Montgomerie proved a tougher proposition. He held sway for another six holes but was overtaken when he three-putted the seventh as Montgomerie made his third birdie from ten feet. Then the 13th again proved unlucky for Jiménez as he repeated his third round error, this time hitting the rocky rim of the pond and seeing his ball rebound across the fairway into a sandy waste.

Although a birdie three at the 14th and a rare Montgomerie error at the next put him back on level terms, Jiménez fatally missed the 16th green from the middle of the fairway and with a one-stroke advantage playing the par five 18th Montgomerie sealed victory with a boldness that underlined his confidence. He struck a driver from the fairway that deposited his ball 15 feet from the flag.

Jiménez could not better the resultant birdie four that gave the Scot a 68 to the Spaniard's 70 and had Montgomerie exclaiming: 'To say I am delighted is an understatement. I could not have asked for a better start and it has made me as full of confidence as I have ever been.'

'It may have been his first tournament of the season but a champion never forgets how to play,' said the admiring Spaniard. Australian Robert Willis, a former golf journalist, was third, just ahead of Couples who shook off the heavy cold that had bothered him all week to close with a 65.

Mike Britten   59

Emirates Golf Club, March 14-17, 1996 • Yardage 7102 • Par 72

Pos	Name	Country	Rnd 1	Rnd 2	Rnd 3	Rnd 4	Total	Prize Money £
1	Colin MONTGOMERIE	(Scot)	67	68	67	68	270	108330
2	Miguel Angel JIMÉNEZ	(Sp)	63	68	70	70	271	72210
3	Robert WILLIS	(Aus)	69	67	70	68	274	40690
4	Fred COUPLES	(USA)	69	69	72	65	275	32500
5	Peter BAKER	(Eng)	71	67	66	72	276	25140
	Raymond BURNS	(N.Ire)	70	68	65	73	276	25140
7	Carl MASON	(Eng)	68	73	70	66	277	15815
	Thomas BJORN	(Den)	70	71	67	69	277	15815
	Ian WOOSNAM	(Wal)	69	69	65	74	277	15815
	Jay TOWNSEND	(USA)	64	71	71	71	277	15815
11	Russell CLAYDON	(Eng)	72	69	69	68	278	10885
	Mark MOULAND	(Wal)	71	69	72	66	278	10885
	Tony JOHNSTONE	(Zim)	71	66	69	72	278	10885
	Joakim HAEGGMAN	(Swe)	68	72	69	69	278	10885
15	Domingo HOSPITAL	(Sp)	69	70	72	68	279	9355
	Stephen AMES	(T&T)	68	72	70	69	279	9355
17	David CARTER	(Eng)	74	68	71	67	280	8406
	Jamie SPENCE	(Eng)	68	68	70	74	280	8406
	Howard CLARK	(Eng)	71	69	70	70	280	8406
20	Eduardo ROMERO	(Arg)	70	70	69	72	281	7410
	Ignacio GARRIDO	(Sp)	67	75	69	70	281	7410
	Peter MITCHELL	(Eng)	71	70	70	70	281	7410
	Mark DAVIS	(Eng)	75	65	70	71	281	7410
	Paul LAWRIE	(Scot)	67	71	73	70	281	7410
25	Niclas FASTH	(Swe)	70	72	72	68	282	6052
	Olle KARLSSON	(Swe)	69	71	69	73	282	6052
	Steven BOTTOMLEY	(Eng)	69	73	70	70	282	6052
	Francisco VALERA	(Sp)	69	71	68	74	282	6052
	Peter FOWLER	(Aus)	74	67	71	70	282	6052
	David GILFORD	(Eng)	68	70	71	73	282	6052
	Paul BROADHURST	(Eng)	69	69	72	72	282	6052
	Gary EVANS	(Eng)	71	71	67	73	282	6052
	Gary EMERSON	(Eng)	72	69	69	72	282	6052
34	Stuart CAGE	(Eng)	70	71	72	70	283	4875
	Gavin LEVENSON	(SA)	72	67	71	73	283	4875
	Barry LANE	(Eng)	70	72	69	72	283	4875
	Wayne RILEY	(Aus)	70	71	70	72	283	4875
	David FEHERTY	(N.Ire)	70	69	73	71	283	4875
	Santiago LUNA	(Sp)	73	69	71	70	283	4875
40	Paul AFFLECK	(Wal)	68	74	70	72	284	3965
	Des SMYTH	(Ire)	71	70	73	70	284	3965
	Phillip PRICE	(Wal)	70	71	68	75	284	3965
	Dean ROBERTSON	(Scot)	70	72	70	72	284	3965
	Andrew OLDCORN	(Scot)	68	71	72	73	284	3965
	Raymond RUSSELL	(Scot)	70	70	74	70	284	3965
	David J RUSSELL	(Eng)	69	73	69	73	284	3965
	Alexander CEJKA	(Ger)	69	73	71	71	284	3965
48	Fabrice TARNAUD	(Fr)	69	69	79	68	285	3185
	Jonathan LOMAS	(Eng)	72	70	72	71	285	3185
	Gordon J BRAND	(Eng)	73	67	72	73	285	3185
	Paul MCGINLEY	(Ire)	69	72	73	71	285	3185
52	Dominique BOULET	(HK)	72	67	73	74	286	2600
	Eamonn DARCY	(Ire)	68	72	73	73	286	2600
	Stephen FIELD	(Eng)	66	73	73	74	286	2600
	Ricky WILLISON	(Eng)	70	72	72	72	286	2600
	Costantino ROCCA	(It)	70	71	66	79	286	2600
57	Andrew COLTART	(Scot)	71	71	74	71	287	2101
	Paul CURRY	(Eng)	69	70	75	73	287	2101
	Mark JAMES	(Eng)	73	69	75	70	287	2101
60	Hendrik BUHRMANN	(SA)	69	70	71	78	288	1950
61	Mats LANNER	(Swe)	71	71	72	75	289	1885
62	Martin GATES	(Eng)	69	72	73	76	290	1755
	Christian CÉVAER	(Fr)	68	72	75	75	290	1755
	Robert KARLSSON	(Swe)	72	70	78	70	290	1755
65	Roger WESSELS	(SA)	70	68	78	75	291	1300
	Fredrik LINDGREN	(Swe)	71	70	78	72	291	1300
67	Seve BALLESTEROS	(Sp)	71	70	74	77	292	972
	Simon HURLEY	(Eng)	69	72	76	75	292	972

THE COURSE

The sumptuous Emirates is now celebrating a new addition to the championship course designed by Karl Litton. An additional nine holes designed by Jeremy Pern and featuring two fresh water lakes, has been added to an existing nine, to provide a second par 72, measuring 7,127 yards.

CELLNET.
THE NET THAT SETS
YOU FREE.

Cellnet is the official supplier of mobile communication services to the PGA European Tour.
Call 0800 21 4000 for details of what Cellnet can do for you.

Riley relishes new lease of life

Wayne Riley broke through last year

for his maiden European Tour victory

and wasted little time in winning again

Wayne Riley, stocky, stubble-shaved and with a dress code that owes more to Crocodile Dundee than Yves St-Laurent, may never have the big fashion houses beating on his front door, but he sure knows how to win at golf.

After 11 years without success in Europe, the 1991 Australian Open Champion showed no fear of failure when Nick Faldo and Colin Montgomerie were snapping at his heels in the 1995 Scottish Open, and that experience of front-running at the highest level stood the 33-year old Surrey-based Sydneyite in good stead against the others vainly trying to catch him the Portuguese Open at Aroeira, a new venue for this historic tournament.

Lined with high pines and looking a cross between Woburn and The Berkshire, this 6,661-yard course won approval from all, though the greens, muddied by a metre of rain since the previous December, ranged from 'frightening' if you had been used to the manicured perfection of Dubai the week before, to 'pretty good' if, like Tour new boy Gary Clark, you had been practising at bleak Pinner Hill.

Designed by Frank Pennink in 1970 and used as a munitions base by the revolutionaries during the 1974 squabbles that set tourism in Portugal back on its heels, Aroeira will host the next two Opens, with the option of two more once a sister course, being designed by Donald Steel, is unveiled in two years.

Riley didn't get the first-day headlines. Those belonged to the weather, a two-hour fog delay meant there was insufficient time left to complete play before nightfall, and to the Swedish player, Klas Eriksson, who birdied nine holes out of 11 to jump into a two-stroke lead with a 63, a score that won him a Johnnie Walker Tour Course Record Award, though he would have to share the booty with Barry Lane, who missed a putt on the 18th to beat it on the final afternoon.

Eriksson, a non-winner on Tour, put it all down to a chat with his father, who told him that when he made one birdie, think two birdies; when you have made two birdies, think three birdies, don't try to play safe, go for it. The word 'bogey' must have got transposed with 'birdie' in the brain programming for the next two days, for

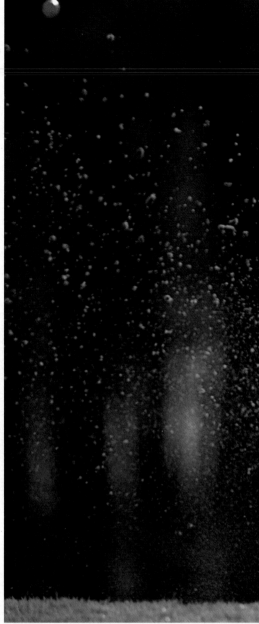

Third round 65 from David Carter (above).

SHOT OF THE WEEK

A toss-up between Riley's five iron pulled round the trees to two feet for an automatic birdie at the seventh hole in round three, or the instinctive pitch from the trees over a bunker to save par at the 13th in the final round and stop the bleeding just when it looked as if things were getting away from him.

young Klas was ten shots worse each time until recovering on the last day to share seventh position.

Riley, who had been Eriksson's main challenger after a 65 on day one, took control as the Swede faded. He opened up a three-shot lead over José Coceres by adding a 67 on day two, and was never headed thereafter. With 11 birdies and a eagle in his first 36 holes, the Australian, who had decided to play only four days earlier, showed just what might have been achieved if Portugal had enjoyed a normal winter and the greens had been up to their normal standard. After that, Riley, a paid-up member at the Surrey club, Camberley Heath, played only as well as he had to.

Only Martin Gates and Mark Davis were able to mount any sort of a charge over the final 36 holes. Midway through round three, Riley had extended his lead to a seemingly insurmountable seven shots, but a double-bogey at the tenth stopped him in his tracks and by Saturday night we still had a golf tournament, with Gates and a second Swede, Olle Karlsson now within two of the lead. They had thrown in a 65 and 66 respectively as Riley struggled, but their catch-up efforts looked doomed to frustration as 18 millimetres of rain brought out the waterhogs

on a bizarre Sunday morning of thunder and lightning.

Dozens of players shook Riley by the hand when it looked as if there was no chance of further play, but the groundstaff did a magnificent job, play resumed, a worthy winner was found by 7pm, and most players, officials and pressmen even managed to weave their way through the Lisbon traffic in time to get their 8.15pm flight. 'I didn't want to win over the short route,' said Riley. 'In our profession, national championships are decided over 72 holes. It is always remembered when you win over three, or two, rounds.'

After the thunder came the wonderful

third before in five years on Tour, missing a tiny putt on the 16th that would have closed the gap to one, and Essex man Davis, twice a winner in Austria, must have got his countries confused as he raced into contention with a 66-67 finish. But his effort broke down on the 72nd hole when, searching for the birdie that would have given him a play-off, he found sand to the right of the green, and had still not reached the putting surface after his third shot. That gave Riley the luxury of having five shots for his second victory in Europe – he needed only four of them.

As he said the day before: 'It's no use worrying what other people are shooting. It's me against the golf course. There's only two things that can happen – you can win or you can lose.' This was one he won, almost a carbon copy of his lead-from-the-front victory at Carnoustie the previous July. Now he would like to win the Open (of course) and 20 or 30 other tournaments before he hangs up his golf gloves.

Outside Riley's victory march, the highspot of the final day was Lane's record-equalling 63 that hoisted him from the supporting cast to a share of fourth spot with Joakim Haeggman. Like Eriksson, he bagged nine birdies in an 11 hole golden spell. 'I just got in the zone,' he explained. 'I missed from four feet, two feet and eight feet as well, and could have played the last 13 holes in 14 under par!'

Lane's day but Riley's week. For the winner of the Open Championships of New Zealand, Australia, Scotland and now Portugal, Wayne's world gets bigger year by year.

Jeremy Chapman

Joint runner-up Martin Gates (above).
Barry Lane (left) stormed home in final round.

sunshine to round off the week as the locals would have wished it. Riley, having had his lead cut to just one, responded with an eagle on the ninth and a chip-and-putt birdie at the tenth, also a par five.

But it wasn't all over yet. In sight of the winning post, the Australian started to stumble, bogeying the 12th and 16th, failing to birdie the par five 15th, and generally looking like an accident waiting to happen. Sadly for them, Gates and Davis had problems of their own, the former, who had never finished higher than

AROEIRA, LISBON, MARCH 21-24, 1996 · YARDAGE 6661 · PAR 71

Pos	Name	Country	Rnd 1	Rnd 2	Rnd 3	Rnd 4	Total	Prize Money £		Pos	Name	Country	Rnd 1	Rnd 2	Rnd 3	Rnd 4	Total	Prize Money £
1	Wayne RILEY	(Aus)	65	67	69	70	271	54160		39	Rolf MUNTZ	(Hol)	69	75	69	71	284	2117
2	Mark DAVIS	(Eng)	72	68	66	67	273	28225			Paul AFFLECK	(Wal)	70	74	70	70	284	2117
	Martin GATES	(Eng)	68	70	65	70	273	28225			Gary ORR	(Scot)	74	69	71	70	284	2117
4	Barry LANE	(Eng)	70	71	71	63	275	15007			Jim PAYNE	(Eng)	69	74	69	72	284	2117
	Joakim HAEGGMAN	(Swe)	67	72	68	68	275	15007			Andrew COLTART	(Scot)	70	72	69	73	284	2117
6	José COCERES	(Arg)	67	68	71	70	276	11375			Jay TOWNSEND	(USA)	69	68	72	75	284	2117
7	Klas ERIKSSON	(Swe)	63	73	73	68	277	7522		45	Retief GOOSEN	(SA)	72	72	69	72	285	1695
	Jamie SPENCE	(Eng)	72	66	71	68	277	7522			Padraig HARRINGTON	(Ire)	72	69	72	72	285	1695
	Jean VAN DE VELDE	(Fr)	74	65	70	68	277	7522			Christian CÉVAER	(Fr)	70	73	71	71	285	1695
	José RIVERO	(Sp)	71	68	69	69	277	7522			Carl MASON	(Eng)	74	70	71	70	285	1695
	Miles TUNNICLIFF	(Eng)	75	66	67	69	277	7522			Per NYMAN	(Swe)	72	68	75	70	285	1695
12	Marcus WILLS	(Wal)	73	69	69	67	278	5410			Daniel SILVA	(Port)	67	74	71	73	285	1695
	Andrew SHERBORNE	(Eng)	72	69	69	68	278	5410			Santiago LUNA	(Sp)	71	72	69	73	285	1695
14	Ricky WILLISON	(Eng)	66	73	71	69	279	4775		52	Francis HOWLEY	(Ire)	72	70	71	73	286	1370
	Des SMYTH	(Ire)	68	73	68	70	279	4775			Angel CABRERA	(Arg)	71	72	72	71	286	1370
	Neal BRIGGS	(Eng)	72	69	68	70	279	4775			Fredrik LINDGREN	(Swe)	68	72	77	69	286	1370
17	Paul LAWRIE	(Scot)	72	69	70	69	280	4126		55	Gary CLARK	(Eng)	73	71	71	72	287	1116
	Miguel Angel JIMÉNEZ	(Sp)	71	71	68	70	280	4126			Paul MCGINLEY	(Ire)	75	69	72	71	287	1116
	Michael JONZON	(Swe)	72	72	65	71	280	4126			Mike MCLEAN	(Eng)	68	73	75	71	287	1116
	Olle KARLSSON	(Swe)	68	69	66	77	280	4126			Richard DINSDALE	(Wal)	70	70	76	71	287	1116
21	Steven BOTTOMLEY	(Eng)	71	73	69	68	281	3550			Patrik SJÖLAND	(Swe)	68	72	76	71	287	1116
	Raymond RUSSELL	(Scot)	74	69	70	68	281	3550		60	Richard BOXALL	(Eng)	70	72	72	74	288	915
	Russell CLAYDON	(Eng)	66	72	73	70	281	3550			Lee WESTWOOD	(Eng)	70	71	74	73	288	915
	Gary EMERSON	(Eng)	73	70	68	70	281	3550			John BICKERTON	(Eng)	72	71	73	72	288	915
	Pedro LINHART	(Sp)	68	72	70	71	281	3550			Mathias GRÖNBERG	(Swe)	68	73	71	76	288	915
	Diego BORREGO	(Sp)	67	71	70	73	281	3550			Thomas GÖGELE	(Ger)	69	70	72	77	288	915
27	Mark MOULAND	(Wal)	75	69	72	66	282	2915		65	Per HAUGSRUD	(Nor)	67	70	76	76	289	570
	Peter MITCHELL	(Eng)	71	72	69	70	282	2915			Hendrik BUHRMANN	(SA)	71	71	72	75	289	570
	Paul WAY	(Eng)	72	70	69	71	282	2915			Ross DRUMMOND	(Scot)	71	70	76	72	289	570
	David FEHERTY	(N.Ire)	70	69	71	72	282	2915			Andrew COLLISON	(Eng)	72	69	76	72	289	570
	Stuart CAGE	(Eng)	71	70	69	72	282	2915		69	Stephen GALLACHER	(Scot)	72	70	71	77	290	479
	Greg CHALMERS	(Aus)	69	70	70	73	282	2915			Peter BAKER	(Eng)	71	69	73	77	290	479
	David CARTER	(Eng)	71	71	65	75	282	2915			Stephen FIELD	(Eng)	73	70	71	76	290	479
34	Jarmo SANDELIN	(Swe)	72	72	70	69	283	2475		72	Dean ROBERTSON	(Scot)	70	72	72	77	291	474
	Mark ROE	(Eng)	70	70	71	72	283	2475			Chris HALL	(Eng)	70	74	71	76	291	474
	Per-Ulrik JOHANSSON	(Swe)	71	70	70	72	283	2475		74	Fernando ROCA	(Sp)	76	68	72	76	292	470
	Tony JOHNSTONE	(Zim)	69	72	70	72	283	2475			Stephen MCALLISTER	(Scot)	71	73	74	74	292	470
	Alexander CEJKA	(Ger)	72	71	67	73	283	2475		76	Iain PYMAN	(Eng)	71	73	75	75	294	467
										77	Ronan RAFFERTY	(N.Ire)	68	76	73	78	295	465
										78	Michel BESANCENEY	(Fr)	68	73	79	77	297	463

THE COURSE

Short at 6,661 yards but tight with encroaching pines that demanded great accuracy. Best hole is the 15th, 505 yards with a lake down the left to grab the greedy second shot and a huge bunker on the right for those who chicken out of the challenge. Excellent fairways and a great credit to the Portuguese after Europe's bad winter.

THE POWER
OF RECOGNITION

Tiffany's Corporate Division offers an array of unforgettable presentation pieces in sterling silver, crystal and gold.

A Tiffany corporate sales professional can help you commemorate outstanding achievements

with exclusive Tiffany designs that will be cherished and proudly displayed. To receive a brochure or learn more

about the rewards of a Tiffany corporate account, call 0171 408 2271.

TIFFANY & CO.

Since 1837

LONDON, 25 OLD BOND STREET W1. 0171-408 2271

Sandelin throttles back to win

Jarmo Sandelin discarded his extra-long driver
and kept the ball in play to record the second
European Tour victory of his career

Jarmo Sandelin went to extraordinary lengths to make a name for himself in 1995. He used a 52-inch 'broomhandle' driver, irons three inches longer than standard, and carried four wedges in his bag to win more than £200,000 and be voted the Sir Henry Cotton Rookie of the Year. He then went on to capture a card at the US Tour school.

Along the way the tall Swede also gained a reputation for zany hitting that often saw him in 'jungle country' rather than on the closely mown grass coveted by the vast majority of professionals.

Yet all that had changed by the time Sandelin had begun his 1996 European Tour campaign in Portugal and arrived at the Madeira Island Open. Macho Jarmo had by then undergone the tough baptism of a spring foray on the US Tour where he made only one cut in six events. The principal lessons he learned was that a big drive and a wedge is not the only way to harvest a birdie, and that discretion is more likely to pay better dividends than daredevil aggression.

Accordingly the 52-inch driver – eight inches longer than standard – had been left out of his golf bag, which was now being fetchingly carried by his girl friend Linda, a nine-handicapper dedicated to the softly-softly approach.

Sandelin's first outing was a 'quiet' 72 and although he followed with 67 to take fourth place at the halfway stage it was a blend of youth and experience in the form of Daniel Chopra and Andrew Oldcorn who were making the early running. Chopra is also Swedish, born in Stockholm, but has an Indian father and was brought up in Delhi where he started playing at the age of eight. A former World Junior champion, he was second on the 1995 Asian circuit before winning his European Tour card. Two eagles in a second round 66 gave him a two-shot lead over Edinburgh's Oldcorn, a former English amateur champion, who is now qualified to play for Scotland. He had an eagle and nine birdies in a 65 he described as 'the most extraordinary round of my life.' 'I felt I could hole anything and it is not often you have that many birdies and feel you have left four shots on the course,' he said.

Sadly the magic soon departed and though Oldcorn added a 71 he closed with 75 to slip to 12th. Chopra on the other hand shot 70 and began the last day holding a three-shot advantage over the Anglo-Scot. Just behind were Spain's Ignacio Garrido and newcomer David Howell, a member of the previous year's victorious Walker Cup team. Sandelin was a further stroke back alongside Stephen McAllister, Phil Golding and Mark Davis,

but only three strokes covered the next 20 players. It was still anybody's title. However, few anticipated just how slippery the climb to the top of the final leaderboard can be, especially at Santo da Serra's heart-pumping 18th.

It measures only 349 yards but it proved heartbreak hill for at least five

players who thought they were likely winners when they stood over birdie putts on the last green. Chopra had gone into a five-stroke lead after almost sinking his second shot at the par five second, but four to get down just short of the innocuous third sent the 22-year old sliding to a 76, and attention switched elsewhere.

For a long time it centred on Irishman Des Smyth who had five birdies in a row in an outward 30 to share the lead at ten under par. Then Howell reached the same mark before slipping back. With no one

efforts on the super-slick upper level, sped downgrain, downslope, and down to the front of the green 15 yards away.

Sandelin admitted he would have followed suit but for experiencing at first

Des Smyth (above) challenged for the title. Patrick Sjöland (below) despairs after a putt.

able to forge a clear lead it looked increasingly likely that the outcome would not be settled until the very last putt.

One by one the contenders trekked up the steep incline to the last green then gasped at a flagstick sited just over the ridge of the two-tier putting surface. Paul Affleck's only blemish in a best of the day 66 for 280 came there when he three-putted to sympathetic applause from the gallery. That was nothing to what followed as one by one the contenders went too boldly for victory.

First Patrik Sjöland five-putted in search of a birdie, then in rapid succession Spaniard Carl Sunesson, Smyth, and David J Russell four-putted as their first

hand the perils of attempting anything more ambitious than merely setting the ball in motion. He went to school on partner McAllister's four-putt misfortune and succeeded in leaving himself a 12-inch uphill tap-in which he thankfully converted to add this title to the Open de Canaries he won in his rookie year.

'I could not have hit my putt more slowly, but I was still praying for it to stop,' said Sandelin, who credited this second victory to his new-found patience. 'I am happier now to make a birdie with a four iron and a seven iron rather than the big stick and a wedge,' he said after his nine under par 279 gave him a one stroke margin over Affleck. Smyth, Russell, Peter Mitchell and David Carter were joint third.

Mike Britten

CAMPO DE GOLFE DA MADEIRA, MARCH 28-31, 1996 • YARDAGE 6606 • PAR 72

Pos	Name	Country	Rnd 1	Rnd 2	Rnd 3	Rnd 4	Total	Prize Money £
1	Jarmo SANDELIN	(Swe)	72	67	71	69	279	50000
2	Paul AFFLECK	(Wal)	72	69	73	66	280	33330
3	David CARTER	(Eng)	71	75	68	67	281	13196
	Des SMYTH	(Ire)	73	71	68	69	281	13196
	Peter MITCHELL	(Eng)	72	66	73	70	281	13196
	David J RUSSELL	(Eng)	73	69	69	70	281	13196
	Daniel CHOPRA	(Swe)	69	66	70	76	281	13196
8	Iain PYMAN	(Eng)	71	74	71	66	282	6427
	Carl SUNESON	(Sp)	71	70	70	71	282	6427
	Diego BORREGO	(Sp)	74	67	70	71	282	6427
	Phil GOLDING	(Eng)	69	71	70	72	282	6427
12	Peter FOWLER	(Aus)	72	72	72	67	283	4448
	Jean VAN DE VELDE	(Fr)	69	71	74	69	283	4448
	Patrik SJÖLAND	(Swe)	72	68	72	71	283	4448
	Thomas GÖGELE	(Ger)	70	70	71	72	283	4448
	Ignacio GARRIDO	(Sp)	70	70	69	74	283	4448
	David HOWELL	(Eng)	71	69	69	74	283	4448
	Andrew OLDCORN	(Scot)	72	65	71	75	283	4448
19	Raymond RUSSELL	(Scot)	71	74	73	66	284	3610
	Bob MAY	(USA)	73	72	70	69	284	3610
	Stephen AMES	(T&T)	72	69	73	70	284	3610
22	Vanslow PHILLIPS	(Eng)	72	74	69	70	285	3285
	Jim PAYNE	(Eng)	70	71	73	71	285	3285
	Andrew SHERBORNE	(Eng)	72	69	71	73	285	3285
	José COCERES	(Arg)	71	73	68	73	285	3285
26	Scott WATSON	(Eng)	70	73	73	70	286	2970
	Fernando ROCA	(Sp)	75	70	72	69	286	2970
	Stephen MCALLISTER	(Scot)	73	67	70	76	286	2970
29	David A RUSSELL	(Eng)	74	69	72	72	287	2616
	David WILLIAMS	(Eng)	70	75	70	72	287	2616
	Russell CLAYDON	(Eng)	72	70	72	73	287	2616
	Ross MCFARLANE	(Eng)	68	74	70	75	287	2616
	Mark DAVIS	(Eng)	72	68	70	77	287	2616
34	Juan Carlos PIÑERO	(Sp)	72	72	72	72	288	2280
	José Maria CAÑIZARES	(Sp)	69	76	72	71	288	2280
	John HAWKSWORTH	(Eng)	69	75	74	70	288	2280
	Ricky WILLISON	(Eng)	75	69	71	73	288	2280
	Paul LAWRIE	(Scot)	71	74	70	73	288	2280
39	Manuel PIÑERO	(Sp)	73	72	71	73	289	1950
	Rolf MUNTZ	(Hol)	75	71	71	72	289	1950
	Andrew COLLISON	(Eng)	76	70	75	68	289	1950
	Ove SELLBERG	(Swe)	72	73	70	74	289	1950
	Santiago LUNA	(Sp)	72	74	69	74	289	1950
	Pedro LINHART	(Sp)	74	71	69	75	289	1950
45	Steven BOTTOMLEY	(Eng)	75	70	72	73	290	1680
	José GARCIA	(Sp)	70	76	72	72	290	1680
	David RAY	(Eng)	73	70	70	77	290	1680
48	John MCHENRY	(Ire)	70	73	73	75	291	1470
	Paul WAY	(Eng)	71	69	77	74	291	1470
	Padraig HARRINGTON	(Ire)	71	73	70	77	291	1470
	Brian MARCHBANK	(Scot)	74	71	66	80	291	1470
52	Paul LYONS	(Eng)	68	72	76	76	292	1260
	Dean ROBERTSON	(Scot)	74	70	73	75	292	1260
	Anders HAGLUND	(Swe)	70	73	77	72	292	1260
55	Steen TINNING	(Den)	74	71	72	76	293	1050
	Michel BESANCENEY	(Fr)	70	72	76	75	293	1050
	Michael ARCHER	(Eng)	73	69	76	75	293	1050
	Mark PULLAN	(Eng)	73	72	75	73	293	1050
59	Glenn RALPH	(Eng)	71	72	73	78	294	885
	Fabrice TARNAUD	(Fr)	73	72	72	77	294	885
	António SOBRINHO	(Port)	72	74	72	76	294	885
	Raphaël JACQUELIN	(Fr)	71	75	73	75	294	885
63	Stephen GALLACHER	(Scot)	69	74	80	72	295	810
64	René BUDDE	(Den)	73	72	73	78	296	765
	Paul BROADHURST	(Eng)	73	72	75	76	296	765
66	Chris HALL	(Eng)	73	73	76	75	297	450
67	Peter HEDBLOM	(Swe)	75	71	72	80	298	446
	Tim PLANCHIN	(Fr)	75	70	75	78	298	446
	Adam HUNTER	(Scot)	71	75	76	76	298	446
70	Philip TALBOT	(Eng)	71	75	74	79	299	442
71	David HIGGINS	(Ire)	71	70	85	76	302	440
72	Christian POST	(Den)	71	74	82	76	303	438

THE COURSE

Santo da Serra, set on a mountainside some 2,000 feet above the capital Funchal, is renowned for its spectacular views, particularly the par five 12th with its card-wrecking deep ravine and clifftop green. But Europe's professionals would now vote the 18th with its steep fairway and lightning fast two-tier green as 'the beast' amid all the beauty.

Russell leads youthful charge

Raymond Russell edged out David Carter in the battle of the youngbloods in Cannes

Time was when a young man coming into tournament golf would have to serve his apprenticeship before he would be allowed to go out and play with the big boys. No more. Youthful winners are becoming the rule rather than the exception on today's European Tour, and Raymond Russell's victory in the Air France Cannes Open in April was a case in point.

Russell, 23 at the moment of his triumph, was playing in only the ninth tournament of his career on the full Tour and his sixth of the 1996 season. Once upon a time he would not have been considered even remotely qualified to win a tournament, but these days the youngsters are not prepared to be wannabees for a nano-second longer than is strictly necessary. They have the game to succeed, they have the desire to do well, and they have the maturity to achieve their aims.

Thus it was that Russell presented a beguiling mix of youthful confidence, precocious calmness under pressure and,

when it was all over, a typically Scottish lack of emotion upon beating the similarly youthful David Carter into second place by a shot with a closing 71 and a total of 272, 12 under par. Carter, whose 73 left

him two strokes adrift, beat Gordon Brand Junior and Ignacio Garrido by two with Costantino Rocca and Jim Payne joint fifth.

Russell had played only three events on the main Tour until the start of 1996 after turning professional following his appearance in the Walker Cup team in 1993. He had finished 19th in the Tour Qualifying School the previous autumn, and a succession of high-profile events on the horizon meant that at the start of this tournament he was not sure when he would get his next start. Now he could play where and when he liked for two years.

Russell went into the final day leading the tournament on ten under par and was playing with Carter in the last group on the course. Like a world-class miler, he bided his time until the last couple of holes, but when he went for the tape he did it with a surge that was as impressive as it was effortless.

The destination of the winner's cheque for £66,660 was kept in doubt

73

THE COURSE

Royal Mougins is a visual delight. In magnificent condition for the tournament, it features undulating fairways, lots of water and heavily contoured greens that can produce agonisingly huge borrows. Colin Montgomerie putted into the lake by the side of the 18th green in 1995. It is a little surprising that he has been the only man to do so in the two years the Air France Cannes Open has been held at the course.

until the dying moments by Carter, who pushed his opponent nearly every step of the way. Russell, from Prestonpans, near Edinburgh, was level with Carter on ten under par as he stepped on to the 17th tee after going into water and dropping a shot at the 16th, where within minutes he was both cursed by the fates and blessed by

them.

A referee ruled that Russell's ball had crossed the margin of a lake before dropping back into the briny, which meant he could take his penalty drop on the green. From that position he was able to two-putt for a bogey six that could have been much worse.

He had wobbled at times, notably when he dropped four shots to par in four holes from the eighth, but the way he played the last two holes would have done credit to Nick Faldo.

At the penultimate hole, a par three of 139 yards, he watched as Carter suffered an adrenaline surge and planted his ball 40

however – a birdie from Carter on the last would mean a play-off. It was not to be. Carter went into a fairway bunker off the tee and found sand again with his second shot. Russell, meanwhile, played the hole immaculately and finished up eight feet from the flag in three as Carter went 25 feet past, also in three.

It was effectively all over when Carter failed to hole that long bunker shot. Russell had two for the title, and needed only one of them for a closing birdie that was as satisfying as it was irrelevant.

Russell kept a low profile early on in the tournament, Carter did not. After Paul McGinley and Philip Walton had taken the lead on the first day, Carter, born and raised in South Africa of British parents and now attached to the driving range near Chesterfield owned by his father, Bryan, a European Seniors Tour player, produced one of the rounds of the European season in the second day.

A 62, it was by a considerable margin the best round of his life and contained ten birdies and only one bogey. He went into a bunker on the last, and had he holed the shot for an eagle he would have

feet beyond the flag, then put his own tee shot nervelessly to six feet. Carter took two putts for par, and Russell calmly rolled his in for a birdie to take a one-stroke lead.

The tournament was still not over,

Gary Orr explodes in Cannes.

David Carter (above) had to give best to Raymond Russell (right).

been in with 60, a feat performed only seven times in the history of the Tour. The fact that he did not, then missed a curly putt of ten feet coming back, did little to take the gloss off a remarkable performance.

Russell started to make his move on the third day and shared pole position with Carter as the last lap started. Russell slipped, Carter slid, they both recov-ered. It was nip and tuck all the way, and it was not totally clear afterwards whether Russell was being quiet and modest or was merely overwhelmed by what he had just achieved. The result was that if you had not known otherwise, you might have thought Russell had just had his pet rabbit run over. He said he was happy, even if he did not show it. They don't go in for dancing in the streets much in Prestonpans.

Mel Webb

Royal Mougins, April 18-21, 1996 · Yardage 6494 · Par 71

Pos	Name	Country	Rnd 1	Rnd 2	Rnd 3	Rnd 4	Total	Prize Money £
1	Raymond RUSSELL	(Scot)	66	68	67	71	272	66660
2	David CARTER	(Eng)	70	62	69	73	274	44440
3	Ignacio GARRIDO	(Sp)	67	68	75	66	276	22520
	Gordon BRAND JNR.	(Scot)	72	73	63	68	276	22520
5	Costantino ROCCA	(It)	70	66	72	69	277	15470
	Jim PAYNE	(Eng)	73	69	68	67	277	15470
7	Carl SUNESON	(Sp)	73	67	68	70	278	12000
8	Paul BROADHURST	(Eng)	70	73	70	66	279	8232
	Rolf MUNTZ	(Hol)	70	68	72	69	279	8232
	Iain PYMAN	(Eng)	70	72	68	69	279	8232
	Padraig HARRINGTON	(Ire)	68	65	72	74	279	8232
	Olivier EDMOND	(Fr)	71	68	68	72	279	8232
13	David FEHERTY	(N.Ire)	72	71	66	71	280	5896
	Peter HEDBLOM	(Swe)	75	64	70	71	280	5896
	Paul AFFLECK	(Wal)	71	68	68	73	280	5896
	Jean VAN DE VELDE	(Fr)	72	71	66	71	280	5896
	Greg TURNER	(NZ)	71	69	69	71	280	5896
18	Ricky WILLISON	(Eng)	68	73	70	70	281	5060
	Miles TUNNICLIFF	(Eng)	67	72	67	75	281	5060
20	Peter MITCHELL	(Eng)	65	71	71	75	282	4500
	Paul MCGINLEY	(Ire)	65	72	71	74	282	4500
	Fernando ROCA	(Sp)	64	75	75	68	282	4500
	Mike MCLEAN	(Eng)	72	73	68	69	282	4500
	Gary ORR	(Scot)	71	68	75	68	282	4500
	Paul EALES	(Eng)	71	70	72	69	282	4500
26	Barry LANE	(Eng)	70	72	71	70	283	3780
	Stuart CAGE	(Eng)	72	67	71	73	283	3780
	Stephen GALLACHER	(Scot)	76	66	74	67	283	3780
	Marc FARRY	(Fr)	70	69	71	73	283	3780
	Santiago LUNA	(Sp)	75	69	72	67	283	3780
	Jon ROBSON	(Eng)	74	70	73	66	283	3780
32	Mark ROE	(Eng)	71	72	68	73	284	3040
	Philip WALTON	(Ire)	65	78	70	71	284	3040
	Tim PLANCHIN	(Fr)	67	69	72	76	284	3040
	Silvio GRAPPASONNI	(It)	71	70	73	70	284	3040
	Domingo HOSPITAL	(Sp)	68	73	73	70	284	3040
	Darren CLARKE	(N.Ire)	68	75	70	71	284	3040
	Raphaël JACQUELIN	(Fr)	71	72	68	73	284	3040
	Richard DINSDALE	(Wal)	70	68	74	72	284	3040
	Anssi KANKKONEN	(Fin)	70	69	71	74	284	3040
41	Michael JONZON	(Swe)	69	70	72	74	285	2560
	Ignacio FELIU	(Sp)	71	74	70	70	285	2560
	David GILFORD	(Eng)	73	68	72	72	285	2560
44	Peter BAKER	(Eng)	71	72	73	70	286	2320
	Per HAUGSRUD	(Nor)	74	71	69	72	286	2320
	Chris HALL	(Eng)	72	69	69	76	286	2320
47	Dean ROBERTSON	(Scot)	71	74	68	74	287	2000
	Neal BRIGGS	(Eng)	73	69	70	75	287	2000
	Fredrik LINDGREN	(Swe)	74	71	72	70	287	2000
	Greg OWEN	(Eng)	73	70	68	76	287	2000
	Andrew COLLISON	(Eng)	71	73	74	69	287	2000
52	Russell CLAYDON	(Eng)	73	70	69	76	288	1560
	Thomas GÖGELE	(Ger)	72	68	73	75	288	1560
	Jonathan LOMAS	(Eng)	75	68	74	71	288	1560
	Jarmo SANDELIN	(Swe)	70	69	69	80	288	1560
	Angel CABRERA	(Arg)	73	71	71	73	288	1560
	David HOWELL	(Eng)	74	69	72	73	288	1560
58	Lee WESTWOOD	(Eng)	71	72	77	69	289	1240
	David A RUSSELL	(Eng)	72	71	71	75	289	1240
	Anders HAGLUND	(Swe)	75	69	72	73	289	1240
61	Roger CHAPMAN	(Eng)	70	72	75	73	290	1140
	Gary CLARK	(Eng)	71	68	74	77	290	1140
63	Stephen MCALLISTER	(Scot)	73	72	74	72	291	1040
	Wayne RILEY	(Aus)	68	75	78	70	291	1040
	Juan Carlos PIÑERO	(Sp)	71	71	76	73	291	1040
66	Fabrice TARNAUD	(Fr)	78	66	71	77	292	599
	Quentin DABSON	(Fr)	72	73	74	73	292	599
68	Per-Ulrik JOHANSSON	(Swe)	71	74	72	76	293	595
	Per NYMAN	(Swe)	71	70	76	76	293	595
70	Christian POST	(Den)	70	74	75	75	294	592
71	Wayne WESTNER	(SA)	75	69	72	79	295	590

SHOT OF THE WEEK

Raymond Russell, 17th hole, final day. All square with David Carter as the tournament approached its climax, Russell knew that the door had opened a crack when Carter put his tee shot 40 feet beyond the flag on the 139-yard hole. Russell calmly drew an eight iron from his bag, took two practice swings and planted the ball six feet from the flag. The birdie putt that followed put Russell one all-important shot ahead playing the last.

Borrego makes it number five

Diego Borrego became the fifth first-time winner on the 1996 European Tour when he defeated Tony Johnstone in a play-off

*L*egend has it that the village of Casares, which sits high on a hilltop above Spain's Costa del Sol, was founded by Julius Caesar. Two thousand years later another Casares inhabitant laid claim to fame when Diego Borrego, who used to play truant to get in some extra golf practice, achieved his European Tour breakthrough by winning the Turespana Masters Open Comunitat Valenciana Paradores de Turismo.

The tournament, moved at short notice from Borrego's home region of Andalucia to Valencia, was played at El Saler, a course held in high esteem by many Tour veterans. Severiano Ballesteros was on hand for only his third European Tour event of the year but the maestro from Pedrena was short of match practice and rounds of 76 and 73 would leave him five strikes the wrong side of the level par halfway cut.

Borrego opened with a 66 to share the first round lead with Fabrice Tarnaud and Ross McFarlane and on the second day

the 24-year old's 67 put him three ahead of Tony Johnstone and Wayne Riley. 'I have changed.' Borrego explained. 'Before, I was a boy. Now I have grown up. I take life more seriously.' The old hands shook their heads. Borrego had failed to retain his Tour card in 1994 and he was back on Tour thanks to a successful Challenge Tour campaign in 1995.

The sceptics expected Diego to fold under the pressure of playing with the leading group. But they were in for a surprise. Two birdies in the first three holes gave him the perfect start to the third round but then Johnstone mounted a determined challenge which brought him to within a stroke after 12 holes. Borrego birdied the 14th but there was a two-stroke swing as the pressure finally took its toll at the par three 17th. Johnstone's birdie attempt from fully 50 feet disappeared into the hole while Borrego missed from 18 inches and they were level. Said Borrego of his lapse: 'I've only had four bogeys so far. Maybe I'm saving them all up for tomorrow.'

In fact he was to concede three more bogeys during the final round but he countered with six birdies and the talk around EL Saler now was of the poise,

SHOT OF THE WEEK

Jose Manuel Lara, the 18-year old amateur from Valencia, may not have set the leaderboards alight in his 'home' debut on the European Tour but during the third round he produced what was surely the shot of the tournament. His sweetly struck two iron at the 515-yard fifth hole flew straight and true over 230 yards to land on the small green just ten feet from the pin and, to the locals' delight, he stroked home the putt for his eagle three.

coaxed home a birdie putt to take the tournament to extra holes.

In the early stages of the play-off Johnstone had the upper hand but was unable to convert his chances and the tide turned after Borrego scrambled par on the 16th with a brave up and down from the greenside bunker. The third play-off hole would unfold over the dramatic setting of the uphill, 215-yard, par three 17th which faces eastwards towards the sea with a green ringed on three sides by massive sand dunes. Johnstone found the green but he was on the lower platform about 20 yards short of the pin. Borrego also

used a wood into the wind but his ball veered left. 'I thought it would be in the bunker,' he said afterwards, 'and from there I would have had no shot.' But the bunker was cheated and Borrego's ball perched precariously on the fringe above. Now, Johnstone charged his putt 12 feet past the hole and Diego took control as his own effort from 40 feet ran confidently up to the flag. And so it ended, suddenly, as these things do. Johnstone missed and Borrego confidently holed out for his first victory. 'Smile,' said the photographers. 'I can't,' said Diego. 'I'm exhausted.'

Jeff Kelly

maturity and sheer cool nerve of the Aloha-based player. Johnstone's short game, meanwhile, was a joy to behold. 'I'm writing a book on the subject and it's helping me to focus,' he explained, and as early as the sixth hole the 39-year old whose declared intent was 'to win again before my 40th birthday next week' had wrested the lead from Borrego.

The youngster's expression never changed though. He simply gritted his teeth and hit back immediately to birdie the next hole and draw level again. Despite flurries from Peter Baker and Ross McFarlane the tournament had become a two-man contest. At the short ninth Borrego hit a superb tee shot to within four feet, but Johnstone turned up the pressure by holing from 25 feet. Diego's nerve held and his birdie putt found the cup.

The pair turned for home neck and neck but at the 12th, a long par three into the wind, Borrego was dismayed to find his hooked tee shot behind a wind-flattened tree. He cancelled out that lapse at the next hole with a superb wedge approach to eight feet but then, on the 14th, disaster struck for Johnstone who uncharacteristically three-putted while his young opponent was hitting a majestic four iron to six feet and sinking the birdie putt. Borrego kept his nose in front until the 18th where a never-say-die Johnstone

Tony Johnstone bowed out in play-off.

El Saler, Valencia, April 25-28, 1996 • Yardage 6950 • Par 72

Pos	Name	Country	Rnd 1	Rnd 2	Rnd 3	Rnd 4	Total	Prize Money £
1	Diego BORREGO	(Sp)	66	67	69	69	271	83330
2	Tony JOHNSTONE	(Zim)	67	69	66	69	271	55550
3	Peter BAKER	(Eng)	67	70	69	69	275	31300
4	Ross MCFARLANE	(Eng)	66	71	72	67	276	25000
5	Fabrice TARNAUD	(Fr)	66	73	70	68	277	21200
6	Ignacio GARRIDO	(Sp)	69	71	68	70	278	17500
7	Domingo HOSPITAL	(Sp)	72	71	68	68	279	12162
	Stuart CAGE	(Eng)	72	71	67	69	279	12162
	Padraig HARRINGTON	(Ire)	71	72	66	70	279	12162
	Greg TURNER	(NZ)	69	68	68	74	279	12162
11	Roger CHAPMAN	(Eng)	69	73	71	67	280	8606
	Costantino ROCCA	(It)	70	73	69	68	280	8606
	Francis HOWLEY	(Ire)	76	64	71	69	280	8606
14	Robert KARLSSON	(Swe)	71	69	73	68	281	7050
	Des SMYTH	(Ire)	71	71	70	69	281	7050
	Gary NICKLAUS	(USA)	72	69	70	70	281	7050
	Neal BRIGGS	(Eng)	67	73	70	71	281	7050
	Sam TORRANCE	(Scot)	73	68	67	73	281	7050
19	Adam HUNTER	(Scot)	72	71	72	67	282	5937
	Richard BOXALL	(Eng)	74	69	69	70	282	5937
	Francisco CEA	(Sp)	70	69	71	72	282	5937
	Per HAUGSRUD	(Nor)	70	70	70	72	282	5937
23	José COCERES	(Arg)	72	69	72	70	283	5100
	Jim PAYNE	(Eng)	71	72	71	69	283	5100
	Jarmo SANDELIN	(Swe)	74	69	73	67	283	5100
	Andrew SHERBORNE	(Eng)	68	72	72	71	283	5100
	Fredrik LINDGREN	(Swe)	72	68	72	71	283	5100
	Mike MCLEAN	(Eng)	72	70	70	71	283	5100
	Joakim HAEGGMAN	(Swe)	71	70	70	72	283	5100
	Jose Manuel LARA (AM)	(Sp)	76	67	71	69	283	
30	David FEHERTY	(N.Ire)	70	72	71	71	284	3862
	Eamonn DARCY	(Ire)	71	73	70	70	284	3862
	Paul LAWRIE	(Scot)	75	69	70	70	284	3862
	Malcolm MACKENZIE	(Eng)	73	71	70	70	284	3862
	Raymond BURNS	(N.Ire)	68	71	75	70	284	3862
	Peter O'MALLEY	(Aus)	74	69	72	69	284	3862
	Mathias GRÖNBERG	(Swe)	71	72	70	71	284	3862
	Steve WEBSTER	(Eng)	74	69	70	71	284	3862
	Jonathan LOMAS	(Eng)	71	71	70	72	284	3862
	Carl SUNESON	(Sp)	69	71	71	73	284	3862
	Wayne RILEY	(Aus)	69	67	74	74	284	3862
	Raymond RUSSELL	(Scot)	73	70	66	75	284	3862
42	David HOWELL	(Eng)	71	68	75	71	285	2900
	Chris HALL	(Eng)	68	75	72	70	285	2900
	Miguel Angel JIMÉNEZ	(Sp)	74	70	72	69	285	2900
	Olivier EDMOND	(Fr)	74	70	72	69	285	2900
	Santiago LUNA	(Sp)	74	70	69	72	285	2900
	Iain PYMAN	(Eng)	69	70	71	75	285	2900
	Andrew COLTART	(Scot)	71	67	68	79	285	2900
49	Ross DRUMMOND	(Scot)	72	71	72	71	286	2250
	Mark DAVIS	(Eng)	71	73	73	69	286	2250
	Ronan RAFFERTY	(N.Ire)	72	71	75	68	286	2250
	Juan Carlos PIÑERO	(Sp)	71	69	72	74	286	2250
	David CARTER	(Eng)	73	70	69	74	286	2250
	Steven BOTTOMLEY	(Eng)	71	70	69	76	286	2250
55	Olle KARLSSON	(Swe)	68	73	73	73	287	1710
	Angel CABRERA	(Arg)	67	76	73	71	287	1710
	Rolf MUNTZ	(Hol)	76	67	74	70	287	1710
	Robert COLES	(Eng)	70	73	75	69	287	1710
	Martin GATES	(Eng)	71	69	72	75	287	1710
60	Mark MOULAND	(Wal)	75	68	73	72	288	1425
	Wayne WESTNER	(SA)	69	74	74	71	288	1425
	Gary EMERSON	(Eng)	73	69	75	71	288	1425
	Per-Ulrik JOHANSSON	(Swe)	73	71	74	70	288	1425
64	Francisco VALERA	(Sp)	72	70	72	75	289	1275
	Peter HEDBLOM	(Swe)	73	71	71	74	289	1275
66	Mark LITTON	(Wal)	71	69	76	74	290	748
	Michel BESANCENEY	(Fr)	71	72	77	70	290	748
	John MCHENRY	(Ire)	74	70	76	70	290	748
69	Lee WESTWOOD	(Eng)	71	73	72	75	291	744
	Antonio PASTRANA (AM)	(Sp)	70	74	78	69	291	
70	David A RUSSELL	(Eng)	75	68	78	71	292	742

THE COURSE

El Saler, regarded as one of the best courses in Europe, offers an intriguing mix of links and woodland golf with the eighth, ninth, 17th and 18th holes spectacularly framed by dunes and the Mediterranean. Any doubts about the health of the course were soon dispelled as it was in excellent condition and basked regally beneath the warm April sun.

Payne Reliever

Jim Payne's recovery from
a career-threatening back injury
was completed with victory in Italy

*T*he banners proclaiming 'Rocca is a legend' and 'Rocca is best' that festooned the fences around the Albenza Club, Bergamo, underlined the esteem with which Italy's premier golfer is regarded in his native city. And when Rocca duly shot 65 to win the pro-am and opened the Conte of Florence Italian Open on his home course with a five under par 66, it looked as though his legions of supporters were merely stating the obvious.

After all, one of Europe's oldest and most prestigious titles, first contested in 1925, had been brought to the prosperous city some 30 miles north east of Milan solely because of Costantino's achievement in becoming his country's first Ryder Cup representative, and in recognition of his status as the figurehead of Italian golf. As Marco Furbetta, the Bergamo club's vice-president remarked: 'We hosted the Open for all those who have worked so hard around here on behalf of golf, but mostly for Costantino because we love him very much and are very proud of him.'

Rocca, whose father Angelo was a quartz miner, was born in the nearby village of San Bartolomeo, and was a teenage caddie at Albenza where he used to sneak on to the course at dusk to play a few holes. At 18, 'Tino' was given a second hand set of clubs and no longer had to

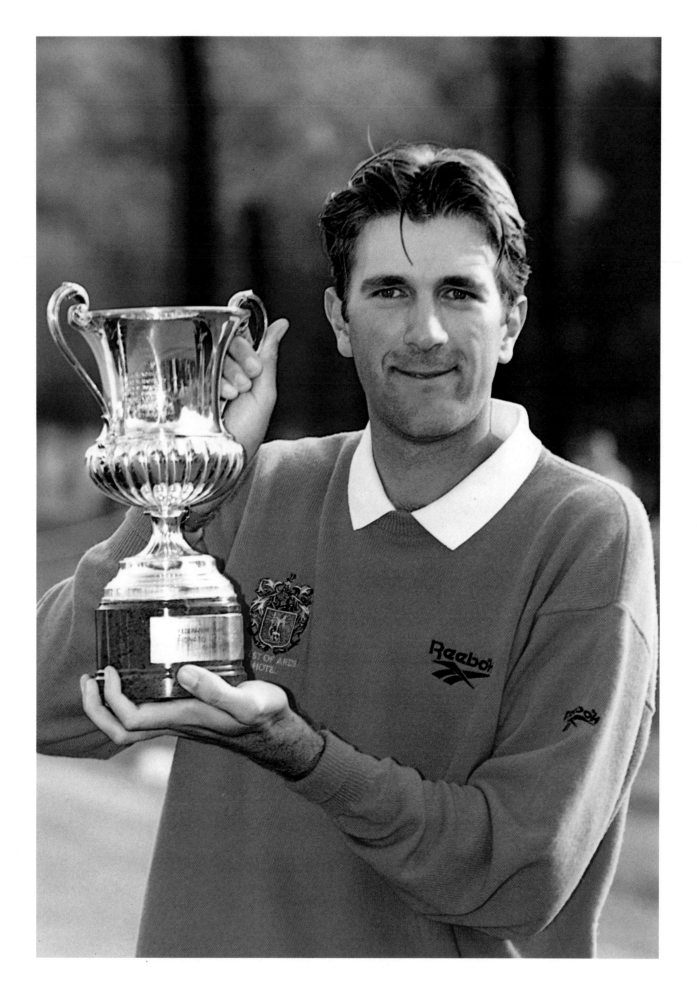

hide from officialdom when he turned to golf during his time off from a local factory where he made polystyrene boxes to help support his widowed mother Maria, sister Rita, and brothers Giuseppe and Alessandro. Then he became the club's caddie-master for two years before setting out to make his name on the European Tour.

He recalled how he carried the bag of Ramon Sota, the uncle of Severiano Ballesteros, when the Radici Open was played at Bergamo in 1972 and was paid seven pounds for his week's work. It was won by a 19-year old Sam Torrance, the first victory of the Scot's career.

The latter's return to the scene of his first glory as defending Italian Open champion was recognised both by the Club, who presented Torrance with a commemorative salver, and Italy's biggest selling sports newspaper La Gazzetta dello sport, which billed the contest between the 1995 Ryder Cup partners as 'Il duello stallare', the duel of the stars.

Home town hero Costantino Rocca.

But Jim Payne, the Lincolnshire lad tipped by Jack Nicklaus to have a great future in the game, had not read that

script. While Torrance opened with rounds of 71 and 69 and Rocca followed his opening 66 with a 71 to enthusiastic acclaim, the slender 26-year old from Grimsby was quietly continuing his rehabilitation from the spinal fusion operation that had threatened to end his career. Payne had been Rookie of the Year in 1992, the year after the Golden Bear had forecast the 6ft 4in former British Youths' and European amateur champion would be a future star of the professional game. The upward graph continued when he won the Open de Baleares in 1993, but then at the 1994 Irish Open Payne began to be plagued by back problems. 'Two vertebrae were out of alignment,' he explained, 'and although doctors believed that I had been born with the problem, playing golf had made it worse.'

Payne reluctantly decided on surgery and the operation was carried out in September 1994. It was six months before he could resume his career and progress

THE COURSE

Sir Henry Cotton designed the L'Albenza course which was opened in 1959, constructing an attractive layout in a woodland setting, its two valleys converging on an imposing clubhouse with a stunning Alpine backdrop. The clever use of streams and small lakes demands accurate tee shots and precise iron play, and the 367-yard par four 17th is perhaps the best example of the architect's emphasis on finesse.

Jonathan Lomas, who won the Sir Henry Cotton Rookie of the Year award two years after Payne, produced the week's biggest gallery pleaser when he sank a wedge shot from 110 yards for an eagle two at the ninth. It was the last shot of a first round 65 that helped the Shropshire golfer tie for third place.

Gary Evans (top) salutes a chip-in. Runner-up Patrick Sjöland (above).

was slow. It was not until October 1995 that he secured a top 20 placing when he had three rounds under 70 in the Mercedes German Masters. Time was running out for Payne when he arrived in Bergamo, for the medical extension he had been granted for the early months of 1996 had only four more weeks to run.

Fate intervened in the form of a series of Alpine thunderstorms which battered the already saturated tree-lined course and so disrupted the schedule that the final two rounds had to be played on Sunday. Payne started the 36 holes marathon sharing 22nd place with 14 others on one under par, six behind halfway leader Gary Evans. Although a morning 67 lifted him to sixth behind Lee Westwood, who had

ten birdies in charging round in 65, Payne was still six shots off the pace when he began the final leg.

When Westwood, another ex-British Youths' champion, birdied his first two holes to move 13 under par, Payne's chance of victory looked slim. But he moved closer with five birdies in an outward 32, and a second 67 gave him a nine under total of 275.

It was a challenging target, but by no means insurmountable. Although Rocca's fragile putting had removed him from the equation, and Torrance had also struggled on the greens, five others were in prime position as they entered the finishing straight. One by one they found the task beyond them. Westwood, Patrik Sjöland

and Miguel Jiménez had the best opportunities. Westwood was in control until the 12th but crashed to an eight there, then Sjöland who was level with Payne on the 18th tee, pushed his four iron approach to the last and failed to make a par four.

Jiménez, with the title in his grasp after a birdie at the 16th elevated him to ten under, dumped his pitch into the pond at the 17th, and three-putted the last, then finally Westwood took six at the 18th.

No one was more surprised, or delighted than Payne who had sat in the clubhouse for more than an hour watching the drama unfold. 'I am amazed because my win was so unexpected,' he said. 'It is one thing being told you will be all right, but quite another proving it. There were times when I wondered whether I would ever play again.'

Mike Britten   85

BERGAMO GC, BERGAMO, MAY 2-5, 1996 · YARDAGE 6609 · PAR 71

Pos	Name	Country	Rnd 1	Rnd 2	Rnd 3	Rnd 4	Total	Prize Money £		Name	Country	Rnd 1	Rnd 2	Rnd 3	Rnd 4	Total	Prize Money
										Angel CABRERA	(Arg)	75	67	74	69	285	4002
										Eric GIRAUD	(Fr)	70	71	72	72	285	4002
1	Jim PAYNE	(Eng)	70	71	67	67	275	85166		Francisco VALERA	(Sp)	69	72	71	73	285	4002
2	Patrik SJÖLAND	(Swe)	66	71	66	73	276	56720	36	Phillip PRICE	(Wal)	68	71	74	73	286	3491
3	Jonathan LOMAS	(Eng)	72	65	71	69	277	26401		Jamie SPENCE	(Eng)	71	73	70	72	286	3491
	Miguel Angel JIMÉNEZ	(Sp)	72	69	63	73	277	26401		Terry PRICE	(Aus)	73	68	73	72	286	3491
	Lee WESTWOOD	(Eng)	68	69	65	75	277	26401		Wayne WESTNER	(SA)	72	71	72	71	286	3491
6	Andrew COLTART	(Scot)	70	68	72	68	278	17884		Mike MCLEAN	(Eng)	69	70	73	74	286	3491
7	Greg TURNER	(NZ)	68	71	71	69	279	13172	41	Andrew COLLISON	(Eng)	72	71	71	73	287	3066
	Paul EALES	(Eng)	71	69	69	70	279	13172		Silvio GRAPPASONNI	(It)	72	69	74	72	287	3066
	Eduardo ROMERO	(Arg)	67	69	70	73	279	13172		Fabrice TARNAUD	(Fr)	75	69	72	71	287	3066
10	Mark MOULAND	(Wal)	69	74	74	63	280	8942		David WILLIAMS	(Eng)	73	71	69	74	287	3066
	David HOWELL	(Eng)	66	70	75	69	280	8942		Oyvind ROJAHN	(Nor)	68	68	72	79	287	3066
	Padraig HARRINGTON	(Ire)	72	71	66	71	280	8942	46	Thomas LEVET	(Fr)	71	70	73	74	288	2597
	Mathias GRÖNBERG	(Swe)	70	69	69	72	280	8942		Dean ROBERTSON	(Scot)	69	74	71	74	288	2597
	Ronan RAFFERTY	(N.Ire)	69	72	67	72	280	8942		Tim PLANCHIN	(Fr)	76	68	71	73	288	2597
15	Mats HALLBERG	(Swe)	73	68	73	67	281	6915		Andrew SHERBORNE	(Eng)	70	73	74	71	288	2597
	David GILFORD	(Eng)	72	69	69	71	281	6915		Alberto CROCE	(It)	68	71	78	71	288	2597
	Gary ORR	(Scot)	70	67	72	72	281	6915		Antoine LEBOUC	(Fr)	72	72	74	70	288	2597
	Barry LANE	(Eng)	69	71	68	73	281	6915	52	Anders FORSBRAND	(Swe)	72	71	72	74	289	2171
	Sven STRÜVER	(Ger)	68	70	69	74	281	6915		Silvano LOCATELLI	(It)	70	72	75	72	289	2171
20	Paul CURRY	(Eng)	69	73	72	68	282	5961		David A RUSSELL	(Eng)	69	75	73	72	289	2171
	Santiago LUNA	(Sp)	71	70	70	71	282	5961		David HIGGINS	(Ire)	72	69	76	72	289	2171
	Chris HALL	(Eng)	69	74	68	71	282	5961	56	Paolo QUIRICI	(Swi)	71	72	72	75	290	1916
	Emanuele BOLOGNESI	(It)	67	73	70	72	282	5961		Mats LANNER	(Swe)	72	72	77	69	290	1916
	Costantino ROCCA	(It)	66	71	72	73	282	5961	58	José RIVERO	(Sp)	71	73	71	76	291	1703
25	Paul BROADHURST	(Eng)	71	71	71	70	283	5280		Robert COLES	(Eng)	69	75	71	76	291	1703
	Emanuele CANONICA	(It)	72	70	68	73	283	5280		Miguel Angel MARTIN	(Sp)	73	68	75	75	291	1703
	Alberto BINAGHI	(It)	68	73	68	74	283	5280	61	Juan Carlos PIÑERO	(Sp)	70	73	71	78	292	1490
28	Rolf MUNTZ	(Hol)	71	73	69	71	284	4684		Massimo SCARPA	(It)	74	70	74	74	292	1490
	Sam TORRANCE	(Scot)	71	69	72	72	284	4684	63	Manuel ZERMAN	(It)	70	74	73	76	293	1362
	Daniel CHOPRA	(Swe)	71	71	70	72	284	4684	64	Jason WIDENER	(USA)	71	73	72	78	294	1277
	Gary EVANS	(Eng)	65	70	76	73	284	4684	65	Pedro LINHART	(Sp)	73	70	74	79	296	1192
32	Ricky WILLISON	(Eng)	68	72	73	72	285	4002	66	Adam MEDNICK	(Swe)	71	72	78	80	301	766

Sam Torrance's 1972 Radici Open win was recognised as was the European Tour's 25th Anniversary with a presentation by Guiseppe Silva of the Italian Golf Federation to Ken Schofield and George O'Grady.

MASTERS OF WEATHERWEAR

Whichever way the barometer swings

PROQUIP 2-LAYER

The new **PROQUIP** 2-layer golf suit uses **GORE-TEX** fabric with its unique membrane system as the outer layer, rather than as a liner on the inside of the garment, so it does not saturate or 'wet' out.

And, because of this **GORE-TEX** fabric, it's guaranteed to be durably waterproof, windproof and very breathable.

In eliminating the bulk normally associated with the traditionally lined waterproof, we have created the ultimate lightweight suit. Which gives you increased comfort and the ability to swing more freely than ever before.

In short, it's serious equipment for serious golfers.

So, if you want to improve your game in the wet, pay a visit to your local professional shop.

MASTERS OF WEATHERWEAR

Proquip International Limited, Wisloe Road, Cambridge, Gloucester GL2 7AF, England.
Tel: (01453) 890707 Fax: (01453) 890826

WL GORE & ASSOCIATES (UK) LTD
Kirkton Campus, Livingston, West Lothian, Scotland EH54 7BH

GORE-TEX is a registered trade-mark of WL Gore & Associates

Then there were six

The run of maiden winners
continued as Padraig Harrington
cruised to victory in Madrid

*P*adraig Harrington became the sixth first-time winner on the 1996 European Tour when he coasted to victory in the rain-affected Peugeot Spanish Open at Club de Campo in Madrid. The 24-year old Dubliner who is a qualified chartered accountant, earned his Tour card at San Roque the previous November after an amateur career which included three Walker Cup appearances.

Harrington arrived in Madrid in good form having secured successive top ten finishes in Cannes, Valencia and Bergamo, yet his opening 70 hardly set the tournament alight. That distinction went to the slightly built 16-year old prodigy and European amateur champion, Sergio Garcia from Castellon, whose card included four birdies for a first round 68. Garcia was thrilled. 'I was disappointed to

miss the cut at El Saler two weeks ago so I've worked hard on my long irons. This 68 in my first Spanish Open means a lot.'

Colin Montgomerie, who had won this tournament in 1994, played the first round but took the next plane home to be with his sick daughter. Defending champion Severiano Ballesteros, gradually regaining his competitive edge, went round in level par 72 but the early leaders

on a first day, in which just over an hour's play was lost to a mid-afternoon electric storm, were Englishman Ian Pyman on 66 and Peter O'Malley (Australia) and Marcus Wills (Wales) on 67.

Harrington sprang to life on Friday when he was off to an early (8.15 a.m.) start. He scrambled a little on the front nine where he spent time visiting trees and bunkers. Even so the Irishman didn't drop a shot and, with his putter working wonders, he managed three birdies. On the back nine Harrington stopped struggling and was rewarded with five more birdies for a round of 64. He was now ten under for the tournament and the rest of the field were to spend a long afternoon chasing those big red double figures on the leaderboard.

Wills and O'Malley kept in touch with 70 apiece and they were joined in second place by Sweden's Per Haugsrud and Scotland's Gordon Brand Junior. Ballasteros made the level par cut with

Miguel Angel Jiménez flags a pitch down.

two to spare and Sergio Garcia had a 73 to reach the halfway stage on three under, level with another young amateur from

the Valencia region, Jose Manuel Lara who had added a 69 to his first round 72.

There was another short hold-up as lightning flickered against the leaden grey of the Madrid skyline, but for the time being the storms kept their distance. It would not last. Saturday dawned even greyer and wet. So wet that play was out of the question and was finally called off altogether. An attempt would be made to play 36 holes on Sunday.

After 24 hours the rain finally stopped and the sun came out, but the rapidly rising temperature shrouded the course in mist, pushing the scheduled early start back another two hours. Harrington took the delay in his stride choosing the third round to stamp his imprint indelibly on the 70th Spanish Open. He made a lot of new friends that Sunday in Madrid. People who had arrived at the course asking 'who is this man Harrington?' would leave later that day with the memory of a fresh-faced

SHOT OF THE WEEK

Riiing! Beep, Beep! 1996 was the year the mobile phone made its presence felt on Tour. Iain Pyman complained after phones rang out on three holes but the Englishman still shot 66 to take the first round lead. The omnipresent beepers didn't affect Fabrice Tarnaud either. The French-man played the shot of the tournament when he holed in one with a three iron at the 210-yard third hole in the second round. Later, new signs – of the times – appeared around the course. 'No mobile phones' they read.

Runner-up Gordon Brand Junior (above).
Spanish prodigy Sergio Garcia (right).

young sportsman with an easy grin and ready smile. Even when he had to repeatedly ask spectators to move out of his line-of-sight as he prepared for an awkward pitch shot at the 16th, he did so with good humour and when one young onlooker reappeared for the umpteenth time from behind a tree Harrington shrugged, smiled again and proceeded to lay his approach dead.

With Club de Campo playing so long, Harrington's third round 67 was a very good score indeed and at 15 under par was now six ahead of Pedro Linhart and seven in front of Gordon Brand, Mathias Gronberg, Per Hagsrud and Peter

O'Malley. Something cataclysmic would have to happen to change the apparent destiny of the Spanish title but when Padraig birdied his 19th hole of the day at the start of the fourth round it became clear he was in no mood to slip.

Eduardo Romero finished with a sparkling 66 and moved up to share of fourth place while Dutchman Rolf Muntz closed with 69 to claim third spot and a place in the following week's Benson and Hedges International. Brand was second and the two young amateurs Garcia and Lara finished 49th and 67th respectively. But the 1996 Peugeot Spanish Open belonged to the smiling, 'delighted and surprised' Padraig Harrington from Dublin.

Jeff Kelly   91

CLUB DE CAMPO, MADRID, MAY 9-12, 1996 · YARDAGE 6939 · PAR 72

Pos	Name	Country	Rnd 1	Rnd 2	Rnd 3	Rnd 4	Total	Prize Money £
1	Padraig HARRINGTON	(Ire)	70	64	67	71	272	91660
2	Gordon BRAND JNR.	(Scot)	70	67	71	68	276	61100
3	Rolf MUNTZ	(Hol)	68	71	70	69	278	34430
4	Eduardo ROMERO	(Arg)	70	71	72	66	279	21637
	Sam TORRANCE	(Scot)	70	71	70	68	279	21637
	Mathias GRÖNBERG	(Swe)	69	70	69	71	279	21637
	Pedro LINHART	(Sp)	70	68	69	72	279	21637
8	Robert ALLENBY	(Aus)	72	70	68	70	280	13015
	Lee WESTWOOD	(Eng)	68	72	72	68	280	13015
10	Fabrice TARNAUD	(Fr)	72	70	71	68	281	11000
11	Roger CHAPMAN	(Eng)	68	74	70	70	282	8983
	Retief GOOSEN	(SA)	74	70	69	69	282	8983
	Miguel Angel MARTIN	(Sp)	71	70	68	73	282	8983
	José COCERES	(Arg)	69	70	71	72	282	8983
	Per HAUGSRUD	(Nor)	68	69	71	74	282	8983
16	Peter BAKER	(Eng)	71	71	71	70	283	7139
	Mark ROE	(Eng)	72	70	69	72	283	7139
	Terry PRICE	(Aus)	70	72	68	73	283	7139
	Stuart CAGE	(Eng)	69	72	69	73	283	7139
	Peter O'MALLEY	(Aus)	67	70	71	75	283	7139
21	Jon ROBSON	(Eng)	70	72	71	71	284	5857
	Diego BORREGO	(Sp)	71	71	73	69	284	5857
	Jean Louis GUEPY	(Fr)	73	70	69	72	284	5857
	Mark MOULAND	(Wal)	73	71	71	69	284	5857
	Stephen AMES	(T&T)	71	70	70	73	284	5857.
	Phil GOLDING	(Eng)	69	72	73	70	284	5857
	Domingo HOSPITAL	(Sp)	72	69	71	72	284	5857
	David CARTER	(Eng)	70	70	72	72	284	5857
29	Andrew COLTART	(Scot)	73	69	70	73	285	4796
	Miles TUNNICLIFF	(Eng)	75	67	70	73	285	4796
	Jean VAN DE VELDE	(Fr)	73	71	69	72	285	4796
	Bob MAY	(USA)	71	68	76	70	285	4796
	Silvio GRAPPASONNI	(It)	71	68	72	74	285	4796
34	Richard BOXALL	(Eng)	73	71	72	70	286	4290
	Emanuele CANONICA	(It)	69	71	75	71	286	4290
	Eamonn DARCY	(Ire)	68	70	73	75	286	4290
37	Stephen GALLACHER	(Scot)	71	71	75	70	287	3685
	Marc FARRY	(Fr)	72	71	74	70	287	3685
	Derrick COOPER	(Eng)	70	73	70	74	287	3685
	Antoine LEBOUC	(Fr)	72	71	72	72	287	3685
	Juan Carlos PIÑERO	(Sp)	72	71	75	69	287	3685
	Manuel PIÑERO	(Sp)	73	71	72	71	287	3685
	Mike HARWOOD	(Aus)	71	70	77	69	287	3685
	Glenn RALPH	(Eng)	71	70	73	73	287	3685
45	Phillip PRICE	(Wal)	71	73	72	72	288	3025
	Ignacio FELIU	(Sp)	71	73	73	71	288	3025
	Andrew SHERBORNE	(Eng)	69	72	72	75	288	3025
	Miguel Angel JIMÉNEZ	(Sp)	73	67	75	73	288	3025
49	Seve BALLESTEROS	(Sp)	72	70	76	71	289	2475
	Santiago LUNA	(Sp)	70	72	76	71	289	2475
	Gary EVANS	(Eng)	72	72	73	72	289	2475
	Robert COLES	(Eng)	73	71	71	74	289	2475
	Gary ORR	(Scot)	69	72	76	72	289	2475
	Marcus WILLS	(Wal)	67	70	75	77	289	2475
	Sergio GARCIA (AM)	(Sp)	68	73	73	75	289	
55	Thomas BJORN	(Den)	69	72	75	74	290	1881
	Christian POST	(Den)	71	72	77	70	290	1881
	Michael CAMPBELL	(NZ)	73	71	73	73	290	1881
	Max ANGLERT	(Swe)	70	71	74	75	290	1881
	Jarmo SANDELIN	(Swe)	70	70	76	74	290	1881
60	Iain PYMAN	(Eng)	66	77	73	75	291	1622
	Russell CLAYDON	(Eng)	71	70	80	70	291	1622
62	Angel CABRERA	(Arg)	69	72	76	75	292	1512
	Ignacio GARRIDO	(Sp)	71	70	72	79	292	1512
64	Anders HANSEN	(Den)	74	70	76	73	293	1402
	Mark LITTON	(Wal)	71	68	75	79	293	1402
66	Gary CLARK	(Eng)	69	72	78	75	294	825
67	Paul EALES	(Eng)	68	74	76	77	295	823
	Jose Manuel LARA (AM)	(Sp)	72	69	79	76	296	
68	Hendrik BUHRMANN	(SA)	72	71	75	79	297	821
69	Emanuele BOLOGNESI	(It)	71	72	78	77	298	818
	Darren CLARKE	(N.Ire)	74	70	76	78	298	818

THE COURSE

'I have never played the course so long,' said Severiano Ballesteros after his first practice round prior to the Peugeot Open de España. The rains had returned to Spain with a vengeance after a long drought and the sun-baked fast-running fairways of the year before were now lush, soft and slow. Club de Campo's sandy sub-soil and an able greens staff quickly dealt with Saturday's downpour enabling a 36-hole finish on Sunday.

sink-it!

No Caffeine, No Sugar, NO LIMITS !

Ames tames the tempest

Stephen Ames kept calm
in stormy conditions to win
his second European Tour title

There is something about the Benson and Hedges International that attracts Mother Nature in her most waspish mood.

Brilliantly staged, staffed by nice people, led by the Special Events Director Jim Elkins, and always with a seriously classy field, the tournament appears to have everything going for it. They even had The Oxfordshire, one of England's finest new courses for a couple of decades, as the tournament's latest spectacular stage in 1996.

And still the weather hammered the event. As bitterly cold winds, gusting up to 50mph, flushed into Thame and its environs in May, The Oxfordshire took the full brunt of a weather system vicious enough to make Michael Fish's personal top ten. Yet, perversely, the more severe the weather turned, the more interesting the golf became.

Few things in life please the average punter more than the opportunity to watch the really big stars battling the sort of conditions they endure every other weekend down at the club. So it proved this time. Naturally it was not fun if you were one of chaps charged with keeping the tented village from stacking somewhere above Heathrow but for the rest it was wonderfully jolly stuff.

Not that Rees Jones's masterpiece requires any outside help in testing anyone's game but the gales that swept across this flat landscape brought another exciting dimension to an already heavily laden table. Added to that, and increasing the

anticipation, from the outset, was the presence of newly crowned US Masters champion Nick Faldo.

This was Faldo's first competitive appearance on British soil since the 1995 Open Championship and he approached the week in upbeat and impressive style. With every member of Europe's victori-

ous Ryder Cup side present Faldo was the superstar attraction even if he was more difficult than usual to spot clad as he was in several layers of finest Pringle, waterproof trousers and a bobble hat worthy of Crans in December.

'Nobody can do anything about the weather so we just have to get on with it.

SHOT OF THE WEEK

While almost any of Stephen Ames' final round 72 is a contender the one that echoed far-thest was Nick Faldo's ace at the 171-yard 13th. This feat was achieved with a seven iron, the ball plopping into the hole in its third bounce. His previous six holes-in-one have all been collected via his six iron.

I've just flown in from 80 something degrees to this so, for me, it's survival,' he said after a creditable first round 70, two under par, a score that included a hole-in-one at the 13th.

This contrasted wildly with playing companion Padraig Harrington's effort at the par five 17th, a hole swiftly christened 'Make your mind up time' by the professionals. Played conservatively – that is, around the lake – it is a neat par five. Played across the water it is either a simple birdie or brutal. Harrington, who won his first European Tour title, the Peugeot Open de España, a week earlier, found that for him it was the latter as he grafted his way to a 13 shot total on this hole. Four times he lashed his ball into the water. This meant he not only missed the cut but came up with a contender for the Irish quote-of-the-year prize when he said: 'I didn't feel embarrassed because I tried on every shot. The problem was that I know I can hit my three wood 250 down-wind but I forgot the first 240 yards were over water.'

Brilliant stuff, and entirely in keeping with this wild and windy week.

Also out after two rounds was Gordon Sherry after an 80 spoiled his Tour debut. 'I really need to chill out a bit

Best finish for Jon Robson.

because my expectations are a bit too high for this stage in my career,' the Scottish skyscraper admitted. But with Faldo still in there, Ian Woosnam playing well and Colin Montgomerie in super form again, the stage was set for a mighty weekend shoot-out.

So it proved. Except that the battle for this title was eventually between three slightly less well-known golfers in Stephen Ames, Jon Robson and Derrick Cooper. The Big Three each came to Sunday well in contention – Montgomerie indeed led by three shots going into his final round – but one by one they fell victim to a mix-ture of the weather and their own

frustration.

Ames, Robson and Cooper, meanwhile, appeared to be in their element. Maybe the fact that none of them has been in contention for a big title helped their concentration on this last day.

But whatever, there is no gainsaying the fact that Ames' par 72 was not only good enough to win this glittering title but was without doubt one of the very best rounds of 1996. The Canada - based player who represents Trinidad and Tobago was, after all, not

Wayne Riley (above) in the sands of The Oxfordshire. Derrick Cooper (below) lined up third place.

only the sole player to match par but one of only 31 in this world-class field to break 80 on Sunday. More than half did not.

His one-shot victory from Robson – who never stopped smiling all week – won Ames £116,660, his second European title and a huge step forward.

'Usually, the weak part of my game is upstairs in the mind but I concentrated on good thoughts and managed to stay focused,' he revealed.

Good enough. It is, as they say, an ill wind that blows nobody any good.

Bill Elliot

THE OXFORDSHIRE, THAME, OXON, MAY 16-19, 1996 • YARDAGE 7205 • PAR 72

Pos	Name	Country	Rnd 1	Rnd 2	Rnd 3	Rnd 4	Total	Prize Money £
1	Stephen AMES	(T&T)	73	71	67	72	283	116660
2	Jon ROBSON	(Eng)	70	70	71	73	284	77770
3	Derrick COOPER	(Eng)	71	70	70	74	285	43820
4	Andrew COLTART	(Scot)	77	67	68	75	287	32320
	Ross DRUMMOND	(Scot)	73	69	70	75	287	32320
6	Miguel Angel JIMÉNEZ	(Sp)	68	70	74	76	288	21000
	Wayne RILEY	(Aus)	73	71	67	77	288	21000
	Paul LAWRIE	(Scot)	71	71	73	73	288	21000
9	Colin MONTGOMERIE	(Scot)	72	68	67	84	291	14163
	Pierre FULKE	(Swe)	74	71	68	78	291	14163
	Stuart CAGE	(Eng)	73	70	71	77	291	14163
12	Richard BOXALL	(Eng)	76	72	70	74	292	10836
	Bernhard LANGER	(Ger)	69	71	73	79	292	10836
	Sam TORRANCE	(Scot)	71	72	72	77	292	10836
	Ian WOOSNAM	(Wal)	72	70	68	82	292	10836
	Nick FALDO	(Eng)	70	73	69	80	292	10836
17	Joakim HAEGGMAN	(Swe)	72	76	69	76	293	9450
18	Eduardo ROMERO	(Arg)	75	72	71	76	294	8456
	Retief GOOSEN	(SA)	75	72	69	78	294	8456
	John BICKERTON	(Eng)	74	73	72	75	294	8456
	Fabrice TARNAUD	(Fr)	75	71	73	75	294	8456
	Robert ALLENBY	(Aus)	74	72	70	78	294	8456
23	Roger CHAPMAN	(Eng)	71	76	69	79	295	7560
	Gary ORR	(Scot)	73	74	74	74	295	7560
	David CARTER	(Eng)	73	73	73	76	295	7560
26	Rolf MUNTZ	(Hol)	73	74	76	73	296	6510
	Peter BAKER	(Eng)	69	74	75	78	296	6510
	Paul MOLONEY	(Aus)	72	74	69	81	296	6510
	Martin GATES	(Eng)	71	76	72	77	296	6510
	Wayne WESTNER	(SA)	72	70	74	80	296	6510
	Seve BALLESTEROS	(Sp)	75	73	71	77	296	6510
	José RIVERO	(Sp)	75	73	72	76	296	6510
33	Paul AFFLECK	(Wal)	72	74	70	81	297	5600
	Roger WESSELS	(SA)	73	72	69	83	297	5600
	Mike HARWOOD	(Aus)	73	75	69	80	297	5600
36	Paul EALES	(Eng)	74	73	70	81	298	4970
	Sandy LYLE	(Scot)	74	73	75	76	298	4970
	Howard CLARK	(Eng)	69	73	75	81	298	4970
	Tim PLANCHIN	(Fr)	74	74	71	79	298	4970
	Pedro LINHART	(Sp)	71	73	74	80	298	4970
	Marc FARRY	(Fr)	78	68	72	80	298	4970
42	Frank NOBILO	(NZ)	75	71	72	82	300	4340
	Barry LANE	(Eng)	76	72	73	79	300	4340
	Malcolm MACKENZIE	(Eng)	72	72	75	81	300	4340
45	Ignacio GARRIDO	(Sp)	71	77	73	80	301	3850
	Peter HEDBLOM	(Swe)	76	71	75	79	301	3850
	Jamie SPENCE	(Eng)	72	73	76	80	301	3850
	Fredrik LINDGREN	(Swe)	74	72	73	82	301	3850
49	Thomas LEVET	(Fr)	77	70	73	82	302	3290
	Greg TURNER	(NZ)	72	75	75	80	302	3290
	Gary EVANS	(Eng)	75	73	74	80	302	3290
	Olle KARLSSON	(Swe)	72	72	75	83	302	3290
53	Andrew SHERBORNE	(Eng)	72	76	73	82	303	2940
54	Mats LANNER	(Swe)	75	72	74	83	304	2590
	Stephen FIELD	(Eng)	74	73	75	82	304	2590
	Jeff HAWKES	(SA)	76	71	72	85	304	2590
	Emanuele CANONICA	(It)	70	73	77	84	304	2590
58	Ronan RAFFERTY	(N.Ire)	70	71	76	88	305	2240
59	Mark MOULAND	(Wal)	72	76	73	85	306	2065
	Timothy SPENCE	(Eng)	74	74	77	81	306	2065
	Klas ERIKSSON	(Swe)	73	74	75	84	306	2065
	Jean VAN DE VELDE	(Fr)	69	77	71	89	306	2065
63	Lee WESTWOOD	(Eng)	74	73	75	85	307	1890
64	Francisco VALERA	(Sp)	72	76	74	87	309	1825
65	Adam HUNTER	(Scot)	73	73	78	88	312	1750

THE COURSE

Designed by Rees Jones, one of legendary architect Robert Trent Jones' two designer sons, The Oxfordshire was completed in 1994. Its rolling parkland lay-out is a result of massive earth-moving and its par 72 is a serious test.

SMOKING WHEN PREGNANT
HARMS YOUR BABY

Chief Medical Officers' Warning
12 mg Tar   0.9 mg Nicotine

Torrance in matchless mood

Sam Torrance swept all before him at
The Oxfordshire to win the largest
cheque of his career

There will be the little matter of $1 million to consider for Sam Torrance during the first week of 1997. This is the first prize in the Andersen Consulting World Championship of Golf and Torrance put himself forward as a strong candidate to win it when he emerged victorious from the European region of the event at The Oxfordshire in late May.

Eight of the European Tour's finest gathered for a tilt at golf's biggest prize, including the 1996 million dollar man himself, Barry Lane, who had defeated David Frost in the final at the Grayhawk Club, Arizona, and thereby started his new year with a flourish.

The first round draw put Lane against Miguel Angel Jiménez, Torrance against Mark James, Colin Montgomerie against Costantino Rocca and Bernhard Langer against Jesper Parnevik.

In the first match, Lane was fighting a losing battle with Jiménez. The defending champion was one ahead when the Spaniard three-putted the first hole. Thereafter there was never more than one hole in it, but then Lane took three putts on the 16th to go one down and could not recover. Torrance produced a spell of seven birdies in nine holes which accounted for James, Montgomerie just edged home against Rocca but Langer and Parnevik had a titanic struggle. Langer was two down with three to play but Parnevik bogeyed the 16th and double-bogeyed the 17th to allow Langer to draw level. Extra holes were needed and Langer came through with a birdie on the 20th.

In the semi-finals Torrance was again in towering form against Jiménez, picking up six birdies in the 14 holes he was required to complete. Montgomerie was also under par in his match against Langer and aided by an eagle at the 11th came home by 4 & 3.

So the final brought together the two men who had made the 1995 battle for European supremacy such a compelling encounter. Could Torrance extract some measure of revenge or would Montgomerie hold all the aces? Quite apart from that, there was also a fairly major difference between first and second place with the winner receiving $300,000 to the runner-up's $150,000.

After six holes the match was all

THE COURSE

Designed by Rees Jones of the famous Jones architectural dynasty, The Oxfordshire is set on rolling land at the foot of the Chiltern Hills. Water comes into play on seven holes and subtle contouring and mounding make this a thinking man's course. The feature hole is the par five 17th (right) which offers two routes to the green depending on the drive. A good drive offers the opportunity to go directly across the water or alternatively, the player can skirt the lake to make it a genuine three-shot hole.

Jesper Parnevik (right) was in caddie mode. Colin Montgomerie (opposite) couldn't hold off Sam Torrance.

square and then Torrance made a decisive move. A drive and seven wood to the 498-yard seventh set up an eagle from seven feet, and birdies at the next two holes meant that Torrance was three up. Montgomerie pegged back one hole when Torrance found water at the tenth, but then probably realised it was not to be his day when Torrance again found water on the 11th, but pitched close enough to save par and gain a half.

The end came at The Oxfordshire's signature hole, the double-dog-leg 17th, where Montgomerie was unable to secure a birdie and graciously conceded Torrance's six feet birdie putt and with it, the match.

'It was a great match,' said Torrance. 'That's what match-play is all about, not shooting a six or seven under par round but just making sure you beat your opponent. Now I'm looking forward to Arizona in January.'

There he faces Scott Hoch, the winner of United States region, with the other semi-final being between Japan's Hisayuki Sasaki and Greg Norman.

In the meantime Torrance can continue to enjoy this golden segment of his career, which now includes the largest cheque of his life with the prospect of an even larger one ahead.

Chris Plumridge

SHOT OF THE WEEK

The outcome of a match can hinge on a single stroke and one that Sam Torrance produced in the final against Colin Montgomerie made all the difference. Torrance had gone three up at the turn but then lost the tenth. He looked like losing the 533-yard 11th as well when his second shot found water. But he dropped under penalty and then hit a glorious wedge shot to nine feet and holed the putt for a par. Montgomerie could only manage a par as well and the psychology of the match was still in Torrance's favour.

La Dolce Vita

Costantino Rocca enjoyed the sweet taste

of success in the European Tour's

flagship event

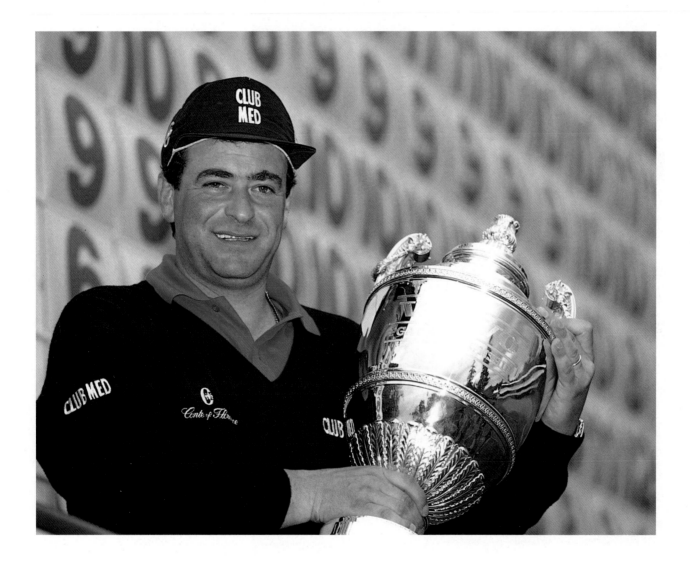

Costantino Rocca is a golfer who wears his heart on his sleeve. There is no doubting how he feels at any time on the golf course, whether it's a resigned shake of the head as a putt fails to drop or whether it's an uninhibited display of joy following success.

The game provides ample opportunities for those twin imposters of triumph and disaster to make an appearance and Rocca has seen them both take centre stage, primarily at the 1995 Open Championship at St Andrews. Here he rode a roller-coaster of emotion, first by

fluffing a chip on the 72nd hole, then by holing a putt of 60 feet to tie for the title and finally losing the play-off to John Daly. Throughout it all though, Rocca kept smiling.

The Open had been one of five runner-up finishes in 1995 for the cheery

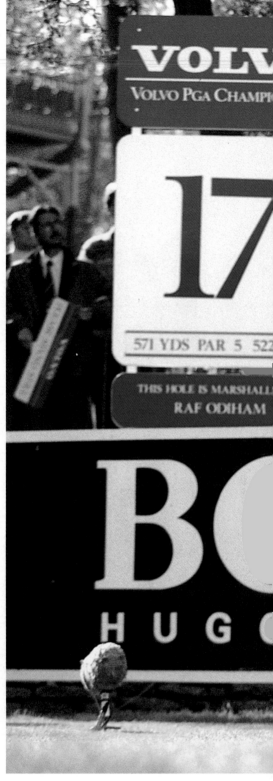

Italian and without a victory since 1993 he wasn't among the favourites for the European Tour's premier event, the Volvo PGA Championship.

Marking the 25th anniversary of the founding of the PGA European Tour, the Championship carried a prize fund of £1 million, a milestone for a 72-hole stroke-play event on these islands, outside the Open Championship.

The quality of the field reflected the quality of the event. Bernhard Langer was defending his title and Colin Montgomerie was seeking the win that would move him back to his normal position at the top of the Volvo Ranking, but the man who was receiving the most attention was Nick Faldo. Following his win in the US Masters when he had come from six shots behind in the final round to over-haul Greg Norman, Faldo was on the

Colin Montgomerie (left) and Mark McNulty (above) were in the thick of the battle.

crest of a wave. His demeanour during that round at Augusta and his sympathy for Norman earned him many admirers and he was certainly the people's favourite at Wentworth.

He did not disappoint them. On a course playing very long in the rain which fell for most of the first day, Faldo was in control of his game. His putter, for so long a cause of frustration was working too, and on three successive holes from the fifth he rattled in putts from 30 feet,

20 feet and 20 feet again. He came to the final hole three under par and drove into prime position leaving himself 225 yards from the flag and playing into a slight breeze. Out came the three wood and the shot covered the pin all the way, finally coming to rest three feet from the hole.

The putt was a formality and Faldo was in the lead with a 67.

Paul Curry, who had missed the cut four times in his last six starts, was back on track with a 68 and he was joined by

and was round in 73, as was Langer.

Faldo was less inspired on the second day and arrived at the 17th at one under par for the round. His second shot to the par five appeared to be heading for the

not in contact with the ground. Two drops followed as the ball bounced nearer the hole and eventually Faldo pitched to within four feet and holed for an unlikely birdie. Another followed at the last and it

Bernhard Langer (left), let go of his consecutive cuts record. Nick Faldo (above) fails narrowly to hole a chip.

Mark McNulty. On 69 were Ignacio Garrido, Robert Allenby and Rocca. Montgomerie struggled with his driving

out-of-bounds on the left but bounced among the spectators, the ball coming to rest on a plastic shopping bag. Faldo was under the impression that he had to place the ball on the spot but rules official Thomas Waldenstedt informed him that he had to take a free drop as the ball was

all added up to a 69 and a total of 136. Joining him on that score was Rocca after a 67, and McNulty after a 68, but the round of the day came from Paul Lawrie who registered a 65 and revealed that his game had been revamped by David Leadbetter. As Rocca, Faldo, McNulty and

Curry were also under the eye of Leadbetter it could be said that the lanky Zimbabwean had achieved something of a tutorial clean sweep at the top of the leader-board.

The cut fell at 144, level par, and among those departing were Severiano Ballesteros and, hold the front page, Bernhard Langer. The man who had, in five years, made 68 consecutive cuts to establish a Tour record, added a 74 to his opening 73 and was gone. 'It had to happen sooner or later ,' said Langer, 'but it is sad that it had to happen here because this is one of our greatest tournaments and a course I like very much.'

The third day of a tournament is usually 'making a move day.' This was more a marking time day as Rocca and McNulty both shot 69 apiece to stay at the head of affairs. Both leaned heavily on the short

THE COURSE

Despite a cold spring and a lack of growth, the West Course at Wentworth was in immaculate condition for the Championship. Heavy rain made the course play every inch of its 6,957 yards but the greens remained true and firm throughout. As usual, the final two holes played a decisive part in the outcome and the newly deepened fairway bunkers to the left of the 18th claimed numerous victims.

Is it a bird? Is it a plane?
No, it's Seve Ballesteros
looking for his ball in a tree,
using John Paramor's
Canon 'image stabilizer'
binoculars.

The Mizuno workshop was a vital facility. Paul Lawrie (right) was joint runner-up.

game, particularly Rocca who opened with a six on the first after a hooked drive which threatened the first tee on the East Course. Within another four holes he had picked up three birdies and was back on track.

For Faldo it was a moving backwards day and his round of 72 was only saved by two birdies in the last three holes. He lay three off the pace. The best golf came from Lawrie who was round in 68 without dropping a shot to move within a stroke of the lead. Others taking closer order

were Eduardo Romero with a 68, to lie three behind and Montgomerie, also with a 68 to get within five shots.

Faldo started the final round in style with a birdie at the first and with a further birdie at the fourth, turned in 33 to Rocca's 34 and was now two shots behind. A birdie at the 11th narrowed the gap again. Both Rocca and Faldo birdied the par five 12th and McNulty was still in there, tied with Rocca for the lead. McNulty failed to save par from the sand on the 13th and then three-putted the

next two greens and was out of contention. Faldo too dropped a shot at the 13th when he three-putted but he recovered with a birdie at the 15th.

Crisis loomed for Rocca at the 15th when he carved his drive into the right-hand trees, but he was able to chip out and a two iron onto the green salvaged a five. Now he was tied with Faldo and it remained to be seen what target Faldo could set. The 17th was crucial. Here Faldo could only manage a five and therefore needed a birdie at the last to apply

SHOT OF THE WEEK

One shot can make a round and in the case of Nick Faldo's second shot to the 18th in the first round, it turned a good round into an outstanding one. Following a good drive, Faldo had 225 yards to the flag, slightly into a breeze and with a steady drizzle falling. It was the optimum distance for his metal three wood. He struck the ball right out of the middle and it flew unerringly at the pin, coming to rest three feet from the hole. The resultant eagle gave him a 67 and the first round lead.

some pressure on the Italian. A huge drive down the last left Faldo with just a six iron to the flag. He went straight for it but the ball caught the front left-hand bunker and he was unable to get down in two more. Faldo's round of 68 set the target at 276 and shortly afterwards Lawrie holed bravely on the last for a birdie to match it.

Could Rocca birdie one of the final two holes to win? He could indeed, in fact he birdied them both.

The 3M physiotherapy unit provided round-the-clock service.

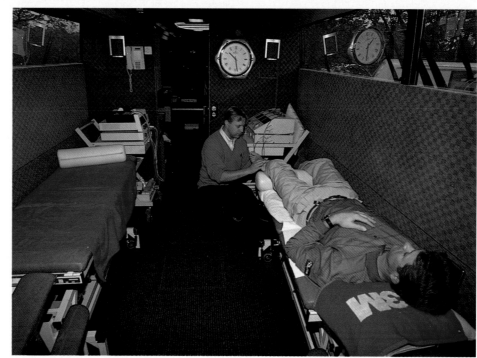

Two good hits down the 17th left him with a short pitch shot, a similar shot to the one he had at St Andrews in the Open. This time there was no doubting his nerve as he floated the ball in to four feet and holed confidently. With the luxury of needing a five at the last to win, Rocca put the icing on the cake by holing from 12 feet on the last for a two-stroke victory.

'I had a lot of pressure today,' said Rocca afterwards, 'because I have not won for three years. This morning when I started, my heart was going 200 and when I play the last hole it was 300. But I just tried to concentrate on each shot.

Unrestrained joy for the winner followed by a Cellnet call home.

I remember reading an interview with Nick Faldo where he said that if he lost a major championship, he wouldn't mind if he was second behind me. This came into my mind when I saw he was 12 under par. I tried to keep him second. This is a great win for me. After the Open Championship, this is the most important tournament in England. I am very happy.'

As he clutched the Volvo PGA Championship silver trophy, Rocca's happiness was plain to see, augmented by the winner's cheque for £166,660. La Dolce Vita? They don't come any sweeter than this.

Chris Plumridge

WEST COURSE, WENTWORTH CLUB, SURREY, MAY 24-27, 1996 · YARDAGE 6957 · PAR 72

Pos	Name	Country	Rnd 1	Rnd 2	Rnd 3	Rnd 4	Total	Prize Money £
1	Costantino ROCCA	(It)	69	67	69	69	274	166660
2	Nick FALDO	(Eng)	67	69	72	68	276	86850
	Paul LAWRIE	(Scot)	73	65	68	70	276	86850
4	Jarmo SANDELIN	(Swe)	70	69	72	67	278	42466
	Mark MCNULTY	(Zim)	68	68	69	73	278	42466
	Andrew SHERBORNE	(Eng)	74	69	70	65	278	42466
7	Gary ORR	(Scot)	71	67	72	69	279	25766
	Colin MONTGOMERIE	(Scot)	73	68	69	69	279	25766
	Patrik SJÖLAND	(Swe)	74	67	72	66	279	25766
10	Eduardo ROMERO	(Arg)	71	69	68	72	280	20000
11	Ian WOOSNAM	(Wal)	73	70	68	70	281	17780
	Lee WESTWOOD	(Eng)	73	70	69	69	281	17780
13	Tony JOHNSTONE	(Zim)	71	72	71	68	282	13872
	Stephen AMES	(T&T)	73	69	74	66	282	13872
	Eamonn DARCY	(Ire)	70	69	71	72	282	13872
	Paul CURRY	(Eng)	68	71	69	74	282	13872
	Mark LITTON	(Wal)	74	68	68	72	282	13872
	Mathias GRÖNBERG	(Swe)	71	71	72	68	282	13872
	Andrew COLTART	(Scot)	71	72	71	68	282	13872
	Padraig HARRINGTON	(Ire)	71	71	72	68	282	13872
21	Jesper PARNEVIK	(Swe)	74	70	70	69	283	10500
	Alexander CEJKA	(Ger)	71	69	71	72	283	10500
	Retief GOOSEN	(SA)	73	71	69	70	283	10500
	Paul EALES	(Eng)	70	69	73	71	283	10500
	Fabrice TARNAUD	(Fr)	72	67	70	74	283	10500
	Paul WAY	(Eng)	71	71	69	72	283	10500
	Miguel Angel JIMÉNEZ	(Sp)	72	66	71	74	283	10500
	Steve WEBSTER	(Eng)	71	73	70	69	283	10500
	Wayne RILEY	(Aus)	75	69	70	69	283	10500
30	David GILFORD	(Eng)	71	71	70	72	284	8242
	José Maria CAÑIZARES	(Sp)	70	69	73	72	284	8242
	Mark JAMES	(Eng)	72	71	73	68	284	8242
	Jean VAN DE VELDE	(Fr)	71	70	73	70	284	8242
	José RIVERO	(Sp)	71	70	70	73	284	8242
	Ross MCFARLANE	(Eng)	72	68	75	69	284	8242
	Niclas FASTH	(Swe)	70	69	74	71	284	8242
37	Phillip PRICE	(Wal)	75	67	71	72	285	7100
	Gordon BRAND JNR.	(Scot)	70	72	71	72	285	7100
	Paul MCGINLEY	(Ire)	73	69	69	74	285	7100
	Steven BOTTOMLEY	(Eng)	74	68	72	71	285	7100
41	Jon ROBSON	(Eng)	71	72	74	69	286	6200
	Mark ROE	(Eng)	73	69	72	72	286	6200
	David FEHERTY	(N.Ire)	73	70	72	71	286	6200
	Roger CHAPMAN	(Eng)	71	67	76	72	286	6200
	Stuart CAGE	(Eng)	70	72	74	70	286	6200
46	David CARTER	(Eng)	71	69	71	76	287	4900
	Philip WALTON	(Ire)	75	67	73	72	287	4900
	Paul BROADHURST	(Eng)	74	69	71	73	287	4900
	Greg TURNER	(NZ)	72	69	73	73	287	4900
	Sam TORRANCE	(Scot)	71	72	71	73	287	4900
	Richard BOXALL	(Eng)	71	72	74	70	287	4900
	Roger WESSELS	(SA)	73	70	72	72	287	4900
	Gary EMERSON	(Eng)	72	69	71	75	287	4900
54	Robert ALLENBY	(Aus)	69	68	75	76	288	3800
	Christy O'CONNOR JNR	(Ire)	74	69	75	70	288	3800
	Steen TINNING	(Den)	71	73	75	69	288	3800
57	Gordon SHERRY	(Scot)	73	71	71	74	289	3233
	Peter O'MALLEY	(Aus)	72	71	73	73	289	3233
	Chris HALL	(Eng)	75	69	73	72	289	3233
60	Marc FARRY	(Fr)	74	70	72	74	290	2750
	Steven RICHARDSON	(Eng)	75	69	71	75	290	2750
	Rodger DAVIS	(Aus)	70	73	76	71	290	2750
	Derrick COOPER	(Eng)	72	70	73	75	290	2750
	Ged FUREY	(Eng)	76	67	75	72	290	2750
	Raymond BURNS	(N.Ire)	72	71	77	70	290	2750
66	Wayne WESTNER	(SA)	70	71	75	75	291	1498
	Olle KARLSSON	(Swe)	71	70	76	74	291	1498
	Domingo HOSPITAL	(Sp)	71	71	74	75	291	1498
69	Pierre FULKE	(Swe)	72	72	75	73	292	1493
	Andrew OLDCORN	(Scot)	72	69	73	78	292	1493
71	Peter MITCHELL	(Eng)	72	72	74	75	293	1490

Lining up at the Volvo PGA Championship were, left to right, George O'Grady, Managing Director, PGA European Tour Enterprises, Jonathan Martin, Head of BBC Television Sports and Events, Ken Schofield, Executive Director, PGA European Tour, and John Shrewsbury, Producer for BBC Television Sports and Events, to announce a new four-year contract between the Tour and BBC Television. The new contract will see the BBC cover the Volvo PGA Championship, the Toyota World Match-Play Championship, the Benson and Hedges International Open and the Loch Lomond World Invitational from 1997 to the year 2000 inclusive.

Flight of the Kiwi

Frank Nobilo soared to the top in
Germany with a stunning exhibition
in the final round

When a player is only a shot off the lead going into the last round and then shoots 66, he could be forgiven for expecting to win. When the player in question is Colin Montgomerie, a very good punter's chance becomes something close to a stone-cold certainty.

If Monty's best is 66, surely nobody is going to beat it, are they? Surely not.

But that is exactly what happened on a fine summer's afternoon in northern Germany at the beginning of glorious June; it was one of the finest rounds of golf seen in Europe all season. It had to be

that good to relegate Montgomerie to second place.

The man with the sublime game, the supreme touch and, last but assuredly not least, the good, old-fashioned bottle to take on and beat maestro Montgomerie was Frank Nobilo, one of the finest golfers to emerge from the tiny population of New Zealand since Bob Charles. A 64 it was, crammed with good shots, brave shots and his total of 270, 18 under par, was good enough to knock Montgomerie off the dais marked 'Winner' by a single stroke.

It was the second time in three months that somebody had shot 64 to beat Montgomerie into second place. In March it had been Fred Couples who had done the dirty on him in the last round of the TPC at Sawgrass. It shouldn't happen to a dog, let alone one of the best players of his generation, and although Montgomerie was naturally disappointed in defeat, even he could not possibly be downhearted after four day's work that at times had seen him very close to his best. 'There always seems to be somebody,' he said with the rueful smile of a man who had lost a pound and found a bent pfennig. 'I don't know what you're supposed to do. But if somebody shoots 64 to beat you, you have to say good luck to him.'

the course, Nobilo and Montgomerie spent most of the day cutting and thrusting, punching and counter-punching as birdies fell to earth like targets at a duck shoot.

Nobilo had two bogeys, but swamped them with an eagle and eight birdies. He

Nobilo dropped a shot at the 12th, but Nobilo got it back at the next. The situation was perfectly set up for the end-game. After a birdie on the 15th, Nobilo got another from six feet at the short 16th, and almost simultaneously Montgomerie bogeyed the 14th. The two-

Good luck never came into it. Nobilo played some marvellous golf on a final day on which the conditions were perfect for low scoring – a gentle breeze, receptive greens, moderate temperature. Nobody could have asked for more.

Although separated by two groups on

came out of the traps at a dead run, picking up five shots in the first six holes, including an eagle three at the third. He was two shots ahead of Montgomerie after eight, but Montgomerie levelled with birdies at the seventh and tenth.

Montgomerie led by one when

stroke swing was to be the final crucial act of the tournament.

Nose in front, Nobilo picked up another shot at the 17th when an exquisitely played bunker shot pulled up four feet from the pin. Confidence sky-high now, he rolled the putt in almost casually.

**Colin Montgomerie
was thwarted again.**

Three birdies on the trot –
Montgomerie now had to
birdie the last two holes to
tie: he could manage only
one.

Nobilo's triumph vindi-
cated his decision to return
to his old clubs after having
had three sets of shafts, none
of them quite to his liking,
fitted to a new set the previous week at the Volvo PGA
Championship. It was the
set that had made him
one of the world's leading
performers in major championships in the 1990s; they
felt right, comfortable like a
favourite pair of carpet slip-
pers. Like reconciled friends,
the clubs and their owner
got on even more famously
than before.

Montgomerie's slimmed-
down but still huge presence
had dominated the tourna-
ment since the day before it
had even started. On pro-am
day on Wednesday he talked
of putting troubles, and the
fact that he had found a putter from his collection of
more than 50 that he
thought might help. It later
proved to be a Ping Pal 4,
although Montgomerie, con-
tracted to another company,
was coy about naming it
while having no objection to
anybody looking into his
bag.

If things were to get
really bad, he was asked,
would be consider trying a
broomhandle putter? 'No,
never,' he said firmly. 'I'd
take up tennis before I'd use
one of those things.' The
feeling was that the Grand
Canyon would freeze over

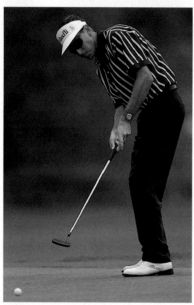

SHOT OF THE WEEK

Frank Nobilo, 16th hole, fourth round. The shot was good enough on its own merits, but in the context of the moment it was absolutely priceless. Montgomerie, two groups behind, had his only bogey of the day when he missed a par putt from 20 feet. Nobilo, meanwhile, pitched to six feet and made the putt for a birdie, The two-stroke swing put him into the lead. He was set for the final push.

Seve Ballesteros (above) showed a return to form. Retief Goosen (above right) and Robert Allenby (right) both finished in the top ten.

before Montgomerie would succumb to the long job, or, for that matter get mixed up in any sport a vital element of which seems to involve thinly-sliced cucumber sandwiches with the crusts cut off.

As Nobilo led with a 65 on the first day, Montgomerie played beautifully in his 71 but did not make anything with his new Pal. That night, frustrated by a round that had bought him little but intense irration, he spent a night of almost monastic solitude in his hotel bedroom in the company of nothing more exciting than a room service menu and about 25 German language television programmes.

As an exercise in self-analysis, it worked a treat, because in the second round he came in with a 65, including five birdies in the first six holes. Nobilo, meanwhile, was completing 36 holes without a bogey and led by two.

Round three saw a welcome return to to form by Severiano Ballesteros, who had his first 66 since he had won the Peugot Spanish Open the previous year, and his first round under 70 since he returned from his self-imposed five-month sabbatical in the winter. Ballesteros's closing 71

left him in a share of 12th place – he was disappointed, but it was a quantum leap forward after his recent travails.

By the end of the third round the stage, with Darren Clarke the leader by a shot, was set for a Montgomerie charge. Clarke had a slightly disappointing 70 to finish third, but Montgomerie produced the expected surge, playing some commanding golf. Not quite commanding enough, though, by Nobilo's lofty standards. Only a 66, eh, Monty? Nice try, but this time, sadly, no cigar.

Mel Webb   119

GUT KADEN, HAMBURG, MAY 30-JUNE 2, 1996 · YARDAGE 7029 · PAR 72

Pos	Name	Country	Rnd 1	Rnd 2	Rnd 3	Rnd 4	Total	Prize Money £
1	Frank NOBILO	(NZ)	65	69	72	64	270	120830.
2	Colin MONTGOMERIE	(Scot)	71	65	69	66	271	80550
3	Darren CLARKE	(N.Ire)	70	67	67	70	274	45400
4	Peter MITCHELL	(Eng)	69	70	71	65	275	30788
	Retief GOOSEN	(SA)	68	67	70	70	275	30788
	Jamie SPENCE	(Eng)	68	69	70	68	275	30788
7	Wayne RILEY	(Aus)	67	71	71	67	276	16791
	Francisco VALERA	(Sp)	68	72	70	66	276	16791
	Robert ALLENBY	(Aus)	66	70	69	71	276	16791
	Stephen AMES	(T&T)	68	68	71	69	276	16791
	Paul MCGINLEY	(Ire)	68	71	68	69	276	16791
12	Michael JONZON	(Swe)	67	75	66	69	277	11743
	Seve BALLESTEROS	(Sp)	70	70	66	71	277	11743
	Carl SUNESON	(Sp)	73	67	68	69	277	11743
15	Per HAUGSRUD	(Nor)	71	69	67	71	278	10213
	Bernhard LANGER	(Ger)	66	70	74	68	278	10213
	Gary ORR	(Scot)	70	66	69	73	278	10213
18	Ross MCFARLANE	(Eng)	69	72	68	70	279	8065
	Olle KARLSSON	(Swe)	69	69	72	69	279	8065
	Paul BROADHURST	(Eng)	69	70	72	68	279	8065
	Richard BOXALL	(Eng)	66	70	71	72	279	8065
	Costantino ROCCA	(It)	72	68	67	72	279	8065
	Anders FORSBRAND	(Swe)	69	68	71	71	279	8065
	Jim PAYNE	(Eng)	70	71	69	69	279	8065
	Mike HARWOOD	(Aus)	68	69	69	73	279	8065
	Russell CLAYDON	(Eng)	71	70	71	67	279	8065
	Miguel Angel MARTIN	(Sp)	68	68	68	75	279	8065
	Thomas BJORN	(Den)	70	69	71	69	279	8065
29	Mark DAVIS	(Eng)	70	68	72	70	280	6207
	Ian WOOSNAM	(Wal)	72	68	72	68	280	6207
	Miguel Angel JIMÉNEZ	(Sp)	68	72	67	73	280	6207
	Fernando ROCA	(Sp)	68	72	72	68	280	6207
	Peter BAKER	(Eng)	68	71	68	73	280	6207
	Stephen MCALLISTER	(Scot)	70	66	73	71	280	6207
35	Greg TURNER	(NZ)	68	71	72	70	281	5335
	José COCERES	(Arg)	67	71	71	72	281	5335
	David WILLIAMS	(Eng)	72	70	68	71	281	5335
	Michael CAMPBELL	(NZ)	69	69	74	69	281	5335
	Terry PRICE	(Aus)	68	73	70	70	281	5335
40	Mark MOULAND	(Wal)	69	73	71	69	282	4682
	Eduardo ROMERO	(Arg)	71	69	71	71	282	4682
	Mark MCNULTY	(Zim)	70	71	72	69	282	4682
	Gary EVANS	(Eng)	69	70	71	72	282	4682
44	Stephen GALLACHER	(Scot)	69	73	72	69	283	3620
	Miles TUNNICLIFF	(Eng)	72	70	71	70	283	3620
	Alexander CEJKA	(Ger)	71	68	71	73	283	3620
	Dean ROBERTSON	(Scot)	72	68	71	72	283	3620
	Daniel CHOPRA	(Swe)	67	71	76	69	283	3620
	Juan Carlos PIÑERO	(Sp)	69	69	74	71	283	3620
	Eric GIRAUD	(Fr)	67	73	72	71	283	3620
	Gary CLARK	(Eng)	69	70	73	71	283	3620
	Gary EMERSON	(Eng)	73	69	70	71	283	3620
	Thomas GÖGELE	(Ger)	71	68	73	71	283	3620
	Malcolm MACKENZIE	(Eng)	67	69	74	73	283	3620
55	Steen TINNING	(Den)	70	69	74	71	284	2336
	Ross DRUMMOND	(Scot)	70	72	71	71	284	2336
	Lee WESTWOOD	(Eng)	66	75	71	72	284	2336
	Domingo HOSPITAL	(Sp)	70	71	73	70	284	2336
	Greg CHALMERS	(Aus)	68	73	71	72	284	2336
	Paul MOLONEY	(Aus)	72	70	71	71	284	2336
	Mark ROE	(Eng)	68	74	71	71	284	2336
	Christian CÉVAER	(Fr)	72	69	73	70	284	2336
	Per NYMAN	(Swe)	66	76	70	72	284	2336
64	Simon BROWN	(Eng)	70	72	73	70	285	1413
	Gordon BRAND JNR.	(Scot)	72	70	72	71	285	1413
	Ricky WILLISON	(Eng)	72	70	71	72	285	1413
	Chris HALL	(Eng)	68	72	71	74	285	1413
	Jarmo SANDELIN	(Swe)	66	76	77	66	285	1413
69	Adam HUNTER	(Scot)	71	71	71	73	286	1079
	Niclas FASTH	(Swe)	67	75	74	70	286	1079
	Mats HALLBERG	(Swe)	71	71	72	72	286	1079
72	Stephen FIELD	(Eng)	71	71	75	70	287	1075
73	Oyvind ROJAHN	(Nor)	66	72	81	73	292	1073
74	Michael WELCH	(Eng)	69	71	78	75	293	1071

THE COURSE

The Gut Kaden course, with its mixture of an old and established front nine and a comparatively new back nine, bought little but praise from the players during a week of more-or-less perfect playing conditions. The mixture of old and new provides an intriguing combination, and the course had the priceless virtue in European Tour terms of identifying the best players and rewarding good golf.

One Market. One Bank.

Deutsche Bank

Allenby's late run clinches the title

Four birdies in the last seven holes

gave Robert Allenby the second

European Tour title of his career

Colin Montgomerie knew exactly what to expect when he pitched up at the Forest of Arden Hotel and Golf Course in early June for the Alamo English Open.

Marriott, owners of the complex, signed the Scot to a three-year deal in 1995 and, as part of this contract, Montgomerie was allowed to help prepare the Warwickshire course. Not physically, of course, but Montgomerie's plan was to advise on how to turn this particular corner of England into something fairly close to that used by the USGA when they set up a US Open course.

As Montgomerie and several other European players were flying off to Detroit and the US Open immediately after competing in the Alamo English Open this seemed like a cracking good idea at the time. So the rough was grown both alongside the fairways and around the greens. Great, clumping bunches of the stuff. Compared to some European Tour courses this was jungle. Easy to get into, horrendously difficult to get out of.

Montgomerie, when he saw it, loved it. Other players had reservations but Colin, was unrepentant.

However, after the first round of this English Open it appeared that Montgomerie had scored something of an own goal when he trudged off the course with a 75 to find himself nine shots off the lead which was held by Andrew Oldcorn. 'I'm not out of it yet. If I score three 68s over the next few days that will put me right back in there,' said Colin.

While the English Open was doing its best to resemble the US Open, Oldcorn is an Englishman who has largely succeeded in disguising himself as a Scot. He represents another Marriott golf hotel, Dalmahoy in Edinburgh, and even manages to speak with a passable burr to his accent. Prior to this 66 he had missed four halfway cuts in five events. He even admitted to being particularly unpleasant to his caddie and added, 'My mental performances have been pathetic. I haven't been able to motivate myself.'

So after day one the big questions were: would Montgomerie manage his three successive 68s and could Oldcorn

Best finish for Ross McFarlane (above).
Sand artistry from
Per-Ulrik Johansson (left).

hang on to his new, positive attitude and add to his 1994 Jersey Open triumph? The answers, in order, turned out to be: yes and no. By the time Sunday dawned he had two of those 68s under his belt, Oldcorn had slipped into a share of second place and the leader going into the final round was Robert Allenby of Australia.

Fast forward a few hours and with two holes of his round left, Montgomerie

was in pole position. When he stood over a five iron approach to the par five 17th it seemed he had a corner at least of the chequered flag in his hand. But then the characteristics which he had helped build into this course struck back at their creator.

His five iron shot flew the green and buried deep in the clag from whence he could only manage a par. He proceeded to find a similar patch of the seriously rough stuff at the par three 18th and once again duffed his attempted pitch, this time dropping a stroke.

It meant he had to settle for a nine

SHOT OF THE WEEK

Ireland's Philip Walton was not the only person with plenty to celebrate after holing in one at the 187-yard 15th hole. His seven iron shot not only won him a jeroboam of Moet & Chandon but earned the Dunblane Appeal £10,000 from the Whitbread Hotel Company.

Peter Mitchell (above left) tangles with some shrubbery and Colin Montgomerie (above right) was in a tangle on the 72nd hole.

English Open was the Australian's to savour after he lagged his penultimate putt up to within six inches from 40 feet away.

'I didn't lose this tournament over the last two holes today, I lost it in the first round. It's always difficult to play catch-up golf,' said Montgomerie almost philosophically as Allenby pocketed a cheque for £108,330.

under par total. Immediately behind him Allenby struck a rich vein of form with three successive birdies from the 14th to move to nine under alongside playing companion Ross McFarlane. 'Even then I expected Colin to birdie the 17th and put the title beyond my reach,' said Allenby.

Instead, both Allenby and McFarlane picked up a stroke at this hole and when McFarlane bogeyed the last, the Alamo

Bill Elliott   125

MARRIOTT FOREST OF ARDEN HOTEL & CC, WARWICKSHIRE, JUNE 6-9, 1996 · YARDAGE 7102 · PAR 72

Pos	Name	Country	Rnd 1	Rnd 2	Rnd 3	Rnd 4	Total	Prize Money £
1	Robert ALLENBY	(Aus)	69	71	69	69	278	108330
2	Colin MONTGOMERIE	(Scot)	75	68	68	68	279	56450
	Ross MCFARLANE	(Eng)	69	71	70	69	279	56450
4	Peter MITCHELL	(Eng)	70	68	73	72	283	27593
	Darren CLARKE	(N.Ire)	71	73	69	70	283	27593
	Per-Ulrik JOHANSSON	(Swe)	72	69	72	70	283	27593
7	Andrew OLDCORN	(Scot)	66	71	73	74	284	16753
	Anssi KANKKONEN	(Fin)	72	72	69	71	284	16753
	Miles TUNNICLIFF	(Eng)	76	69	69	70	284	16753
10	Hendrik BUHRMANN	(SA)	72	70	75	68	285	12480
	Joakim HAEGGMAN	(Swe)	72	72	70	71	285	12480
12	Michael WELCH	(Eng)	72	69	72	73	286	9635
	Greg TURNER	(NZ)	76	68	70	72	286	9635
	Retief GOOSEN	(SA)	74	69	68	75	286	9635
	Thomas BJORN	(Den)	72	70	69	75	286	9635
	Phillip PRICE	(Wal)	75	67	76	68	286	9635
	Mike HARWOOD	(Aus)	71	73	71	71	286	9635
	Robert COLES	(Eng)	76	69	73	68	286	9635
19	Steve WEBSTER	(Eng)	72	68	73	74	287	7618
	Chris HALL	(Eng)	68	76	71	72	287	7618
	Philip WALTON	(Ire)	73	71	73	70	287	7618
	Jim PAYNE	(Eng)	73	69	72	73	287	7618
	Niclas FASTH	(Swe)	71	72	69	75	287	7618
24	Mark DAVIS	(Eng)	70	73	72	73	288	6435
	Domingo HOSPITAL	(Sp)	70	71	72	75	288	6435
	David GILFORD	(Eng)	73	73	73	69	288	6435
	David CARTER	(Eng)	75	71	74	68	288	6435
	Steen TINNING	(Den)	70	68	75	75	288	6435
	Gary EVANS	(Eng)	73	70	75	70	288	6435
	Eric GIRAUD	(Fr)	71	70	76	71	288	6435
31	Richard DINSDALE	(Wal)	76	66	71	76	289	5557
	Michael CAMPBELL	(NZ)	71	73	72	73	289	5557
33	Dean ROBERTSON	(Scot)	73	71	76	70	290	4940
	Pierre FULKE	(Swe)	70	70	74	76	290	4940
	Joe HIGGINS	(Eng)	72	70	76	72	290	4940
	Stephen AMES	(T&T)	72	71	75	72	290	4940
	Mats LANNER	(Swe)	74	72	72	72	290	4940
	Michel BESANCENEY	(Fr)	70	69	76	75	290	4940
	José Maria CAÑIZARES	(Sp)	73	73	74	70	290	4940
40	Mathias GRÖNBERG	(Swe)	71	74	74	72	291	4225
	Malcolm MACKENZIE	(Eng)	72	72	71	76	291	4225
	Raymond RUSSELL	(Scot)	71	72	74	74	291	4225
	Paul AFFLECK	(Wal)	67	74	76	74	291	4225
44	Roger WESSELS	(SA)	73	71	77	71	292	3380
	Mark ROE	(Eng)	73	73	73	73	292	3380
	Ricky WILLISON	(Eng)	69	72	72	79	292	3380
	Paul MCGINLEY	(Ire)	69	73	75	75	292	3380
	Tony JOHNSTONE	(Zim)	74	71	72	75	292	3380
	Raymond BURNS	(N.Ire)	69	73	77	73	292	3380
	Mike MCLEAN	(Eng)	74	69	72	77	292	3380
	Jon ROBSON	(Eng)	70	73	74	75	292	3380
	Phil GOLDING	(Eng)	74	72	75	71	292	3380
53	Gary EMERSON	(Eng)	76	69	77	71	293	2535
	Mark JAMES	(Eng)	74	67	75	77	293	2535
	Ross DRUMMOND	(Scot)	75	71	76	71	293	2535
	Angel CABRERA	(Arg)	75	69	75	74	293	2535
57	Paul CURRY	(Eng)	74	72	72	76	294	2063
	Barry LANE	(Eng)	73	73	71	77	294	2063
	Derrick COOPER	(Eng)	70	76	76	72	294	2063
	Olle KARLSSON	(Swe)	78	67	73	76	294	2063
61	Silvio GRAPPASONNI	(It)	73	72	73	77	295	1755
	Andrew SHERBORNE	(Eng)	70	75	73	77	295	1755
	Russell CLAYDON	(Eng)	72	71	76	76	295	1755
	Jay TOWNSEND	(USA)	69	76	74	76	295	1755
	Miguel Angel MARTIN	(Sp)	70	76	77	72	295	1755
66	Iain PYMAN	(Eng)	70	72	75	79	296	972
	David A RUSSELL	(Eng)	73	71	77	75	296	972
	Fernando ROCA	(Sp)	72	73	75	76	296	972
	Fredrik LINDGREN	(Swe)	76	70	70	80	296	972
70	Antoine LEBOUC	(Fr)	74	72	80	71	297	966
	Greg CHALMERS	(Aus)	72	74	71	80	297	966
72	Per HAUGSRUD	(Nor)	74	72	80	72	298	960
	Michael JONZON	(Swe)	72	69	79	78	298	960
	Thomas GÖGELE	(Ger)	69	77	79	73	298	960
	Mark MOULAND	(Wal)	73	68	82	75	298	960
76	Richard BOXALL	(Eng)	74	72	75	78	299	955
77	Jeff HAWKES	(SA)	77	69	80	75	301	953
78	Marc FARRY	(Fr)	71	74	72	85	302	951

THE COURSE

Typical English parkland course which boasts deer, pheasant, ducks and geese among its pleasures. Tremendously improved over the last few years, The Forest of Arden is now widely admired for its challenge as well as its aesthetic appeal. The back nine especially provides a resolute challenge to golfers of all abilities.

The key to a perfect drive

Vauxhall Corsa 1.2 LS.

You can now drive out of over 200 locations across the
UK and Europe with Alamo. Simply call 0800 272 300.

OFFICIAL SPONSORS OF THE 1996 ENGLISH OPEN

Alamo features Vauxhall cars

Seventh heaven for Goosen

Retief Goosen became

the seventh first-time winner

of the 1996 European Tour

R etief Goosen came to Slaley Hall in a relaxed mood and ended up a winner. The 27-year old South African led from the start to finish for his debut win in the European Tour's newest event.

Naturally, Goosen's victory – he became the seventh first-time winner on the European Tour – was important to him, but perhaps what was more important was the return of big-time golf to the north-east. Sixteen years is too long a gap for an area as sports-mad as Tyneside to miss out on tournament golf.

Clashing as it did with the European soccer championships and the US Open – which with the best will in the world meant a quality field but without some of the cream – inevitably affected attendances.

However, Paresh Kotecha, Slaley Hall's Managing Director and head of the Aston Group of Hotels, made it clear he and his colleagues were more than happy. 'We weren't really expecting big crowds for this particular year. Crowds are determined by the field and US Open took the limelight, but we've had a decent turn-out.

We have to prove ourselves first on terms of the quality of the course, the players and how well we can organise a tournament in the north-east before we can move forward.'

'We're here for the long-term,' emphasised Kotecha who has given the go-ahead for work to start on a second course at Slaley designed by Neil Coles, quite a turnaround for a complex which went into receivership for three years until Aston Hotels rescued it and completed the five-star hotel.

The 'Gleneagles of the North' is Slaley's claim and it certainly showed itself in all its glory with the late spring turning into summer on the eve of the tournament with the blossoming rhododendrons among the pines giving an almost Augusta-like quality.

'I'd heard Slaley was a nice resort,' said Goosen, 'and went there with my girlfriend looking for a relaxing week. Perhaps I should try relaxing more often, it's obviously good for my game.' Goosen could have arrived at Slaley already a win-

ner on Tour having been in contention the previous week at the Forest of Arden, but the long-hitting former South African Open champion blew his chance in the space of four holes in the middle of the final round. 'I wasn't too worried. Sure, I was concerned that I'd played four holes badly and lost my chance, but it's not something I was going to let myself get really worried about – it just made me more determined to play well at Slaley,' said Goosen, who reckoned his game was beginning to reap the rewards of working with his coach Sam Frost. 'He's expensive, but he's worth it and we worked mainly on course management and made only some small changes to my swing.'

Goosen admitted his easy-going atti-

over here. Winning at Slaley and in Europe is a really important milestone for me and also coming down the stretch with just a one stroke lead and doing the business is also very important.'

Goosen's opening 66 set the tone for the tournament and gave him a two-stroke lead over Juan Carlos Piñero and the personable South African was never headed as scores tumbled in the brilliant sunshine.

A second day 66 from Ross McFarlane matched by Angel Cabrera in the third round set a new record before Scot Ross Drummond emerged as a serious challenger to Goosen on the final day with a charging 65, containing six birdies and an eagle to take the £3,000 Johnnie Walker

Heinz-Peter Thul's four iron for a hole-in-one at the 179-yard 14th might well have qualified for shot of the week had he done it at the 17th. He would have picked up a £17,000 car from Minories if he'd saved his ace for the 182-yard penultimate hole. David Jones' eagle two, another four iron straight into the cup, at the notorious 18th and Retief Goosen's spin back into the 565-yard 11th hole after hitting a wedge from 110 yards on day three were also candidates. But the shot of the week was almost the last one with Goosen knowing he needed to play the 18th in no worse than five to edge out Ross Drummond. The South African hit the perfect approach with a mid-iron to 12 feet from the flag at the 18th and took the two putts to win by two from Drummond.

Spirited challenge from Ross Drummond.

tude caused people to think him unconcerned when things went badly. 'I'm not as laid back as people think – I get as nervous as anyone else until I settle down. I probably got a bit lazy after I came to England and didn't progress as much as I thought I would, but I was buying a house and my mind really wasn't on golf, but I'm pretty much settled in now. I like it on the European Tour and enjoy it

Tour Course Record Award.

It also shot Drummond up the leaderboard to nine under par and within reach of Goosen who was showing the first signed of stumbling by dropping three shots in four holes.

Drummond, in fact, came within a shot of Goosen. 'I got on a lovely roll on the front nine and stayed on it,' said Drummond, whose work with sports psy-

chologist Jos Vanstiphout certainly paid dividends with winnings of £36,000 from his trip to the north-east.

'I was watching the leaderboard and keeping my eye on how things were going and when Ross finished nine under par I knew it was my tournament to win or lose,' said Goosen. 'I dropped three shots in four holes but I kept my cool and kept my head down and to win makes me feel great.'

Alan Hedley

SLALEY HALL GC, HEXHAM, JUNE 13-16, 1996 · YARDAGE 7003 · PAR 72

Pos	Name	Country	Rnd 1	Rnd 2	Rnd 3	Rnd 4	Total	Prize Money £
1	Retief GOOSEN	(SA)	66	69	70	72	277	50000
2	Ross DRUMMOND	(Scot)	74	71	69	65	279	33330
3	Robert LEE	(Eng)	71	71	67	72	281	18780
4	Heinz P THÜL	(Ger)	72	69	72	70	283	11800
	Gary EVANS	(Eng)	72	71	70	70	283	11800
	Andrew OLDCORN	(Scot)	71	69	71	72	283	11800
	David HOWELL	(Eng)	69	72	72	70	283	11800
8	Paul WAY	(Eng)	74	72	69	69	284	7500
9	Padraig HARRINGTON	(Ire)	70	71	72	72	285	6070
	Jamie SPENCE	(Eng)	73	74	69	69	285	6070
	John BICKERTON	(Eng)	72	72	72	69	285	6070
12	Ross MCFARLANE	(Eng)	77	66	72	71	286	4644
	Peter MITCHELL	(Eng)	74	71	71	70	286	4644
	Paul MCGINLEY	(Ire)	74	73	70	69	286	4644
	René BUDDE	(Den)	72	75	70	69	286	4644
	John MELLOR	(Eng)	79	68	69	70	286	4644
17	Andrew COLTART	(Scot)	75	70	69	73	287	3880
	Angel CABRERA	(Arg)	75	71	66	75	287	3880
	Gary CLARK	(Eng)	72	75	72	68	287	3880
20	David A RUSSELL	(Eng)	72	76	69	71	288	3420
	Adam HUNTER	(Scot)	69	76	72	71	288	3420
	Stephen DODD	(Wal)	71	70	76	71	288	3420
	Michel BESANCENEY	(Fr)	74	70	75	69	288	3420
	Juan Carlos PIÑERO	(Sp)	68	75	71	74	288	3420
25	Lee WESTWOOD	(Eng)	70	71	74	74	289	3015
	Paul BROADHURST	(Eng)	71	75	73	70	289	3015
	Roger CHAPMAN	(Eng)	77	68	73	71	289	3015
	Hendrik BUHRMANN	(SA)	70	70	75	74	289	3015
29	Andrew BEAL	(Eng)	76	72	71	71	290	2655
	Patrik SJÖLAND	(Swe)	72	74	71	73	290	2655
	David J RUSSELL	(Eng)	73	72	75	70	290	2655
	Magnus PERSSON	(Swe)	72	76	72	70	290	2655
33	Michael URE	(Eng)	70	77	72	72	291	2400
	Christian POST	(Den)	75	71	71	74	291	2400
	Miles TUNNICLIFF	(Eng)	70	73	75	73	291	2400
36	Jon ROBSON	(Eng)	71	73	76	72	292	2070
	Malcolm MACKENZIE	(Eng)	71	72	78	71	292	2070
	John HAWKSWORTH	(Eng)	75	71	70	76	292	2070
	Gordon J BRAND	(Eng)	69	72	77	74	292	2070
	Glenn RALPH	(Eng)	72	74	72	74	292	2070
	Richard DINSDALE	(Wal)	72	70	76	74	292	2070
	Mark PLUMMER	(Eng)	71	74	73	74	292	2070
	Ged FUREY	(Eng)	73	72	73	74	292	2070
44	Anders HANSEN	(Den)	73	73	75	72	293	1680
	David LYNN	(Eng)	76	72	72	73	293	1680
	Mike CLAYTON	(Aus)	76	69	76	72	293	1680
	Per NYMAN	(Swe)	73	71	74	75	293	1680
	David R JONES	(Eng)	73	73	72	75	293	1680
49	Michael ARCHER	(Eng)	74	73	73	74	294	1410
	Howard CLARK	(Eng)	76	71	76	71	294	1410
	David HIGGINS	(Ire)	73	75	72	74	294	1410
	Chris HALL	(Eng)	72	76	68	78	294	1410
53	Anthony PAINTER	(Aus)	75	72	73	75	295	1110
	Jeremy ROBINSON	(Eng)	72	74	77	72	295	1110
	Steven BOTTOMLEY	(Eng)	71	76	74	74	295	1110
	Peter FOWLER	(Aus)	74	74	73	74	295	1110
	Max ANGLERT	(Swe)	72	72	73	78	295	1110
	Jason WIDENER	(USA)	74	73	74	74	295	1110
59	Carl SUNESON	(Sp)	77	67	79	73	296	915
	Tim PLANCHIN	(Fr)	73	73	70	80	296	915
61	Carl MASON	(Eng)	74	70	78	75	297	840
	George RYALL	(Eng)	74	72	79	72	297	840
	Daniel CHOPRA	(Swe)	72	75	74	76	297	840
64	Anssi KANKKONEN	(Fin)	74	72	77	75	298	660
	Anders SORENSEN	(Den)	75	73	70	80	298	660
	Derrick COOPER	(Eng)	74	73	77	74	298	660
67	Neal BRIGGS	(Eng)	74	73	81	75	303	448
68	Ian SPENCER	(Eng)	78	69	77	80	304	446

THE COURSE

Dave Thomas was very pleased when he designed the 7,003-yard course. A spectacular mix of imposing pines, rolling moorland and water with stunning views of the Tyne Valley, Slaley is a typical Thomas course with massive bunkers and raised greens. It has three tough holes in succession around the turn with the seventh involving a drive with a lake on the left and a massive tree on the right and then an uphill approach to a two-tier green. The eighth is a downhill dog-leg right with a stream ready to catch those unwise to use a driver off the tee. Then there is the 452-yard ninth – Slaley's signature hole (right), described by Slaley's touring pro, Ronan Rafferty as an 'Augusta-like par four played over water through an avenue of towering pines and dense rhododendrons to a sloping green.' And there is the 18th – a superb closing hole where the tee shot is all-important. Too long and you have a downhill lie for your second across the stream to a green guarded by three bunkers on the left and one on the right; too short and you may need a fairway wood to reach the green.

Farry's finest hour

As rain shortened
the tournament to 36 holes,
Marc Farry was buoyant in Munich

Rain can be a blessing at times. It can soften up hard, fast greens and make them more manageable, but too much of it can create a nightmare for the tournament organiser. In Munich this year the organisers of the BMW International Open, who run one of the best events on the Tour, were foiled by the one thing over which they had no control.

The rain sweeping down from the Alps made play impossible over the weekend and their event, despite the heroic work of the green-keeping staff, had to be cut to 36 holes. Tarpaulins were draped over tees and greens in a bid to keep them playable but such was the intensity of the downpour that all efforts to play were finally thwarted and the event, which had enjoyed glorious weather in its first seven years, became another victim of the weather.

No fewer than ten of the early events were affected one way or another by rain, strong winds, thunder and lightning but the problems in Munich turned out to be a godsend to one golfer, halfway leader Marc Antoine Farry. When he stepped forward to pick up his first prize cheque of £87,495, 75 per cent of what he would have received had the event gone the full distance, it was, truly, an emotional moment.

After all, the stylish Frenchman, who had to visit the Qualifying School five times, might well have quit tournament play had it not been for the encouragement of his wife Isabelle. He had won 15 times on the French National circuit, but it was she who insisted that he continue to compete against the best in European golf. It was she who encouraged him to stay on despite the disappointments. It was she who, initially, could not speak when Marc telephoned to tell her that after eight full years on Tour, during which time he had never finished better than 91st in the Volvo Ranking and only once managed a top three finish, in Austria in 1991, he was at last a winner.

Yet 36-year old Farry, who taught golf in Florida for four years at one point in his career, does not plan on his breakthrough win at St Eurach Land und Golf Club, a fast drive along the motorway to Munchengladbach and close

Runner-up Richard Green secured his card for 1997.

Marc Farry's maiden European Tour victory was gained by the narrowest of margins – one shot. In this context, the shot that made the difference was his third to the par four 12th in the second, and ultimately, final round when his wedge shot from 130 yards dived into the hole for an eagle. It made the vital difference.

by the spa resort of Baden Baden, being his only Tour success.

For Farry, whose prematurely grey hair gives him the look of a diplomat and whose career has been dogged by back trouble, the win was overdue although others have waited longer to enjoy the delights of making that winner's speech. Singapore-based American Peter Teravainen waited 20 years for his dream to come true at Mariánské Lázne in the

Czech Republic and Englishman Carl Mason, who joined the Tour in 1974, waited just as long before he won the Turespaña Masters Open de Andalucia at Montecastillo. Having done so, Mason went on the same year to win the Bell's Scottish Open over the King's course at Gleneagles.

In some respects Farry's win was surprising. He had no early form to boast about as he headed to Munich for the

tournament that would raise him to a new status on Tour. He had missed the cut in the first five events he played in Singapore, Australia and South Africa. His early season putting had been appalling. He had struggled so much on the greens that it had affected his long game and, coming into the BMW International, the best he had managed in 14 starts was 26th, behind another first time winner Raymond Russell in the Air France Cannes Open.

Step forward Patrick Leglise, former

St Eurach Land und Golf Club is situated in the foothills of the Bavarian Alps, approximately 40 kilometres from Munich. Built in the early 1970s by the English architect Donald Harradine, the course runs through rolling countryside with nine of the holes tracking through narrow forest lanes. Water comes into play on four holes and the course features a tough final three holes of 585 yards, 219 yards and 432 yards respectively.

St Eurach Land und Golf Club, Munich, June 20-23, 1996 · Yardage 7035 · Par 72

Pos	Name	Country	Rnd 1	Rnd 2	Rnd 3	Rnd 4	Total	Prize Money £
1	Marc FARRY	(Fr)	65	67			132	87495
2	Richard GREEN	(Aus)	67	66			133	58327
3	Russell CLAYDON	(Eng)	69	65			134	27115
	Padraig HARRINGTON	(Ire)	68	66			134	27115
	David HIGGINS	(Ire)	64	70			134	27115
6	Francisco CEA	(Sp)	70	65			135	15750
	Raymond RUSSELL	(Scot)	69	66			135	15750
	Ignacio GARRIDO	(Sp)	67	68			135	15750
9	Phil GOLDING	(Eng)	65	71			136	10622
	Gary CLARK	(Eng)	72	64			136	10622
	Mathias GRÖNBERG	(Swe)	67	69			136	10622
12	Pierre FULKE	(Swe)	75	62			137	8308
	Fabrice TARNAUD	(Fr)	69	68			137	8308
	Francis HOWLEY	(Ire)	69	68			137	8308
	Lee WESTWOOD	(Eng)	65	72			137	8308
16	David HOWELL	(Eng)	70	68			138	6503
	Mats HALLBERG	(Swe)	70	68			138	6503
	David GILFORD	(Eng)	67	71			138	6503
	Bernhard LANGER	(Ger)	69	69			138	6503
	Mark MOULAND	(Wal)	67	71			138	6503
	Marcus WILLS	(Wal)	66	72			138	6503
	Alexander CEJKA	(Ger)	70	68			138	6503
	Emanuele CANONICA	(It)	68	70			138	6503
24	John BICKERTON	(Eng)	70	69			139	5197
	Patrik SJÖLAND	(Swe)	70	69			139	5197
	Mark LITTON	(Wal)	73	66			139	5197
	Miles TUNNICLIFF	(Eng)	69	70			139	5197
	Peter FOWLER	(Aus)	71	68			139	5197
	Richard DINSDALE	(Wal)	70	69			139	5197
	Stephen MCALLISTER	(Scot)	69	70			139	5197
31	Frank NOBILO	(NZ)	73	67			140	3889
	Mark MCNULTY	(Zim)	72	68			140	3889

Pos	Name	Country	Rnd 1	Rnd 2	Total	Prize Money £
	Mark JAMES	(Eng)	67	73	140	3889
	Ignacio FELIU	(Sp)	71	69	140	3889
	Daniel CHOPRA	(Swe)	69	71	140	3889
	Peter BAKER	(Eng)	68	72	140	3889
	Jim PAYNE	(Eng)	71	69	140	3889
	Emanuele BOLOGNESI	(It)	69	71	140	3889
	Tim PLANCHIN	(Fr)	67	73	140	3889
	Jeremy ROBINSON	(Eng)	70	70	140	3889
	David WILLIAMS	(Eng)	72	68	140	3889
	Chris HALL	(Eng)	71	69	140	3889.
	John MELLOR	(Eng)	70	70	140	3889
44	Carl SUNESON	(Sp)	70	71	141	2782
	Malcolm MACKENZIE	(Eng)	69	72	141	2782
	David CARTER	(Eng)	71	70	141	2782
	Mark ROE	(Eng)	69	72	141	2782
	Seve BALLESTEROS	(Sp)	71	70	141	2782
	Ronan RAFFERTY	(N.Ire)	69	72	141	2782
	Pedro LINHART	(Sp)	72	69	141	2782
	Angel CABRERA	(Arg)	69	72	141	2782
52	Scott WATSON	(Eng)	70	72	142	1669
	Paul EALES	(Eng)	70	72	142	1669
	Gordon BRAND JNR.	(Scot)	73	69	142	1669
	Heinz P THÜL	(Ger)	73	69	142	1669
	Christian CÉVAER	(Fr)	74	68	142	1669
	Thomas BJORN	(Den)	72	70	142	1669
	Domingo HOSPITAL	(Sp)	71	71	142	1669
	Darren CLARKE	(N.Ire)	71	71	142	1669
	Robert ALLENBY	(Aus)	74	68	142	1669
	Raymond BURNS	(N.Ire)	70	72	142	1669
	Antoine LEBOUC	(Fr)	74	68	142	1669
	Eric GIRAUD	(Fr)	73	69	142	1669
	Per HAUGSRUD	(Nor)	71	71	142	1669
	Jeff CRANFORD	(USA)	70	72	142	1669
	Sven STRÜVER	(Ger)	75	67	142	1669

amateur international, now professional at Chantilly just outside Paris. He reminded Farry that he had been used to putting with the ball further forward, something that helped him take his shoulders out of the equation. Doing that made him more dependent on his hands and he had made the necessary changes.

There was something else in his favour as he headed for Bavaria. Some players and their games are well suited to some courses. Farry with rounds of 67, 67 on Thursday and Friday in 1995 indicated he was comfortable among the pines, eventually finishing seventh behind New Zealand's Frank Nobilo. In 1996, relying on his old putting technique, he shot 65, 67 for 132, the highlight being an eagle at the 12th, on the second day when ironically he did not need to putt. He holed a 130-yard wedge shot.

It meant he finished a shot clear of Richard Green from Australia, who did enough in the event to make sure of his Tour card for 1997. His second prize of £58,827 shooting him well past the anticipated amount required to finish in the top 117 of the Volvo Ranking at the end of the season. Of course, Farry would have had a tough weekend with Russell Claydon, Padraig Harrington, winner of the Peugeot Open de España earlier in the season, and David Higgins, son of former Tour big-hitter Liam Higgins from Waterville, just two behind. Raymond Russell, winner in Cannes, fancied his chances over the weekend and there was considerable interest in the impressive performance of Francisco Cea, who like Claydon had shot 65 on the second day,

while 25-year old Pierre Fulke had geared up for the weekend in the best possible way with a ten-birdie 62 which was 13 shots better than his disappointing opening round. His score which earned him the £3000 Johnnie Walker Tour Course Award prize, was his best on Tour and beat the record set the previous year by another Swede, Jarmo Sandelin.

The heavy showers, sweeping in every so often to further saturate the course, meant they did not get a chance to challenge over the weekend leaving Farry, like Paul Lawrie in Catalonia earlier in the season, a winner over 36 holes. 'It would have been nice to prove to my peers that I could have won over 72 holes,' said Farry. 'But a win is a win and this is my dream come true.'

Renton Laidlaw

Allenby clinches second title

Robert Allenby's victory over Bernhard Langer in a play-off gave him his second win of the season

*I*n the early days of the European Tour it was dangerous to make too many predictions. Certainly, nobody dared to forecast that come 1996 the Tour would welcome the 50th member of its very own Millionaires' Club. But, just 20 years on from a season when total prize-money amounted to less than £900,000 and Severiano Ballesteros was the leading money-winner with £39,504, it happened. At the Peugeot Open de France. And it happened, appropriately, in the grand manner, with the player concerned crashing through the seven-figure barrier by taking the prestigious title. It was his second in four weeks.

Young Australian Robert Allenby enjoyed quite a June. An awesome one, in fact. He climbed from 71st place to third in the Volvo Ranking, from 63rd to 38th in the Sony Ranking and in 14 rounds was under par in 13 of them. Little surprise then that he was named the Johnnie Walker Golfer of the Month.

The 24-year old, who had come up with a storming finish to pip Colin Montgomerie and Ross McFarlane in the Alamo English Open, left it even later this time. Eleven of Europe's victorious 1995

Ryder Cup by Johnnie Walker side (all but Nick Faldo) assembled at Le Golf National for an event whose proud history dates back to 1906 and whose list of winners includes Walter Hagen, Henry Cotton, Roberto de Vicenzo, Byron Nelson, Bobby Locke, Greg Norman and Faldo.

Ballesteros was there to try to equal Audrey Boomer's record five victories, 19 years after his first. Bernhard Langer was there as well to attempt to repeat his success at St Cloud in 1984 and Colin Montgomerie was there to try to go one better than he had in his previous two European starts.

In 1995, fierce rough and a strong wind had made L'Albatros course something of a monster. The halfway cut then was six over par and nothing all season was higher. If it did not exactly leave some of the world's top players in fear and trepidation – Paul Broadhurst, after all, shot a record 63 in the final round to

Top ten finish for Paul Broadhurst.

SHOT OF THE WEEK

Tempting though it is to go straight to Robert Allenby's birdie putt, up and over a ridge, which decided the play-off, the shot which forced the play-off was even more memorable. Needing a birdie four at the 18th to catch Bernhard Langer, Allenby made his task much harder by pushing his drive. It forced him to lay up short of the lake, but he then hit a 70-yard pitch to three feet. 'I felt very comfortable over it,' he said, 'but it was still a great shot.'

win by eight – it certainly earned their respect.

But this time things were different. Springtime in Paris had seen little or no rain and as a result the rough was much less intimidating and the course played a lot shorter. The cut mark came down from 150 to 141, three under par and the lowest of the season to date, and among those who did not make it was Montgomerie, despite an eagle three at the 513-yard 18th.

Six players fired 66s on the opening day and on the second England's Steve Richardson became the first of three men in the week to equal Broadhurst's course record of 63. Richardson, the 1991 Volvo Ranking runner-up, had missed the cut on ten of his previous 11 starts, but had not lost sight of the fact that 'we've got a great job, haven't we?' He played the last ten holes of his second round in eight under par, chipping in from 30 yards for eagle at the long ninth and then coming home in 30, and at halfway he led on 131 (13 under) by two from Ulsterman Raymond Burns and three from defending champion Broadhurst, Ian Woosnam and Retief Goosen, winner of his first Tour title a fortnight earlier.

A wind returned for the third round and Richardson began by going into the lake at the first two holes. A nightmare loomed, but he got his act together and a drive and seven iron to four feet for a

Differing emotions on the green from (above, left to right) Bernhard Langer, Seve Ballesteros and Colin Montgomerie. Steven Richardson (left) tied the course record.

closing eagle put him back in front.

Woosnam fell out of the picture with a 78, but Allenby moved into second place with a 68 and Langer's 67 for joint fourth spot showed that after talk of yips and even possible retirement he was still alive and kicking.

If any further proof were needed it came with Langer's stunning start to the last round. Six birdies in the first

seven holes: 'Some of the best golf I've ever played,' he said, and another on the 11th swept him from four behind to two in front and on course for maintaining a remarkable record that had seen him win at least once every year since 1979.

It was enough to see off Richardson, but Allenby proved a tougher nut to crack and after Langer double-bogeyed the 12th, the Melbourne golfer saw his chance. He was rock solid as the event built to its climax, whereas the German dropped another shot on the 17th. They were level then and after Langer two putted the 514-yard last for a birdie four, Allenby, forced to lay up short of the lake after pushing his drive, hit a 70-yard pitch to three feet

to force sudden-death.

The play-off did not last long. Langer hit his approach to the 421-yard 15th, the first extra hole, to around 12 feet, but from more than twice as far Allenby holed and Langer, suddenly needing his to stay alive, missed.

'It was a lucky putt, but in play-offs things like that happen all the time,' commented Allenby, his satisfaction at winning all the greater because of whom he had beaten. 'Bernhard is one of the great players in the world – I'm very happy to see him doing well again, but I feel I am mentally very tough.'

Mark Garrod

NATIONAL GC, PARIS, JUNE 27-30, 1996 · YARDAGE 7119 · PAR 72

Pos	Name	Country	Rnd 1	Rnd 2	Rnd 3	Rnd 4	Total	Prize Money £
1	Robert ALLENBY	(Aus)	70	65	68	69	272	100000
2	Bernhard LANGER	(Ger)	69	70	67	66	272	66660
3	Retief GOOSEN	(SA)	66	68	72	68	274	37560
4	Steven RICHARDSON	(Eng)	68	63	71	73	275	27700
	Paul MCGINLEY	(Ire)	70	67	75	63	275	27700
6	Lee WESTWOOD	(Eng)	67	68	73	68	276	21000
7	Frank NOBILO	(NZ)	67	68	71	71	277	15480
	Greg TURNER	(NZ)	66	70	70	71	277	15480
	Paul BROADHURST	(Eng)	70	64	70	73	277	15480
10	Philip WALTON	(Ire)	67	71	68	72	278	11106
	Peter MITCHELL	(Eng)	70	70	69	69	278	11106
	Miles TUNNICLIFF	(Eng)	70	70	75	63	278	11106
13	Gary ORR	(Scot)	70	65	75	69	279	9410
	Raymond BURNS	(N.Ire)	67	66	75	71	279	9410
15	Malcolm MACKENZIE	(Eng)	71	65	76	68	280	7960
	Per-Ulrik JOHANSSON	(Swe)	68	67	78	67	280	7960
	Gordon BRAND JNR.	(Scot)	67	70	72	71	280	7960
	Ronan RAFFERTY	(N.Ire)	66	70	74	70	280	7960
	Mark MOULAND	(Wal)	70	71	66	73	280	7960
	Sven STRÜVER	(Ger)	69	67	76	68	280	7960
21	André BOSSERT	(Swi)	69	72	71	69	281	6480
	Santiago LUNA	(Sp)	69	71	72	69	281	6480
	Costantino ROCCA	(It)	66	72	70	73	281	6480
	Francisco CEA	(Sp)	70	70	74	67	281	6480
	Ian WOOSNAM	(Wal)	69	65	78	69	281	6480
	Olle KARLSSON	(Swe)	70	67	76	68	281	6480
	David HOWELL	(Eng)	67	70	72	72	281	6480
28	Roger CHAPMAN	(Eng)	68	72	74	68	282	5106
	Bradley HUGHES	(Aus)	74	65	74	69	282	5106
	José COCERES	(Arg)	70	66	76	70	282	5106
	Paul CURRY	(Eng)	69	71	72	70	282	5106
	Gary CLARK	(Eng)	69	68	71	74	282	5106
	Sam TORRANCE	(Scot)	71	68	72	71	282	5106
	Wayne RILEY	(Aus)	72	69	71	70	282	5106
	Miguel Angel MARTIN	(Sp)	70	70	70	72	282	5106
	Thomas BJORN	(Den)	66	71	76	69	282	5106
37	Max ANGLERT	(Swe)	71	65	78	69	283	4380
	Andrew COLTART	(Scot)	72	66	72	73	283	4380
39	Glenn RALPH	(Eng)	71	70	73	70	284	3900
	Richard GREEN	(Aus)	71	70	72	71	284	3900
	Sandy LYLE	(Scot)	70	70	72	72	284	3900
	Pierre FULKE	(Swe)	68	72	72	72	284	3900
	Joakim HAEGGMAN	(Swe)	70	68	79	67	284	3900
	Bob MAY	(USA)	72	68	77	67	284	3900
45	Russell CLAYDON	(Eng)	72	69	70	74	285	3120
	Mark MCNULTY	(Zim)	73	67	75	70	285	3120
	Jim PAYNE	(Eng)	71	69	74	71	285	3120
	Klas ERIKSSON	(Swe)	70	66	74	75	285	3120
	Tim PLANCHIN	(Fr)	71	69	71	74	285	3120
	Eric GIRAUD	(Fr)	71	68	75	71	285	3120
	Angel CABRERA	(Arg)	70	70	72	73	285	3120
52	Daniel CHOPRA	(Swe)	67	70	72	77	286	2400
	Jay TOWNSEND	(USA)	71	66	78	71	286	2400
	Ignacio GARRIDO	(Sp)	71	67	76	72	286	2400
	Mark JAMES	(Eng)	70	70	75	71	286	2400
	Francisco VALERA	(Sp)	69	72	73	72	286	2400
57	Seve BALLESTEROS	(Sp)	72	66	71	78	287	2040
58	Jon ROBSON	(Eng)	70	69	75	74	288	1860
	Fredrik LINDGREN	(Swe)	72	67	76	73	288	1860
	David HIGGINS	(Ire)	69	70	76	73	288	1860
	Christophe RAVETTO (AM)	(Fr)	68	73	78	69	288	
61	Francis HOWLEY	(Ire)	73	67	79	70	289	1710
	Eduardo ROMERO	(Arg)	71	68	78	72	289	1710
63	Antoine LEBOUC	(Fr)	71	68	78	73	290	1395
	Jean VAN DE VELDE	(Fr)	74	67	78	71	290	1395
	John BICKERTON	(Eng)	71	68	80	71	290	1395
	Per HAUGSRUD	(Nor)	66	71	81	72	290	1395
67	Neal BRIGGS	(Eng)	70	71	78	72	291	898
68	Gabriel HJERTSTEDT	(Swe)	73	68	77	74	292	896
69	Jeff REMESY	(Fr)	67	72	79	76	294	894

THE COURSE

Le Golf National just outside Paris was sculptured from 1.6million cubic metres of earth, brought from the nearby EuroDisney site in 400 giant tipper trucks every day for two years. It has been the dramatic setting for the Peugeot Open de France since 1991 and is widely regarded as one of the best layouts on the European Tour, both for players and spectators. L'Albatros course builds to a climax in which everything is possible from eagles to double figures. Water, water everywhere.

1 Sometimes the best laid plans need a little help.

2 We help deliver.

Scotch™ Magic™ Tape from 3M has been helping people for years. When we learned that farmers were taping cracked eggs so they could hatch, we knew yet another great use had been born. From attaching wings to aircraft, to pin-striping cars, people trust Scotch™ brand tapes for strength, consistency and value.

It all comes from our unique corporate spirit–which lets us make the leap

from need to...

3M *Innovation*

For more information call (071) 5 450 450

Montgomerie consolidates at the top

Victory in Ireland strengthened Colin Montgomerie's position at the top of the Volvo Ranking

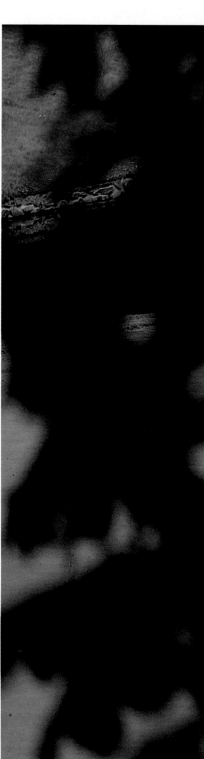

*T*he Druid's Glen was the sixth, and most spectacular, venue for the Murphy's Irish Open since the championship was revived in 1975, but it was young, untried and certainly unexposed to the considerable talents of Europe's top players. It was tough and it was tight, and the weather cocktail of strong winds, rain, thunder and lightning and even a hail storm, rarely included the more pleasant ingredients normally associated with mid-summer.

Thus, the splendour of the place was diminished, and the local slogan 'The Garden of Eden in the Garden of Ireland' was hardly relevant for this particular week, but The Druid's Glen is a special place and it could not have produced a better winner. Colin Montgomerie returned from a frustrating 13th place in the US Open and promptly missed the cut in his next outing at the Peugeot Open de France.

The European number one needed a boost to his morale, in preparation for his assault on his native Scottish Open, which he had never won, and the Open at Royal Lytham & St. Annes in the following weeks. The Murphy's Irish Open provided the tonic. He liked the course from the start despite a cruel opening blow in the first round when his triple-bogey seven at the 13th (his 4th) included the first fresh air shot of his professional career. Tournament Director Andy McFee's set up of the course entailed reduction of the par for the sixth and 18th holes from five to four, narrowing the fairways and growing collars of rough around the greens for an overall tough par of 71.

Seve Ballesteros couldn't recover his form.

'This course suits me,' declared Montgomerie. 'This is the way all courses should be set up for tournaments in Europe. It is a pleasure to come and play here.'

The Scot did not hit all the fairways or all the greens but he hit more than most. One he missed was the 13th

SHOT OF THE WEEK

The 17th is an island green approached from a tunnel of trees 200 yards away. Club selection is always difficult. Hitting the green is paramount, making birdie is, in the final round, a bonus with the pin tucked to the left back. Montgomerie chose a six iron and hit it perfectly to 25 feet and picked up the bonus. It gave him the chance of a lifetime. Without it he might not have won the tournament.

on the first day. This signature hole was carved out of several feet of a rock face to make a dog-leg from an elevated tee to a fairway bordered on the right by a stream and on the left by a cliff-like bank of scrub. The second shot demands accuracy to a narrow target across a pond. Montgomerie's tee shot finished on the bank of the stream and in the act of extricating it his foot slipped and he produced a fresh air shot followed by a fluff into the water incurring a penalty drop, all of which led him to a seven after only his fourth hole of the tournament. It says much for his resilience and determination that he covered the remaining 68 holes in eight under, and that included a third round 73 which cost him the lead to the man he was eventually to beat by one shot, the luckless Andrew Oldcorn.

Grateful for victory, Montgomerie had the grace to acknowledge the plight of the vanquished. 'This is my 11th victory on the European Tour and this was the most fortunate. My heart goes out to Andrew as a fellow Scot. This Tour is very close. We fly together, share cars, stay in the same hotels and see each other in bars and restaurants. We all saw what happened out there and it was a shame. He had it in the bag and I was playing for second place.'

He was, until Oldcorn took a double-bogey six at the 18th. He had moved into the third round lead at three

Padraig Harrington (left) was up a tree and in the drink.
Celtic cross points the way for Bernhard Langer (above).

under with a blistering back nine of four under for a round 70, one clear of Montgomerie, Lee Westwood and Miguel Angel Martin and two ahead of Carl Mason, Wayne Westner, Joakim Haeggman and Ricky Willison. Oldcorn held command on the final day until the last hole by virtue of the fact that his pursuers had fallen by the wayside, and that

included Montgomerie after he three-putted the eighth and ninth to drop three behind.

The final six holes at The Druid's Glen present a stern finish, and Montgomerie covered them in two under par, the feature being a brilliant birdie on the island green at the 17th to pile on the pressure. Sitting in the clubhouse at four

145

THE COURSE

'Build the best inland course in Ireland,' was the brief given to architects Pat Ruddy and Tom Craddock. The Woodstock estate 25 miles from Dublin and set between the Wicklow Mountains and the Irish Sea had already been acquired and money was not a problem. The name, The Druid's Glen, comes from a water-laden wooded valley in which lie two spectacular par threes, the eighth and 12th with, history tells us, an ancient stone Druid's altar to the side of the latter. The 13th, a dog-leg carved out of solid rock, is the signature hole and the course is a test for the best, and the rest.

Johnnie Walker Tour Course Record Award went to Wayne Riley.

under was the Australian Wayne Riley who had cracked Bernhard Langer's first day record of 67 with a superb 66. Riley would readily agree with Montgomerie insofar as the tougher the course the better he likes it. 'Those 24-under-pars don't suit me. I like to tack my way around a course.'

The big Scot finished five under par leaving Oldcorn with a par to win and bogey to tie. The green is separated from the fairway by a cascade of water dropping over three falls and when he pulled his drive into a dreadful lie in the left rough,

THE DRUID'S GLEN GC DUBLIN, JULY 4-7, 1996 • YARDAGE 7025 • PAR 71

Pos	Name	Country	Rnd 1	Rnd 2	Rnd 3	Rnd 4	Total	Prize Money £
1	Colin MONTGOMERIE	(Scot)	69	69	73	68	279	127551
2	Andrew OLDCORN	(Scot)	72	68	70	70	280	66459
	Wayne RILEY	(Aus)	73	68	73	66	280	66459
4	Miguel Angel MARTIN	(Sp)	71	68	72	70	281	38265
5	Ignacio GARRIDO	(Sp)	71	69	74	69	283	29602
	Raymond RUSSELL	(Scot)	74	70	71	68	283	29602
7	Phillip PRICE	(Wal)	76	70	70	68	284	17712
	Wayne WESTNER	(SA)	70	70	72	72	284	17712
	Robert ALLENBY	(Aus)	74	69	71	70	284	17712
	Lee WESTWOOD	(Eng)	70	71	70	73	284	17712
	Ricky WILLISON	(Eng)	72	69	71	72	284	17712
12	Carl MASON	(Eng)	74	68	70	74	286	12107
	Joakim HAEGGMAN	(Swe)	71	72	69	74	286	12107
	Ernie ELS	(SA)	73	70	71	72	286	12107
	Bernhard LANGER	(Ger)	67	76	71	72	286	12107
16	David HOWELL	(Eng)	73	73	73	68	287	10785
17	Peter MITCHELL	(Eng)	72	72	71	73	288	9164
	Jay TOWNSEND	(USA)	76	70	71	71	288	9164
	Malcolm MACKENZIE	(Eng)	75	70	70	73	288	9164
	Ronan RAFFERTY	(N.Ire)	74	72	72	70	288	9164
	Sandy LYLE	(Scot)	75	71	68	74	288	9164
	Ian WOOSNAM	(Wal)	71	70	73	74	288	9164
	Raymond BURNS	(N.Ire)	72	74	71	71	288	9164
	Domingo HOSPITAL	(Sp)	75	70	72	71	288	9164
25	Roger CHAPMAN	(Eng)	72	73	76	68	289	7346
	Peter O'MALLEY	(Aus)	75	70	74	70	289	7346
	Frank NOBILO	(NZ)	71	72	72	74	289	7346
	Peter BAKER	(Eng)	74	70	75	70	289	7346
	Andrew COLTART	(Scot)	72	68	76	73	289	7346
	Marcus WILLS	(Wal)	73	70	74	72	289	7346
	Peter HEDBLOM	(Swe)	71	68	75	75	289	7346
32	Jarmo SANDELIN	(Swe)	74	73	72	71	290	5969
	Paul MCGINLEY	(Ire)	73	71	70	76	290	5969
	Sam TORRANCE	(Scot)	71	72	76	71	290	5969
	José COCERES	(Arg)	71	72	75	72	290	5969
	Daniel CHOPRA	(Swe)	73	73	69	75	290	5969
	Rolf MUNTZ	(Hol)	73	70	72	75	290	5969
	Miles TUNNICLIFF	(Eng)	76	69	72	73	290	5969
39	Carl SUNESON	(Sp)	76	71	72	72	291	5127
	Stephen AMES	(T&T)	71	74	72	74	291	5127
	David A RUSSELL	(Eng)	71	73	76	71	291	5127
	John BICKERTON	(Eng)	76	71	73	71	291	5127
43	Russell CLAYDON	(Eng)	71	77	70	74	292	4438
	Michael CAMPBELL	(NZ)	73	71	76	72	292	4438
	Darren CLARKE	(N.Ire)	79	69	69	75	292	4438
	Mark ROE	(Eng)	75	71	71	75	292	4438
	Jim PAYNE	(Eng)	77	69	72	74	292	4438
48	David CARTER	(Eng)	77	71	73	72	293	3596
	Per-Ulrik JOHANSSON	(Swe)	69	75	80	69	293	3596
	Roger WESSELS	(SA)	72	75	73	73	293	3596
	Bradley HUGHES	(Aus)	74	74	74	71	293	3596
	Brenden PAPPAS	(SA)	70	78	70	75	293	3596
	Steen TINNING	(Den)	72	72	73	76	293	3596
54	Paul BROADHURST	(Eng)	75	73	75	71	294	2634
	José RIVERO	(Sp)	76	71	75	72	294	2634
	Gary MURPHY	(Ire)	70	71	81	72	294	2634
	Tony JOHNSTONE	(Zim)	73	70	75	76	294	2634
	Paul LAWRIE	(Scot)	76	72	75	71	294	2634
	Ross MCFARLANE	(Eng)	73	75	75	71	294	2634
	Eric GIRAUD	(Fr)	75	71	70	78	294	2634
61	Fredrik LINDGREN	(Swe)	70	74	76	75	295	2142
	Philip WALTON	(Ire)	76	72	73	74	295	2142
	Ross DRUMMOND	(Scot)	72	72	74	77	295	2142
64	Per HAUGSRUD	(Nor)	77	71	72	76	296	1951
	Gary EVANS	(Eng)	76	69	77	74	296	1951
66	David WILLIAMS	(Eng)	74	73	79	71	297	1148
67	Barry LANE	(Eng)	76	72	74	76	298	1143
	Silvio GRAPPASONNI	(It)	74	74	72	78	298	1143
	Patrik SJÖLAND	(Swe)	75	73	75	75	298	1143
	Mats HALLBERG	(Swe)	76	70	73	79	298	1143
71	Gordon SHERRY	(Scot)	73	74	69	83	299	1137
	Mike CLAYTON	(Aus)	76	71	74	78	299	1137

Despair for Andrew Oldcorn as he three-putts the final green.

reaching it in two was out of the question. Making the fairway was the priority leaving a pitch and putt for victory or even two putts for a tie. Unfortunately his third came up short of the ridge on the green and rolled back. The first putt from 25 feet up the hill went three feet past but that too was missed to his grief and the crowd's groan. Nobody gloated. It was a cruel way to lose but Oldcorn was positive in his reflection. 'I don't feel I bottled it. I'm really proud of the way I played. I just got one terrible lie on the last hole.'

Colm Smith

147

Scottish triple for Woosnam

Ian Woosnam took his third
Scottish Open title with a
bravura display at Carnoustie

I an Woosnam overcame a brutal wind
and a tough and treacherous golf
course to record his third Scottish Open
success in the last decade. Coincidentally,
it was also his third win of the 1996
European Tour season and was achieved
in a manner which recalled the time in the
late 1980s when the Welshman won the
US Masters and, for a short while at least,
was the undisputed world's number one.

Woosnam went into the final round
over the venerable championship course
at Carnoustie with a three-shot lead and
in the end he was to increase his advantage to four after registering a three over
par 75 on the final afternoon. In different
circumstances such a score in the mid-70s
would have meant a fall from grace but on
this occasion it was actually an excellent
performance in winds gusting up to

40 mph and gave the Welshman a four-shot margin over Scotland's Andrew Coltart, who closed with a 74, and a five-shot lead over Sweden's Mats Hallberg, who at one stage through the turn had actually shared the lead before Woosnam eagled the par five 12th for the second successive round to prise an advantage he was never to relinquish.

An illustration of the difficulties involved is that Woosnam's one over par 289 total was no less than 13 shots higher than the aggregate which Australia's Wayne Riley posted while winning the same tournament over the same course 12 months before. It was also the first time that a score above par had been good enough to win a European Tour event since Sandy Lyle prevailed in the Open at Royal St George's in 1985 although the Welshman's winning aggregate was still some eight shots lower than the total South Africa's Harold Henning posted while winning the Pringle of Scotland

THE COURSE

There was a time when Carnoustie's reputation as one of Britain's finest seaside courses was jeopardised by reports of its poor condition but those problems have long since been solved under the guidance of Course Superintendent John Philp and his staff and it deserves to regain its rightful place among Britain's best once more. During the Scottish Open a stream of competitors queued up to lavish praise on the course, and their approval, both of James Braid's layout and the condition in which it was presented, was not dampened even when gale force winds caused their scores to soar. Carnoustie is scheduled to stage its sixth Open Championship in 1999. It is more than two decades since America's Tom Watson defeated Australia's Jack Newton in an 18-hole play-off in its last Open in 1975 and it promises to be a real treat for competitors and spectators alike.

tournament at Carnoustie in 1964.

The Angus course is a tough test in benign conditions and can become almost unmanageable when the wind is gusting as it was for most of the Scottish Open. In both of the first two rounds the best scores posted were 70s while at the other end of the leaderboard no less than 73 golfers succumbed to scores in the 80s. It meant that the cut fell at nine over par, or just six shots short of the European Tour record set at the Italian Open at Pevero in 1978 and equalled at the Portuguese Open at Troia in 1983, with the aforementioned Riley, Ryder Cup colleagues Per-Ulrik Johansson and Costantino Rocca, and the

Americans Tiger Woods, Tim Herron and Jim Furyk among the most notable casualties.

The wind did abate during the penultimate round, and the scores improved accordingly, but it was to prove to be a temporary reprieve for the competitors because it returned in earnest in time for the final round causing 24 out of the 71 golfers on the course to post scores in the 80s and meaning that Retief Goosen was the only man to manage to break 70 during the final round. Indeed, Goosen's 69 made him a member of an extremely exclusive club because during the whole of the championship the Carnoustie

course yielded a mere five scores in the 60s with Sandy Lyle (68) and Andrew Coltart, Jim Payne and Jesper Parnevik (all 69s) all taking advantage of the calmer conditions in the third round to make considerable inroads on the leaderboard.

In such taxing conditions, and on a course as tough as Carnoustie, a class golfer was always liable to emerge victorious and that's exactly what Woosnam proved to be. The Welshman has made a career out of winning on tough courses but it has been quite a while since he prevailed in such an impressive fashion.

During the first round Woosnam was fortunate in as much as his 70 was com-

utes after receiving his £80,000 winner's cheque. 'The course is great. Before I went out today I thought 76 would be good enough to win. It was really tough out there. Putting from four or five feet was a nightmare. I was trying to hit the ball so low that I topped it three times. You just have to accept your bad shots and try to take advantage of your good ones.

'It was a game of patience,' he added and one to which he adapted brilliantly.

Colin Callander

S H O T   O F   T H E   W E E K

Ian Woosnam hit a succession of spectacular shots while winning his third Scottish Open but arguably his finest was the masterful three iron he hit to ten feet at the par five 12th during the final round. The Welshman had just been caught at the top of the leaderboard by Sweden's Mats Hallberg but the shot set up an eagle three and restored his advantage just when it mattered most.

piled before the wind was at its strongest but he received no such advantage during the other three rounds when he relied on a combination of a sure touch round the greens and his innate ability to hit iron shots under the wind to compile rounds of 74, 70 and 75 and leave the rest of the field struggling in his wake.

Woosnam himself was in no doubt about the severity of the conditions and alluded to the fact that it was the strength of the wind rather than a mechanical fault which had caused him to hit a few loose shots during the final round.

'This has played like a true links course all week,' the champion said min-

CARNOUSTIE, ANGUS, SCOTLAND, JULY 10-13, 1996 · YARDAGE 7187 · PAR 72

Pos	Name	Country	Rnd 1	Rnd 2	Rnd 3	Rnd 4	Total	Prize Money £
1	Ian WOOSNAM	(Wal)	70	74	70	75	289	80000
2	Andrew COLTART	(Scot)	74	76	69	74	293	53280
3	Mats HALLBERG	(Swe)	75	71	73	75	294	30050
4	Diego BORREGO	(Sp)	72	78	72	73	295	22175
	Lee WESTWOOD	(Eng)	73	74	76	72	295	22175
6	Malcolm MACKENZIE	(Eng)	72	76	71	77	296	15600
	Peter MITCHELL	(Eng)	75	74	73	74	296	15600
8	Andrew SHERBORNE	(Eng)	76	75	71	75	297	10783
	Russell CLAYDON	(Eng)	72	72	73	80	297	10783
	Silvio GRAPPASONNI	(It)	74	72	74	77	297	10783
11	José RIVERO	(Sp)	71	78	73	76	298	7841
	Bob ESTES	(USA)	72	76	75	75	298	7841
	Paul LAWRIE	(Scot)	71	74	73	80	298	7841
	Sandy LYLE	(Scot)	79	74	68	77	298	7841
	Mathias GRÖNBERG	(Swe)	76	76	72	74	298	7841
16	Jay TOWNSEND	(USA)	72	72	74	81	299	5383
	Colin MONTGOMERIE	(Scot)	70	77	71	81	299	5383
	Retief GOOSEN	(SA)	75	77	78	69	299	5383
	Raymond RUSSELL	(Scot)	76	76	73	74	299	5383
	Paul BROADHURST	(Eng)	71	76	72	80	299	5383
	Mark JAMES	(Eng)	74	75	72	78	299	5383
	Peter BAKER	(Eng)	74	71	74	80	299	5383
	Rolf MUNTZ	(Hol)	78	70	70	81	299	5383
	Robert KARLSSON	(Swe)	75	74	74	76	299	5383
	Brian MARCHBANK	(Scot)	76	76	72	75	299	5383
	Jesper PARNEVIK	(Swe)	74	78	69	78	299	5383
	Sam TORRANCE	(Scot)	76	77	75	71	299	5383
	Ernie ELS	(SA)	76	77	71	75	299	5383
	Stuart CAGE	(Eng)	73	76	70	80	299	5383
	Greg TURNER	(NZ)	76	71	72	80	299	5383
31	Domingo HOSPITAL	(Sp)	75	74	75	76	300	3935
	Phillip PRICE	(Wal)	74	75	73	78	300	3935
	Bradley HUGHES	(Aus)	78	74	71	77	300	3935
	Robert ALLENBY	(Aus)	71	75	80	74	300	3935
	Pierre FULKE	(Swe)	77	72	77	74	300	3935
36	Jim PAYNE	(Eng)	79	72	69	81	301	3592
	Steven RICHARDSON	(Eng)	72	75	79	75	301	3592
38	José COCERES	(Arg)	72	77	75	78	302	3307
	Eduardo ROMERO	(Arg)	80	71	74	77	302	3307
	Stephen MCALLISTER	(Scot)	78	74	73	77	302	3307
	Peter O'MALLEY	(Aus)	73	75	74	80	302	3307
42	Andrew OLDCORN	(Scot)	77	76	74	76	303	2880
	Paul MOLONEY	(Aus)	72	78	73	80	303	2880
	Carl MASON	(Eng)	72	74	74	83	303	2880
	Carl SUNESON	(Sp)	75	76	72	80	303	2880
	Gordon BRAND JNR.	(Scot)	74	77	74	78	303	2880
47	David GILFORD	(Eng)	74	77	75	78	304	2310
	Olle KARLSSON	(Swe)	74	79	72	79	304	2310
	Eamonn DARCY	(Ire)	76	77	75	76	304	2310
	Mike MCLEAN	(Eng)	74	77	73	80	304	2310
	Neal BRIGGS	(Eng)	75	78	76	75	304	2310
	Dean ROBERTSON	(Scot)	76	75	76	77	304	2310
	Christian CÉVAER	(Fr)	76	76	74	78	304	2310
54	Des SMYTH	(Ire)	75	75	75	80	305	1740
	Thomas GÖGELE	(Ger)	74	76	80	75	305	1740
	Tony JOHNSTONE	(Zim)	77	72	76	80	305	1740
	David J RUSSELL	(Eng)	71	81	73	80	305	1740
	Patrik SJÖLAND	(Swe)	75	78	74	78	305	1740
59	Ross DRUMMOND	(Scot)	73	79	73	81	306	1475
	Euan MCINTOSH	(Scot)	76	73	80	77	306	1475
61	Richard BOXALL	(Eng)	74	77	71	85	307	1350
	Martin GATES	(Eng)	76	75	78	78	307	1350
	Paul MCGINLEY	(Ire)	75	76	79	77	307	1350
64	David CURRY	(Eng)	75	77	80	76	308	1225
	Paul EALES	(Eng)	78	75	77	78	308	1225
66	Klas ERIKSSON	(Swe)	73	80	78	79	310	719
	Ronan RAFFERTY	(N.Ire)	77	76	80	77	310	719
68	David FEHERTY	(N.Ire)	74	78	79	82	313	715
	Marc FARRY	(Fr)	76	76	78	83	313	715
70	Tommy TOLLES	(USA)	76	77	79	83	315	712
71	Andrew COLLISON	(Eng)	72	78	82	88	320	710

Andrew Coltart was runner-up to Ian Woosnam for the second time in the season.

HOW BI-METAL TECHNOLOGY LED TO THE CONQUEST OF SPACE

INNER SPACE

WILSON ENGINEERS STARTED FROM THE INSIDE OF THE CLUBHEAD AND WORKED THEIR WAY OUT. THEY DEVISED A SUPERIOR WEIGHT DISTRIBUTION BY COMBINING TWO METALS: TITANIUM AND STAINLESS STEEL. WILSON REPLACED THE CONVENTIONAL STEEL HOSEL WITH A SPACE AGE "TITANIUM SLEEVE". BY NESTLING THIS NEARLY WEIGHTLESS DEVICE DEEP INTO A STAINLESS STEEL CLUBHEAD, THEY WERE ABLE TO REDISTRIBUTE A FULL 12% OF THE WEIGHT FROM THE HOSEL INTO THE PERIMETER, DELIVERING MAXIMUM FORGIVENESS.

TITANIUM SLEEVE STABILIZES HEAD WHILE IMPROVING WEIGHT DISTRIBUTION.

OUTER SPACE

BI-METAL TECHNOLOGY ENABLED OUR ENGINEERS TO DESIGN INVEX TO BE THE MOST AERODYNAMIC ON EVERY PLANE; HENCE, THE MYSTERIOUS UFO-LIKE APPEARANCE. YET, INVEX STILL RETAINS A CLASSIC LOOK FROM THE PLAYING POSITION. MULTIPLANE AERODYNAMICS REDUCE THE DRAG IN YOUR SWING BY 85%. BECAUSE OF THIS SUPERIOR DESIGN, INVEX ENABLES YOU TO GENERATE MORE CLUBHEAD SPEED WITHOUT SWINGING HARDER. GREATER CLUBHEAD SPEED EQUALS GREATER DISTANCE. INVEX. MORE DISTANCE WITH LESS EFFORT.

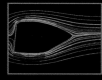

INVEX DESIGN SLICES CLEANLY THROUGH THE AIR IN VIRTUAL WIND TUNNEL TESTS.

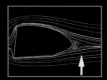

OTHER CLUBHEADS EXPERIENCE AIR TURBULENCE AS INDICATED BY BLUE SWIRLS.

Wilson.
The Right Equipment Makes The Difference™

INVEX™  INVASION.

TODAY THE BRITISH OPEN. TOMORROW THE WORLD

Lehman rides the big one

Tom Lehman opened his
major championship account
at Royal Lytham & St Annes

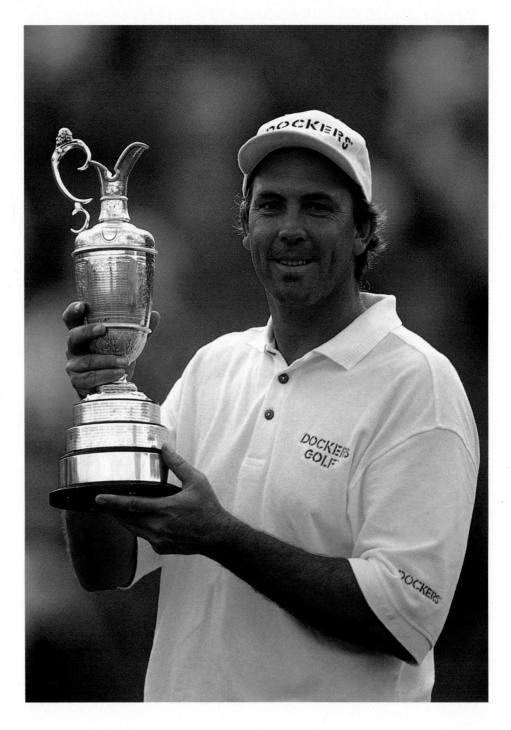

A couple of miles down the road from Royal Lytham & St Annes lies the gaudy seaside resort of Blackpool, home of the famous tower, candyfloss and kiss-me-quick hats. One of its main attractions is a huge roller-coaster which soars 80 feet into the sky and is affectionately known as The Big One.

It is a title that sat equally comfortably on the reputation of the Open Championship as once again the oldest major championship in the world provided a roller-coaster of thrills, spills and emotion.

Even the weather was in a holiday mood with temperatures touching 90 degrees during the week and the sun baking the fairways. There was almost a complete absence of wind and the old links had never been more vulnerable to the skills of the world's best players.

Before a stroke was hit in anger, Nick Faldo predicted that if the conditions remained benign then the

American contingent would dominate. The course wasn't quite West Palm Beach with dunes but with the greens running at an easy pace it was primed for low scores.

It was a fairly accurate prediction from Faldo as on the first day, seven of the first 14 places were filled by Americans with three other players, Faldo, Ernie Els and Nick Price being full-time participants on the US Tour. The player at the head of affairs however, was definitely not American. Paul Broadhurst, who in the 1988 Open at Lytham had won the silver

medal as leading amateur, was still hunting happily on this ground and with four birdies and an eagle at the seventh was round in 65 to tie Severiano Ballesteros' course record set in the final round eight years ago.

This put Broadhurst two strokes ahead of a plalanx of players including Fred Couples, Mark McCumber, Loren Roberts, Mark Brooks and, significantly, Tom Lehman whose 67 contained a double-bogey six on the 13th, the shortest par four on the course.

Faldo was round in 68 and left it a little late to make his score with birdies on the 15th and 18th. On the same score were Carl Mason, Els, Price and Padraig Harrington who did himself proud playing with Couples and McCumber.

Other notable names fared less well. Defending champion John Daly sprinted to the turn in 31, five under par, and then limped home in 39. Colin Montgomerie, still trying to find his swing after the buffeting it received at Carnoustie the previous week, was round in 73 after tak-

155

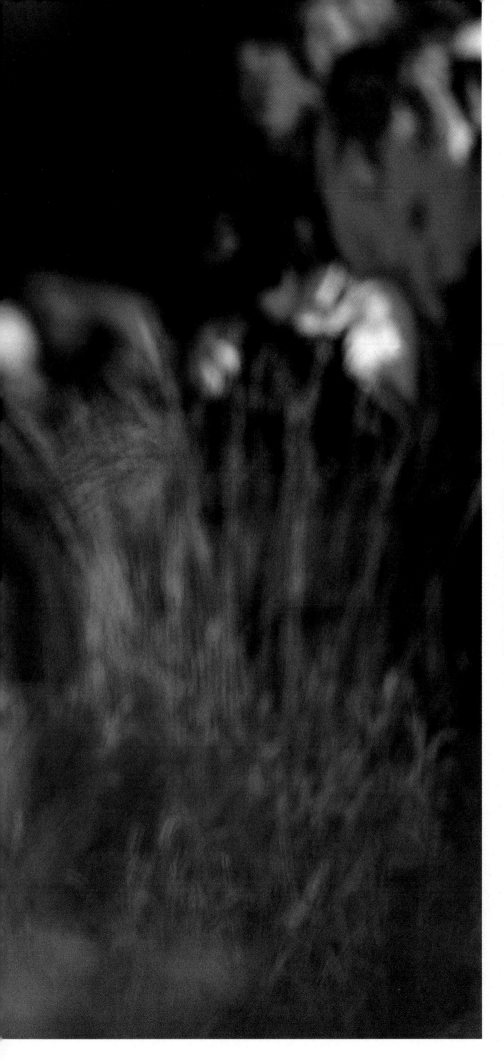

**New Tiger, vintage Bear.
Jack Nicklaus (left),
and Tiger Woods (above).**

ing two from a bunker on the 18th. Ian
Woosnam, the victor in the Scottish
Open, took eight at the 17th and was
round in 74 and Ballesteros, the sentimen-
tal favourite, had to make some brilliant
recoveries to keep his score at 74.

When it came to sentiment however,
one man stole the scene on the second
day. Having opened with a creditable 69,
Jack Nicklaus wound back the clock 20

157

years by producing a second round of 66 which had the crowd on its feet. Five birdies fell to his clubs and for a 56-year old man with back trouble it was a remarkable achievement.

It thrust Nicklaus right into the thick of things as he lay just one stroke off the lead. This had been established earlier in the day by Paul McGinley who, with the aid of a hole-in-one at the ninth, had reached the turn in 29 and after a few

adventures had returned home in level par. No one could overtake the Irishman but Lehman, with another 67 joined him later. Accompanying Nicklaus were Peter Hedblom after a 65 and Ernie Els after a 67.

Faldo stayed in touch with another 68 and he was joined by Vijay Singh, Corey Pavin, Loren Roberts, Mark O'Meara, McCumber and Harrington, all of whom lay two strokes off the pace. First round

A tale of three bunkers:
Mark McCumber (top)
Robert Allenby (left) and
Greg Norman (above).

leader Broadhurst fell back with a 72.

It is often said that although you can't win a tournament in the third round, you can certainly lose it. In this Championship, Tom Lehman blew that piece of philosophy out of the window. Almost every time he stood over the ball with his putter, the hole got in the way. Five birdies were gleaned in the first nine

holes and three more when he stood on the 18th tee. Here he suffered his one blemish by driving into a bunker and could only manage a five. It all added up to a 64, a new course record, but more importantly, it had opened up a six-stroke lead on the field as Lehman set a new 54-hole record of 198 for the Championship.

The significance of the lead and the

man in second place was not lost on those whose memories were flicking back to the US Masters in April. Faldo was the man who made up precisely that defecit on Greg Norman and here he was again in the same position. However, to state the obvious, Tom Lehman is not Greg Norman and Lytham is not Augusta. As long as the weather remained

159

dented his confidence. Meanwhile Lehman was heading for a 73, and he averted any crisis with a birdie at the 12th and a brilliant save from a bunker at the 15th.

It was all over bar the prize-giving as Lehman completed a two-stroke victory over Els and McCumber and became the first American professional to win at Lytham. It had been a long haul to the top for the 37-year old from Austin, Minnesota, a road that took him to the Far East, to South Africa and various satellite tours. At the end of 1992 he decided to have one last shot at the Hogan Tour in America and finished top of the money list to qualify for the main US Tour. In

**No joy for Ernie Els (left)
nor Nick Faldo (above).**

placid it seemed unlikely that Lehman would go into freefall and it would take something extraordinary from the nearest challengers to produce an upset.

As it turned out, the final round was something of an anti-climax. Lehman struggled early on but Faldo, with whom he was playing, could not take advantage. Ahead of them Couples went to the turn in 30 to draw within two strokes of Lehman, but staggered home in 41. Els also made a run with four birdies in the space of five holes from the tenth, but he too ran out of steam by dropping shots at the 15th and 18th. McCumber had started the day nine shots off the pace and he closed to within two strokes with a final round of 66.

Faldo had missed putts on the first, fifth, sixth and seventh, all of which

1994 he was runner-up in the US Masters, last year he was third in the US Open and a month prior to Lytham he finished one stroke behind his close friend, Steve Jones, the new US Open champion.

Now he had landed the big one and at Royal Lytham & St Annes Tom Lehman was riding higher than any holiday-maker on Blackpool's roller-coaster.

Chris Plumridge

THE COURSE

Lytham's claws were drawn for this Open as the wind failed to materialise and the prolonged sunshine baked the fairways. The fearsome final five holes still exacted some retribution and the numerous bunkers claimed some notable victims.

SHOT OF THE WEEK

Tom Lehman was two strokes ahead of his nearest challengers in the final round when he bunkered his second shot to the 15th. The ball finished at the back of the bunker on a downhill lie with the pin only 15 feet away. He was unable to obtain any backspin but played a marvellous shot to around six feet and holed the putt to preserve his lead.

ROYAL LYTHAM & ST. ANNES, JULY 18-21, 1996 · PAR 71 · YARDS 6892

Pos	Name	Country	Rnd 1	Rnd 2	Rnd 3	Rnd 4	Total	Prize Money £
1	Tom LEHMAN	(USA)	67	67	64	73	271	200000
2	Mark MCCUMBER	(USA)	67	69	71	66	273	125000
	Ernie ELS	(SA)	68	67	71	67	273	125000
4	Nick FALDO	(Eng)	68	68	68	70	274	75000
5	Jeff MAGGERT	(USA)	69	70	72	65	276	50000
	Mark BROOKS	(USA)	67	70	68	71	276	50000
7	Fred COUPLES	(USA)	67	70	69	71	277	35000
	Greg TURNER	(NZ)	72	69	68	68	277	35000
	Greg NORMAN	(Aus)	71	68	71	67	277	35000
	Peter HEDBLOM	(Swe)	70	65	75	67	277	35000
11	Vijay SINGH	(Fij)	69	67	69	73	278	27000
	Alexander CEJKA	(Ger)	73	67	71	67	278	27000
	Darren CLARKE	(N.Ire)	70	68	69	71	278	27000
14	David DUVAL	(USA)	76	67	66	70	279	20250
	Paul MCGINLEY	(Ire)	69	65	74	71	279	20250
	Shigeki MARUYAMA	(Jap)	68	70	69	72	279	20250
	Mark MCNULTY	(Zim)	69	71	70	69	279	20250
18	Padraig HARRINGTON	(Ire)	68	68	73	71	280	15500
	Loren ROBERTS	(USA)	67	69	72	72	280	15500
	Michael WELCH	(Eng)	71	68	73	68	280	15500
	Rocco MEDIATE	(USA)	69	70	69	72	280	15500
22	Mark JAMES	(Eng)	70	68	75	68	281	11875
	Jay HAAS	(USA)	70	72	71	68	281	11875
	Steve STRICKER	(USA)	71	70	66	74	281	11875
	Carl MASON	(Eng)	68	70	70	73	281	11875
	Tiger WOODS (AM)	(USA)	75	66	70	70	281	
26	Tom KITE	(USA)	77	66	69	70	282	9525
	Paul BROADHURST	(Eng)	65	72	74	71	282	9525
	Frank NOBILO	(NZ)	70	72	68	72	282	9525
	Ben CRENSHAW	(USA)	73	68	71	70	282	9525
	Corey PAVIN	(USA)	70	66	74	72	282	9525
	Peter MITCHELL	(Eng)	71	68	71	72	282	9525
32	David GILFORD	(Eng)	71	67	71	74	283	7843
	Tommy TOLLES	(USA)	73	70	71	69	283	7843
	Hidemichi TANAKA	(Jap)	67	71	70	75	283	7843
	Brad FAXON	(USA)	67	73	68	75	283	7843
	Mark O'MEARA	(USA)	67	69	72	75	283	7843
	Eamonn DARCY	(Ire)	73	69	71	70	283	7843
	Scott SIMPSON	(USA)	71	69	73	70	283	7843
	Eduardo ROMERO	(Arg)	70	71	75	67	283	7843
40	David FROST	(SA)	70	72	71	71	284	7150
	Phil MICKELSON	(USA)	72	71	72	69	284	7150
	Mark CALCAVECCHIA	(USA)	72	68	76	68	284	7150
	Klas ERIKSSON	(Swe)	68	75	72	69	284	7150
44	Payne STEWART	(USA)	70	73	71	71	285	6400
	Bradley HUGHES	(Aus)	70	69	75	71	285	6400
	Bill MAYFAIR	(USA)	70	72	74	69	285	6400
	Jesper PARNEVIK	(Swe)	72	69	69	75	285	6400
	Peter JACOBSEN	(USA)	72	70	74	69	285	6400
	Richard BOXALL	(Eng)	72	70	71	72	285	6400
	Jack NICKLAUS	(USA)	69	66	77	73	285	6400
	Jim FURYK	(USA)	68	71	72	74	285	6400
	Craig STADLER	(USA)	71	71	75	68	285	6400
	Nick PRICE	(Zim)	68	73	71	73	285	6400
	Todd HAMILTON	(USA)	71	70	74	70	285	6400
55	Robert ALLENBY	(Aus)	74	68	71	73	286	5687
	Jim PAYNE	(Eng)	72	71	73	70	286	5687
	Stephen AMES	(T&T)	71	72	69	74	286	5687
	Sandy LYLE	(Scot)	71	69	73	73	286	5687
59	D A WEIBRING	(USA)	71	72	72	72	287	5475
	Jeff SLUMAN	(USA)	72	70	70	75	287	5475
	Brian BARNES	(Scot)	73	70	69	75	287	5475
	Michael JONZON	(Swe)	69	73	73	72	287	5475
63	Costantino ROCCA	(It)	71	70	74	73	288	5300
	Carl SUNESON	(Sp)	73	69	74	72	288	5300
	Gordon LAW	(?)	74	69	71	74	288	5300
66	Brett OGLE	(Aus)	70	73	73	73	289	5150
	John DALY	(USA)	70	73	69	77	289	5150
	David A RUSSELL	(Eng)	70	72	74	73	289	5150
69	Howard CLARK	(Eng)	72	71	76	71	290	5050
70	Bob CHARLES	(NZ)	71	72	71	77	291	5000
71	Roger CHAPMAN	(Eng)	72	70	70	80	292	4875
	Curtis STRANGE	(USA)	71	72	72	77	292	4875
	Rick TODD	(Can)	74	69	73	76	292	4875
	Domingo HOSPITAL	(Sp)	75	68	77	72	292	4875
75	Retief GOOSEN	(SA)	72	71	74	76	293	4750
76	Arnaud LANGENAEKEN	(Bel)	72	71	77	78	298	4700

Champion and caddie share the moment of triumph.

Unisys and The PGA European Tour

Unisys is a major information management company providing solutions and systems integration for business and government worldwide. As part of our sports marketing programme we are delighted to be the Official Provider of Information Services to the PGA European Tour.
http://www.unisys.com

UNISYS

THE INFORMATION MANAGEMENT COMPANY

McNulty's welcome return

Eight years after he first played at
Hilversumsche, Mark McNulty found
the course was still ideal for his game

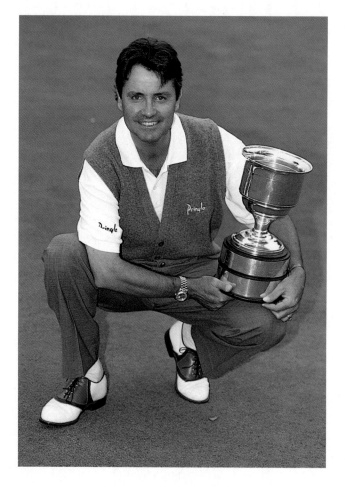

When Mark McNulty finished eighth in the 1988 Dutch Open at Hilversumsche, he made a mental note: 'could do better'. The tight, tree-lined course with tricky greens had been made for him, and if he got another chance, he vowed, he would not under-achieve the next time.

When the Zimbabwean, now 42 and with six further European Tour successes behind him since last visiting Hilversumsche, recognised the entrance to the course, he was delighted. He would hardly have a better chance to chalk up a 14th European victory.

With a worrying knee injury now given the all-clear by the specialists for a 'psychological boost', the way was surely open to a second win of the year. There would be obstacles to surmount, like keeping at bay a determined defending champion Scott Hoch, but McNulty's 'good vibes' for Hilversumsche, were not misread.

His victory in the end came down to a putt. But not one of McNulty's renowned silky-smooth strokes. A miss from six feet for birdie by Hoch on the 72nd hole finally ended the hopes of the American, whose outrageous chip-in eagle from heavy rough on the long 12th had given him the chance for back-to-back victories. Hoch, who equalled Jerry Anderson's 1987 record 63 the day before, closed with a five-under-par 66, but it was one shot light of forcing a play-off with McNulty, who carded 68 to be 18 under par for the tournament and earn the £108,330 first prize.

When the week began, though, it was a pair of Irishman and their broomhandle putters, and a Frenchman, who made the early running. Evergreen Des Smyth, aim-ing for his eighth title towards his dream of ten before reaching 50, led the way on day one, and kept his lead on Friday. Just a year and a week after switching to the broomhandle, a putter which he consid-ered 'stress-free' compared to the orthodox one, Smyth led by a stroke with a 64.

David Feherty had only a couple of weeks' experience with his long putter, given to him by long-time friend Sam Torrance, who had won five events with it. Jean Van de Velde stayed orthodox and matched Feherty's 65 but both faded the next day, when a bold finish by Smyth,

Hilversumsche, roaring home in just 29 strokes, birdieing the last four holes. Unerring accuracy was the key and Smyth observed wryly that: 'If you lost your nerve through missing the fairways, you could shoot millions'.

John Daly highlighted Smyth's hyper-

without any thought of handing a priceless advantage to a possible arch-rival, was happy to help.

As Smyth perished in a flurry of mistakes around the turn in the third round, Nobilo's birdie from 40 feet on the first filled him with confidence. The New

Frank Nobilo (left), and Raymond Russell (above) finished tied for third place.

although not quite as spectacular as his eagle finale of Thursday, took him past McNulty by a shot on 11 under par.

By then the Zimbabwean had proved his penchant for

bole with an 89 to balloon 22 over par and miss the cut by 23 shots. New Zealander Frank Nobilo, playing alongside Daly, was unabashed at his partner's many arborial visits, but was dismayed by his own wayward putting which held him back. He thus sought the help of McNulty, who,

Zealander moved up to second place with Hoch, who surged through the field with a 63 in which he picked up six shots over the first nine holes.

The American had been criticised for missing the Open by some of his fellow-countrymen. But he pointed out that he

Scott Hoch watches his putt to tie slide agonisingly past.

might never have been able to put up such a determined defence of his Dutch title if his game, not suited to links, had been laid low by Lytham. Hoch praised his caddie Pete Coleman, on sabbatical from injured Bernhard Langer's bag. 'Pete's helping me get into the clubhouse', joked the low-profile American, who lost to Nick Faldo in the 1989 US Masters play-off.

A 63 made Hoch far from anonymous for the final round, but McNulty began it three strokes ahead of him and Nobilo. The Zimbabwean, playing with Hoch, looked unruffled until the 12th. Visibly shaken by the chip-in which momentarily drew Hoch level, McNulty faced a fast putt of 35 feet for his eagle. He left

SHOT OF THE WEEK

Shot of the week came in the third round on the long 12th when Mark McNulty punched a two iron 180 yards through a funnel of trees and under overhanging branches just 12 feet past the flag to save par and preserve his lead. 'We'd had to wait on the tee,' said McNulty. 'I lost my rhythm and hit my widest and worst shot I can remember, before then hitting my best of the week.' His birdie putt from ten feet on the same hole in the final round, however, was definitely the most important of the week.

it ten feet short. Calmly, though, he holed out for birdie and held on to his one-shot advantage to the last. Here McNulty had already sold himself short for birdie by the time the door was ajar for Hoch. Hoch, though, missed from six feet and the deserving McNulty had 'done better'.

'When I played alongside Mark Mouland in 1988 at Hilversumsche and he shot 65 to win,' he said, 'I kicked myself because I knew I could have done that. The course is built for my game and I'd been waiting to come back to do what I should have done then. When I realised where I was, I just knew I had a chance to win.'

Norman Dabell

HILVERSUMSCHE GC, HILVERSUM, JULY 25-28, 1996 • PAR 71 • YARDS 6636

Pos	Name	Country	Rnd 1	Rnd 2	Rnd 3	Rnd 4	Total	Prize Money £
1	Mark MCNULTY	(Zim)	67	65	66	68	266	108330
2	Scott HOCH	(USA)	70	68	63	66	267	72210
3	Raymond RUSSELL	(Scot)	68	68	67	66	269	36595
	Frank NOBILO	(NZ)	69	68	64	68	269	36595
5	John HUSTON	(USA)	69	65	69	69	272	25140
	Jean VAN DE VELDE	(Fr)	65	70	69	68	272	25140
7	Phillip PRICE	(Wal)	67	72	69	65	273	19500
8	Daniel CHOPRA	(Swe)	69	70	68	67	274	14586
	Ross MCFARLANE	(Eng)	68	68	68	70	274	14586
	Greg CHALMERS	(Aus)	72	66	71	65	274	14586
11	Lee WESTWOOD	(Eng)	71	69	67	68	275	11570
	David HOWELL	(Eng)	71	65	69	70	275	11570
13	Peter O'MALLEY	(Aus)	67	69	70	70	276	9577
	Mike MCLEAN	(Eng)	73	67	69	67	276	9577
	Jamie SPENCE	(Eng)	71	67	69	69	276	9577
	Tony JOHNSTONE	(Zim)	69	68	69	70	276	9577
	Andrew COLTART	(Scot)	73	68	67	68	276	9577
18	Sam TORRANCE	(Scot)	70	71	67	69	277	7642
	Paul LAWRIE	(Scot)	73	68	66	70	277	7642
	Retief GOOSEN	(SA)	70	66	72	69	277	7642
	Wayne RILEY	(Aus)	68	71	69	69	277	7642
	Darren CLARKE	(N.Ire)	69	70	67	71	277	7642
	Paul EALES	(Eng)	68	72	71	66	277	7642
	Carl SUNESON	(Sp)	68	67	71	71	277	7642
25	Des SMYTH	(Ire)	64	67	75	72	278	6435
	Stephen FIELD	(Eng)	66	73	70	69	278	6435
	Roger CHAPMAN	(Eng)	68	72	66	72	278	6435
	Pedro LINHART	(Sp)	70	69	67	72	278	6435
	Thomas BJORN	(Den)	71	66	71	70	278	6435
30	Diego BORREGO	(Sp)	72	68	68	71	279	5655
	David GILFORD	(Eng)	68	67	72	72	279	5655
	Rodger DAVIS	(Aus)	68	70	69	72	279	5655
33	Paul BROADHURST	(Eng)	71	69	67	73	280	5135
	Paul CURRY	(Eng)	74	67	71	68	280	5135
	Paul AFFLECK	(Wal)	70	70	71	69	280	5135
	Mark ROE	(Eng)	71	69	67	73	280	5135
37	Iain PYMAN	(Eng)	69	72	67	73	281	4420
	Peter BAKER	(Eng)	72	69	67	73	281	4420
	Rolf MUNTZ	(Hol)	71	70	69	71	281	4420
	David CARTER	(Eng)	71	69	69	72	281	4420
	Mike CLAYTON	(Aus)	70	69	71	71	281	4420
	Philip WALTON	(Ire)	69	68	70	74	281	4420
	Anders HAGLUND	(Swe)	68	70	69	74	281	4420
44	Santiago LUNA	(Sp)	69	69	75	69	282	3705
	Juan Carlos PIÑERO	(Sp)	71	69	72	70	282	3705
	Mark MOULAND	(Wal)	71	68	71	72	282	3705
	Stuart CAGE	(Eng)	67	67	73	75	282	3705
	Maarten LAFEBER (AM)	(Hol)	70	70	65	77	282	
48	Stephen AMES	(T&T)	71	68	70	74	283	3185
	Christian CÉVAER	(Fr)	68	72	72	71	283	3185
	Jim PAYNE	(Eng)	70	71	67	75	283	3185
	Howard CLARK	(Eng)	70	69	72	72	283	3185
52	Per NYMAN	(Swe)	70	71	73	70	284	2600
	Robert COLES	(Eng)	71	70	74	69	284	2600
	Carl MASON	(Eng)	69	69	71	75	284	2600
	Roger WESSELS	(SA)	71	69	73	71	284	2600
	Adam HUNTER	(Scot)	70	70	70	74	284	2600
57	Fabrice TARNAUD	(Fr)	75	66	73	71	285	2210
58	Steven RICHARDSON	(Eng)	68	73	75	70	286	1982
	Russell CLAYDON	(Eng)	66	73	77	70	286	1982
	Phil GOLDING	(Eng)	69	70	75	72	286	1982
	Gary EMERSON	(Eng)	70	71	73	72	286	1982
62	Chris HALL	(Eng)	69	71	75	73	288	1755
	David FEHERTY	(N.Ire)	65	71	73	79	288	1755
	David WILLIAMS	(Eng)	69	71	73	75	288	1755
65	Miles TUNNICLIFF	(Eng)	72	68	73	76	289	1625
66	Joost STEENKAMER	(Hol)	69	69	76	76	290	975

THE COURSE

Rain in the weeks before the Sun Dutch Open made Hilversumsche longer but much less hard and bouncy than in the previous two years. This took away the occasional element of chance off the tee. As in any year, though, the accurate tee-shot was rewarded. Errant shots were heavily punished by the glorious fully blooming trees which line the undulating 6,636-yard, par-71, course.

Westwood Ho!

Lee Westwood fulfilled the promise
he had shown as a junior when he joined
the swelling ranks of new winners

*L*ee Westwood arrived in Gothenburg unheralded, unsung, and unrecognised to the extent that he was even denied a drink by a hotel barman on the grounds that he looked too young.

He departed chuckling at the rebuff, celebrating a first European Tour victory, and clutching a six-figure cheque that ensured his face would be one of the most easily recognisable to the millions of Swedish sports fans. Westwood may have looked cherubic on his Saturday evening stroll in Sweden's second city, but European number one Colin Montgomerie, Ian Woosnam, and 1995 Open champion John Daly can all testify to the maturity of the 23-year old Englishman's golf which had left them trailing among the also-rans in the sixth Volvo Scandinavian Masters. So, too, can Paul Broadhurst and Russell Claydon who were caught by Westwood's birdie at the 71st hole on the breezy Forsgardens course and then mastered in the play-off by their baby-faced countryman.

All three had closed with a final round of 68 to tie on a seven under par total of 281, but when they again returned to the 449-yard 18th Broadhurst was the first to depart. On the second visit Claydon was despatched by Westwood's birdie putt from 50 feet and the youngster from Worksop had taken his place among the 1996 crop of new Tour champions.

He had threatened to join them at Bergamo back in May, yet when he needed a par at the last hole to force a play-off for the Conte of Florence Italian Open, had taken six, and been forced to settle for third place. But the lessons of that frustrating afternoon had been well learned, and Westwood, steeled by a run of seven subsequent top 12 finishes, was much more confident in his ability to handle last day pressure when he again found himself in contention.

He had begun with a solid 69, the same as Montgomerie and Woosnam, and also Daly, who subsequently had two penalty shots added to his score for unwittingly contravening Rule 13-2 by removing loose sand from in front of his ball at the ninth. A golfer is permitted to do so on the green, but not off the putting surface where Daly's ball had landed after his recovery chip, so his bogey five became a seven, and the American lost much of the benefit of his five birdies.

A buffeting wind tested everyone on the second day, but Dane Thomas Bjorn, who along with Spaniard Santiago Luna

SHOT OF THE WEEK

It could have been a mammoth John Daly drive to the fringe of the green at the 383-yard third, or any of the many who hit their tee shots onto the 334-yard 15th. But the precision shot that meant the most was Lee Westwood's title-winning putt from 50 feet on his third trip to the 18th. 'It was so long it was just a blur as it went into the hole,' said the new Scandinavian Master.

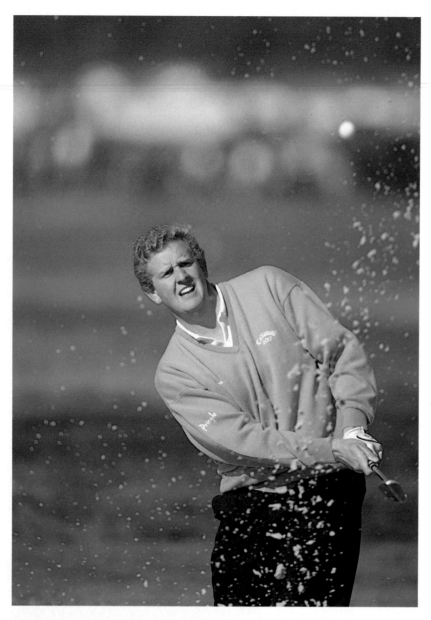

THE COURSE

Set in undulating, partly-wooded terrain some 20 kilometres north of Gothenburg, Forsgardens was extensively upgraded for its second staging of Volvo's Scandinavian showcase. Feature holes are the par five seventh and short eighth where water is always in play, but the toughest par four is the semi-dog-leg 449-yard 18th, usually played into a stiff breeze.

Colin Montgomerie (opposite), Santiago Luna (left),
Bernhard Langer (right) and Paul Broadhurst (below)
all had to give best to Lee Westwood.

had equalled the course record of 67 in the first round, scarcely noticed. He added another six birdies for a 68 that took him to nine under par at the halfway stage and into a three-stroke lead over Luna who had recently switched to a long putter, with Claydon holding third place. Bjorn, who like Westwood had enjoyed an outstanding amateur career, had scored four victorious in being number one on the 1995 Challenge Tour. Having secured his 1997 card the previous week in Holland, he was playing with rare freedom on a familiar course close to home, and was not a golfer to be disregarded. Montgomerie (76) was ten behind, Woosnam (79) even further back, and with Daly still in a state of shock after his 89 in the previous week's Sun Dutch Open, and not able to improve on his opening 71, the stage was set for further surprises.

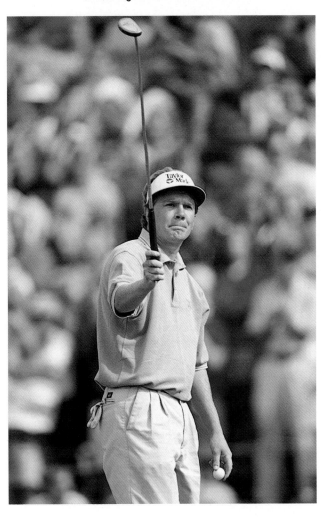

On the third day they were provided principally by Steven Bottomley, the Yorkshireman who had finished third, one stroke behind champion Daly and Costantino Rocca in the Open at St Andrews 12 months previously. The Bradford golfer had qualified for the final 36 holes on the exact four over par mark, but such is the strength in depth on the European Tour that 24 hours later he was celebrating a Johnnie Walker Tour Course Record Award of £3,000 after shooting 65. It was also a career-best, one lower than his previous best mark set in Stockholm six years earlier. Bottomley had only 25 putts while making eight birdies, five of them in and inward 31 to join Westwood, Jim Payne, Broadhurst, Claydon and Italy's Silvio Grappasonni in sharing second spot at three under. Bjorn, despite slipping to a 76, retained the lead, although it had been

FORSGÅRDENS, GOTEBORG, AUGUST 1-4, 1996 · PAR 72 · YARDS 6899

Pos	Name	Country	Rnd 1	Rnd 2	Rnd 3	Rnd 4	Total	Prize Money £
1	Lee WESTWOOD	(Eng)	69	75	69	68	281	116660
2	Paul BROADHURST	(Eng)	72	70	71	68	281	60795
	Russell CLAYDON	(Eng)	68	71	74	68	281	60795
4	Santiago LUNA	(Sp)	67	71	76	68	282	35000
5	Jean VAN DE VELDE	(Fr)	72	68	74	70	284	29640
6	Iain PYMAN	(Eng)	71	73	70	71	285	24500
7	Thomas BJORN	(Den)	67	68	76	75	286	16198
	Carl SUNESON	(Sp)	72	72	71	71	286	16198
	Philip WALTON	(Ire)	77	69	70	70	286	16198
	Roger WESSELS	(SA)	73	72	72	69	286	16198
	Steven BOTTOMLEY	(Eng)	74	74	65	73	286	16198
12	Miguel Angel MARTIN	(Sp)	68	72	77	70	287	10605
	Colin MONTGOMERIE	(Scot)	69	76	72	70	287	10605
	Per NYMAN	(Swe)	70	78	71	68	287	10605
	Fernando ROCA	(Sp)	70	71	74	72	287	10605
	Silvio GRAPPASONNI	(It)	70	70	73	74	287	10605
	Pierre FULKE	(Swe)	71	73	76	67	287	10605
18	Mark MOULAND	(Wal)	70	75	71	72	288	8230
	Ignacio GARRIDO	(Sp)	72	70	73	73	288	8230
	Per HAUGSRUD	(Nor)	75	71	71	71	288	8230
	Padraig HARRINGTON	(Ire)	69	77	72	70	288	8230
	John DALY	(USA)	71	71	76	70	288	8230
	Mark ROE	(Eng)	71	73	73	71	288	8230
	John BICKERTON	(Eng)	68	73	76	71	288	8230
25	Jim PAYNE	(Eng)	70	73	70	76	289	7035
	Jonathan LOMAS	(Eng)	71	73	74	71	289	7035
	Gary CLARK	(Eng)	73	71	73	72	289	7035
	Peter BAKER	(Eng)	70	76	71	72	289	7035
	Martin ERLANDSSON (AM)	(Swe)	73	75	70	71	289	
29	Peter HEDBLOM	(Swe)	75	72	74	69	290	6020
	José RIVERO	(Sp)	71	76	73	70	290	6020
	Paul EALES	(Eng)	70	73	72	75	290	6020
	Per-Ulrik JOHANSSON	(Swe)	70	73	73	74	290	6020
	Ian WOOSNAM	(Wal)	69	79	72	70	290	6020
	Wayne RILEY	(Aus)	77	71	70	72	290	6020
35	Peter O'MALLEY	(Aus)	71	77	70	73	291	5390
	Mats HALLBERG	(Swe)	70	72	75	74	291	5390
	Christoffer HANELL (AM)	(Swe)	72	76	73	70	291	
37	Glenn RALPH	(Eng)	75	72	74	71	292	4620
	Juan Carlos PIÑERO	(Sp)	71	74	73	74	292	4620
	Dean ROBERTSON	(Scot)	73	73	74	72	292	4620
	Rolf MUNTZ	(Hol)	77	68	75	72	292	4620
	Martin GATES	(Eng)	69	77	73	73	292	4620
	Derrick COOPER	(Eng)	73	75	75	69	292	4620
	Gary EVANS	(Eng)	72	76	74	70	292	4620
	Raymond RUSSELL	(Scot)	75	72	74	71	292	4620
	Ronan RAFFERTY	(N.Ire)	73	74	73	72	292	4620
46	Stuart CAGE	(Eng)	71	76	73	73	293·	3710
	Bernhard LANGER	(Ger)	74	74	75	70	293	3710
	Richard BOXALL	(Eng)	72	74	73	74	293	3710
	Robert KARLSSON	(Swe)	75	72	74	72	293	3710
50	Mark LITTON	(Wal)	70	75	75	74	294	2940
	Pedro LINHART	(Sp)	72	73	78	71	294	2940
	Francis HOWLEY	(Ire)	70	73	77	74	294	2940
	Stephen MCALLISTER	(Scot)	74	74	73	73	294	2940
	Adam HUNTER	(Scot)	71	76	74	73	294	2940
	Barry LANE	(Eng)	72	76	73	73	294	2940
	Roger CHAPMAN	(Eng)	71	76	76	71	294	2940
57	Gabriel HJERTSTEDT	(Swe)	70	78	77	70	295	2073
	Mathias GRÖNBERG	(Swe)	72	75	75	73	295	2073
	Bob MAY	(USA)	73	72	75	75	295	2073
	Sven STRÜVER	(Ger)	71	75	79	70	295	2073
	Brian MARCHBANK	(Scot)	71	77	75	72	295	2073
	Max ANGLERT	(Swe)	73	74	77	71	295	2073
	Gary EMERSON	(Eng)	70	75	76	74	295	2073
	Mike CLAYTON	(Aus)	76	72	75	72	295	2073
65	Ricky WILLISON	(Eng)	73	72	73	78	296	1400
	Anders FORSBRAND	(Swe)	74	73	77	72	296	1400
67	Michael JONZON	(Swe)	76	72	76	73	297	1045
	Lian-Wei ZHANG	(Chi)	70	77	75	75	297	1045
	Carl MASON	(Eng)	73	75	75	74	297	1045
	Paul MOLONEY	(Aus)	74	72	78	73	297	1045
71	Paul WAY	(Eng)	68	78	79	73	298	1038
	Adam MEDNICK	(Swe)	75	71	79	73	298	1038
	Eric GIRAUD	(Fr)	72	76	74	76	298	1038
74	Olle NORDBERG	(Swe)	75	73	75	76	299	1032
	David FEHERTY	(N.Ire)	75	73	77	74	299	1032
	Jesper PARNEVIK	(Swe)	72	74	79	74	299	1032
77	David A RUSSELL	(Eng)	73	75	77	75	300	1027
	Steen TINNING	(Den)	70	76	77	77	300	1027
79	Steven RICHARDSON	(Eng)	72	76	75	78	301	1024
80	Joakim NILSSON	(Swe)	72	76	79	75	302	1021
	Mike MCLEAN	(Eng)	73	74	79	76	302	1021

reduced to only two shots.

It was anybody's title on another bright and breezy final afternoon, but it looked like Claydon's when he had five birdies in eight holes around the turn to take the lead at seven under with five holes remaining. He clung on doggedly, sinking a par saver from six feet at the 15th, and making his four at the last, despite driving into sand and leaving himself 130 yards short of the flag for his third shot. Claydon holed from 20 feet for his

68 to set the target.

It was just beyond Luna who also had 68, and also Bjorn who collapsed to an inward 39 and shot 75, but Broadhurst pulled level with three birdies in his last five holes to be home in 33, as was Westwood after beating par at the 11th, from 50 feet, 12th and 17th.

The play-off was a triumph for the former Youths' champion whose slide-rule putt clinched not only a top prize of £116,660, but also made him odds-on to

finish the year in Europe's elite top 15. Ahead lay a first appearance in England's team for the Alfred Dunhill Cup, and the chance to again demonstrate the more aggressive approach urged by new coach Peter Cowen, a former Tour player. Experienced caddie John Graham has also helped to put an old head on those broad young shoulders. Only a certain Gothenburg bartender still believes that Lee Westwood is a boy in a man's game.

Mike Britten

BOSS
HUGO BOSS

Photograph by Richard Avedon

McGinley's magnificent finale

A last round 62 swept Paul McGinley

to his first European Tour title

*P*aul McGinley, four times second but never the champion, gave one of the great performances of the year when he finally gained his first European Tour victory at the Hohe Brücke Open at Litschau.

Forget the fact that most of the top Europeans were competing at the USPGA championship the same week. Few of them could have lived with 29-year old McGinley as he blazed round the picturesque Waldviertel course with a final round 62 for a winning aggregate of 269, 19 under par.

It was just enough to give him a one shot victory over Spaniard Juan Carlos Pinero, the third round leader, and former England amateur international David Lynn. Yet, what was most remarkable about the Irishman's success was that he began the final round eight shots off the pace. Pinero, younger brother of Ryder Cup star Manuel, was three shots ahead of the field at the start of the fourth round and McGinley was joint 21st, seemingly out of contention. Even McGinley, who shot an opening 73, had dismissed his chances by the end of the third round. 'After my bad first round I thought I had blown it,' he said. 'But I shot 20 under par for the last three rounds and I just can't explain how delighted I am.'

McGinley, whose four second places included the Heineken Classic in Perth,

THE COURSE

The Waldviertel Golf Club at Litschau is an undulating, parkland-type course, 6,937 yards in length, par 72. Several natural lakes serve as hazards, particularly at the third, fourth and 11th holes. Out of bounds on the right has to be avoided when driving from the tenth and 18th and trees and thick rough behind many of the greens are added dangers.

SHOT OF THE WEEK

American Bob May produced the shot of the week when he eagled the 377-yard 18th hole in the second round. May, 76 yards from the pin after a two iron tee shot down the hill, holed out with his lob wedge, the ball, landing on the front of the green, checked once and then rolled straight into the hole. As May said 'It was a great pity. From where I was, I couldn't see it.'

the European Tour these days. The halfway cut was made at three under par and that speaks volumes for the exceptional standard we have. You had to shoot 13 under par just to finish in the top ten.'

True, 99 of the 144-strong field were under par for two rounds on a course 6,937 yards long and very tight in places. Certainly, the European Tour has never been healthier.

Scott Watson led the field after day one with an eight under par 64 with Pinero and Italian Massimo Scarpa one shot behind. McGinley was joint 97th at this stage. Pinero took over the lead on 131 after a second round 66 and was two

Juan Carlos Pinero (right) and David Higgins (below) succumbed to Paul McGinley's last round spectacular.

Australia, in February, added: 'I've been near so many times I knew my time had to come. I was joint leader after two rounds at the Open Championship and after shooting a 65 at Royal Lytham I knew I had it in me to win very soon. People said the Hohe Brücke Open had a very weak field because most of the top guys were at the USPGA. Well, there are no weak fields on

ahead of Scarpa and rookie Irishman David Higgins. McGinley shot 66 to move up to joint 33rd.

Following the third round, Pinero, with a 68 for 199, had increased his lead to three shots with Higgins second on 202 and Sweden's Max Anglert in third spot after a superb 64. McGinley, with 68, was now tied 21st. That night Pinero telephoned brother Manuel in

GC WALDVIERTEL, LITSCHAU, AUSTRIA, AUGUST 8-11, 1996 · YARDAGE 6937 · PAR 72

Pos	Name	Country	Rnd 1	Rnd 2	Rnd 3	Rnd 4	Total	Prize Money £
1	Paul MCGINLEY	(Ire)	73	66	68	62	269	41660
2	David LYNN	(Eng)	66	68	70	66	270	21710
	Juan Carlos PIÑERO	(Sp)	65	66	68	71	270	21710
4	Adam HUNTER	(Scot)	67	74	67	64	272	11550
	Gary CLARK	(Eng)	66	68	70	68	272	11550
6	Phil GOLDING	(Eng)	67	69	70	67	273	8125
	Per NYMAN	(Swe)	70	66	69	68	273	8125
8	Max ANGLERT	(Swe)	71	68	64	71	274	6250
9	Andrew BARNETT	(Wal)	69	67	70	69	275	4555
	Rolf MUNTZ	(Hol)	67	69	74	65	275	4555
	Anders HAGLUND	(Swe)	70	71	66	68	275	4555
	Daniel CHOPRA	(Swe)	69	69	70	67	275	4555
	David HIGGINS	(Ire)	66	67	69	73	275	4555
	Stephen DODD	(Wal)	67	67	71	70	275	4555
15	Scott WATSON	(Eng)	64	70	70	72	276	3378
	Bob MAY	(USA)	70	68	68	70	276	3378
	Per HAUGSRUD	(Nor)	67	68	71	70	276	3378
	Massimo SCARPA	(It)	65	68	71	72	276	3378
	Steve WEBSTER	(Eng)	66	69	71	70	276	3378
20	Thomas GÖGELE	(Ger)	68	67	69	73	277	2962
	Andrew SHERBORNE	(Eng)	67	70	70	70	277	2962
22	Raymond BURNS	(N.Ire)	68	71	69	70	278	2812
	Marcus WILLS	(Wal)	69	70	70	69	278	2812
24	Mats LANNER	(Swe)	67	69	72	71	279	2365
	Matthew MCGUIRE	(Eng)	70	67	69	73	279	2365
	Mikael PILTZ	(Fin)	71	67	74	67	279	2365
	Mark LITTON	(Wal)	69	68	68	74	279	2365
	Greg CHALMERS	(Aus)	69	70	67	73	279	2365
	Michael WELCH	(Eng)	71	70	69	69	279	2365
	Ronan RAFFERTY	(N.Ire)	72	69	69	69	279	2365
	Roger WESSELS	(SA)	69	72	67	71	279	2365
	Brian MARCHBANK	(Scot)	67	71	68	73	279	2365
	Jonathan LOMAS	(Eng)	68	66	74	71	279	2365
34	Rudi SAILER	(Aut)	70	70	72	68	280	1900
	Barry LANE	(Eng)	69	66	71	74	280	1900
	Lee S JAMES	(Eng)	70	66	76	68	280	1900
	Silvio GRAPPASONNI	(It)	67	70	72	71	280	1900
	Francisco CEA	(Sp)	70	67	75	68	280	1900
39	Matthias DEBOVE	(Fr)	70	71	72	68	281	1625
	Brenden PAPPAS	(SA)	67	72	70	72	281	1625
	Anssi KANKKONEN	(Fin)	68	71	71	71	281	1625
	André BOSSERT	(Swi)	67	71	74	69	281	1625
	Antoine LEBOUC	(Fr)	70	70	68	73	281	1625
	David R JONES	(Eng)	68	70	72	71	281	1625
45	Simon BROWN	(Eng)	71	68	73	70	282	1375
	Andrew COLLISON	(Eng)	73	67	67	75	282	1375
	Fredrik LARSSON	(Swe)	70	66	73	73	282	1375
	Johan RYSTRÖM	(Swe)	71	66	70	75	282	1375
49	Stephen PULLAN	(Eng)	68	72	72	71	283	1125
	Gordon J BRAND	(Eng)	68	72	68	75	283	1125
	Olle NORDBERG	(Swe)	72	69	69	73	283	1125
	Heinz P THÜL	(Ger)	66	73	72	72	283	1125
	Roger WINCHESTER	(Eng)	73	66	73	71	283	1125
	Brian DAVIS	(Eng)	71	69	74	69	283	1125
55	Nic HENNING	(SA)	70	67	75	72	284	875
	Olivier EDMOND	(Fr)	71	70	71	72	284	875
	Gabriel HJERTSTEDT	(Swe)	69	70	76	69	284	875
	John MELLOR	(Eng)	72	68	73	71	284	875
59	Greg OWEN	(Eng)	67	73	73	72	285	750
	Mark STEVENSON	(Eng)	75	64	70	76	285	750
	Frédéric GROSSET-GRANGE	(Fr)	72	69	73	71	285	750
62	Bill LONGMUIR	(Scot)	71	69	72	74	286	700
63	Tim PLANCHIN	(Fr)	68	72	77	70	287	675
64	Robert COLES	(Eng)	70	71	78	69	288	650
65	Oyvind ROJAHN	(Nor)	69	72	73	75	289	625
66	Claude GRENIER	(Aust)	73	68	72	80	293	400

Marbella and said: 'Manuel told me to play my normal game in the final round and I would win easily. I think it is easier to win when you are on the telephone.'

McGinley had one great advantage on the final day. He began seven matches ahead of Pinero and birdied seven of the first eight holes. By the time the Spaniard began, as last man out, he knew the Irishman was only one shot behind. Lynn, too, was one behind Pinero at this point with four birdies in his first six holes.

McGinley dropped his only shot of the round at the short ninth where he three putted from 40 feet but he birdied

Massimo Scarpa pitched in with a top ten finish.

the 11th, 13th and 16th to go to 18 under. Pinero birdied the first and bogeyed the fourth and fifth but further birdies at the 12th and 14th took him to 19 under. Lynn, with three holes to play, was 17 under.

Then came the real drama. McGinley missed the 17th green but holed a crucial 20 foot putt to save par and an immaculate sand wedge to three feet at the last gave him his 11th birdie of the day to enable him to catch Pinero at 19 under. Lynn birdied the last to finish on 270, one behind McGinley, but Pinero, coming up behind, looked certain to force a play-off. But he three putted the 17th from 50 feet and just missed a putt at the last to allow the man from Dublin his victory.

John Oakley

Lomas graduates with honours

Former Rookie of the Year Jonathan Lomas
secured his first European Tour victory
with a closing round of 66

The beautiful spa town of Mariánské Lázne, now restored to its former grandeur after years of neglect under a communist regime, was the romantic setting for the third Chemapol Trophy Czech Open when a former tennis star shared centre stage at the beginning of the week and a golf star of the future took the final bow by registering his maiden European Tour victory, and with it a prize of £125,000.

Ivan Lendl, winner of eight majors in the world of tennis, made his European Tour debut as a golf professional but it was Cheshire-based Jonathan Lomas who claimed the limelight with four sub-70 scores on the lovely 6,758-yard Mariánské Lázne course set among the trees at an altitude of 2,000 feet.

Lomas, 28, paced himself like a thoroughbred and came through on the rails for a thrilling one-stroke victory over Sweden's Daniel Chopra with a 72-hole total of 12 under par 272. It was a well-deserved win and he revealed afterwards the reasons why he had not fulfilled his earlier promise. After the 1994 Open championship at Turnberry, Lomas began to suffer sciatica pains in both legs, a condition which baffled doctors. 'I saw all sorts of specialists about it but every test was clear and they didn't believe I had pain,' explained Lomas. 'The doctors' advice was to keep playing, to play my way through it and they were proved right. It cleared up as quickly and as mysteriously as it had come during the Conte of Florence Italian Open.'

A graduate of the 1993 European Challenge Tour after four unsuccessful Qualifying School attempts, Lomas won the Sir Henry Cotton Rookie of the Year Award in his first season in 1994 with 32nd place in the Volvo Ranking, despite the sciatica pains which began in the second half of the season. In 1995, he slipped to 101st in the Ranking and his struggle continued in 1996 until the pain disappeared at the Italian Open. Then he quietly began climbing the Ranking list and his opening rounds of 69, 68 at Mariánské Lázne ensured he hit his first target of the year, retaining his playing rights for 1997.

Lomas had no way of knowing at the

Best finish for Daniel Chopra.

time that his maiden European Tour win was just around the corner. After the first round, he was two shots behind joint leaders Dean Robertson, Jamie Spence, Andew Coltart and big-hitting Italian Emanuele Canonica, and at the halfway stage he was still two behind the pace-setting Robertson and England's Peter Mitchell, whose second round 65 equalled the best of the week. A 69 in the third round maintained his position and he went into Sunday's final round on a gloriously sunny day two behind Chopra, who scored a third round 65, and Scot Gary Orr, who had a 66.

Mitchell was still in touch, just one behind the leaders, and there were some significant moves up the field from Spain's Domingo Hospital, defending champion Peter Teravainen and Lee Westwood, who only just made the halfway cut after an opening 75 but was now only four shots off the lead. Indeed, as the final round got under way there were 14 players in with a chance of winning, among them local favourite Alexander Cejka and rookie Raymond Russell, who set the field a clubhouse target of eight under par by scoring a last round 66.

Hospital's closing 67 set a new target of ten under par and Westwood came racing through the field with seven birdies in 11 holes to become joint leader with Lomas. Double bogeys at both the 16th and 17th

Winning your first tournament is always a thrill but to win in style makes it even sweeter. At the 431-yard 72nd hole in Mariánské Lázne, Jonathan Lomas hit what he later described as a 137-yard flying wedge second shot which landed the ball 12 inches from the hole for a tap-in birdie, and victory.

Gary Orr (above left) hits out. Ivan Lendl (left) featured in the tournament promotion.

THE COURSE

The Mariánské Lázne course, 2,000 feet above sea level and set among beautiful woodland, was opened in 1905 by King Edward VII, who regularly visited the spa town to take the waters. The people of the town managed to keep the course open during the communist era and now it has hosted a third Chemapol Trophy Czech Open.

183

Mariánské Lázne, Czech Republic, Auguust 15-18, 1996 • Par 71 • Yards 6758

Pos	Name	Country	Rnd 1	Rnd 2	Rnd 3	Rnd 4	Total	Prize Money £
1	Jonathan LOMAS	(Eng)	69	68	69	66	272	125000
2	Daniel CHOPRA	(Swe)	70	69	65	69	273	83320
3	Domingo HOSPITAL	(Sp)	68	70	69	67	274	46940
4	Raymond RUSSELL	(Scot)	69	70	71	66	276	37500
5	Peter TERAVAINEN	(USA)	73	69	69	66	277	24817
	Jamie SPENCE	(Eng)	67	71	69	70	277	24817
	Lee WESTWOOD	(Eng)	75	67	66	69	277	24817
	Peter MITCHELL	(Eng)	70	65	70	72	277	24817
9	Gary ORR	(Scot)	71	67	66	74	278	13663
	Gary EVANS	(Eng)	70	68	71	69	278	13663
	Dean ROBERTSON	(Scot)	67	68	75	68	278	13663
	Miles TUNNICLIFF	(Eng)	70	69	68	71	278	13663
	Paul BROADHURST	(Eng)	69	70	69	70	278	13663
	Martin GATES	(Eng)	69	72	66	71	278	13663
15	Mark ROE	(Eng)	72	68	71	68	279	10138
	Gary CLARK	(Eng)	69	72	69	69	279	10138
	Carl SUNESON	(Sp)	74	69	68	68	279	10138
	Richard BOXALL	(Eng)	68	70	74	67	279	10138
	Emanuele CANONICA	(It)	67	71	72	69	279	10138.
20	John HAWKSWORTH	(Eng)	71	69	68	72	280	8662
	Roger WESSELS	(SA)	70	69	69	72	280	8662
	Alexander CEJKA	(Ger)	73	68	67	72	280	8662
	Malcolm MACKENZIE	(Eng)	70	71	69	70	280	8662
24	Robert ALLENBY	(Aus)	70	71	71	69	281	7537
	Russell CLAYDON	(Eng)	68	68	74	71	281	7537
	Andrew COLTART	(Scot)	67	69	73	72	281	7537
	Patrik SJÖLAND	(Swe)	71	69	68	73	281	7537
	Steven BOTTOMLEY	(Eng)	75	67	71	68	281	7537
	Pedro LINHART	(Sp)	71	71	71	68	281	7537
30	Phillip PRICE	(Wal)	69	69	74	70	282	6182
	David HIGGINS	(Ire)	68	71	73	70	282	6182
	Philip WALTON	(Ire)	70	70	74	68	282	6182
	Paul LAWRIE	(Scot)	72	70	66	74	282	6182
	Howard CLARK	(Eng)	74	68	71	69	282	6182
	Angel CABRERA	(Arg)	73	69	71	69	282	6182
	Andrew SHERBORNE	(Eng)	74	68	68	72	282	6182
37	Retief GOOSEN	(SA)	70	68	71	74	283	5400
	José RIVERO	(Sp)	72	70	71	70	283	5400
	Bob MAY	(USA)	68	71	74	70	283	5400
40	Gary EMERSON	(Eng)	68	70	74	72	284	4500
	Nic HENNING	(SA)	74	68	72	70	284	4500
	Peter BAKER	(Eng)	69	67	76	72	284	4500
	Stephen FIELD	(Eng)	72	70	73	69	284	4500
	Jim PAYNE	(Eng)	75	66	74	69	284	4500
	Jarmo SANDELIN	(Swe)	72	70	70	72	284	4500
	Joakim HAEGGMAN	(Swe)	68	68	75	73	284	4500
	David A RUSSELL	(Eng)	69	70	74	71	284	4500
	Robert COLES	(Eng)	69	71	74	70	284	4500
49	Thomas GÖGELE	(Ger)	70	73	71	71	285	3600
	Greg CHALMERS	(Aus)	68	73	72	72	285	3600
	Paul AFFLECK	(Wal)	68	73	75	69	285	3600
52	Ross DRUMMOND	(Scot)	69	73	74	70	286	3300
53	Tim PLANCHIN	(Fr)	69	71	70	77	287	3150
54	Pierre FULKE	(Swe)	69	73	72	74	288	2850
	Mats HALLBERG	(Swe)	70	73	70	75	288	2850
	Eric GIRAUD	(Fr)	72	69	72	75	288	2850
57	Stuart CAGE	(Eng)	71	72	71	75	289	2550
58	David CARTER	(Eng)	71	71	73	75	290	2212
	Paul MCGINLEY	(Ire)	71	72	72	75	290	2212
	Glen HUTCHESON	(SA)	71	72	76	71	290	2212
	Mathias GRÖNBERG	(Swe)	70	69	80	71	290	2212
	Andrew BARNETT	(Wal)	71	71	74	74	290	2212
	Brian MARCHBANK	(Scot)	74	68	73	75	290	2212
64	Neal BRIGGS	(Eng)	73	70	73	75	291	1912
	Thomas LEVET	(Fr)	70	71	75	75	291	1912
66	Anders HAGLUND	(Swe)	69	72	75	77	293	1123
	Michel BESANCENEY	(Fr)	69	71	80	73	293	1123
	Andrew COLLISON	(Eng)	74	69	74	76	293	1123
69	Mike CLAYTON	(Aus)	72	71	76	75	294	1119
70	Fredrik LARSSON	(Swe)	70	72	79	74	295	1117

Hometown boy Alexander Cejka.

ended Westwood's challenge, though, and as the tournament came to a close only two players were left in the race, Lomas and Chopra. The Englishman, playing in the penultimate group and experiencing the pressures of leading a tournament for the first time, handled the situation magnificently and birdied the final hole to post a 12 under par mark. Chopra, meanwhile, was on course to snatch victory when his second shot to the 521-yard 17th with a three wood finished four feet from the hole. But he missed the eagle putt and came to the 18th needing a birdie to force a play-off. It was not to be and Lomas was the champion.

In the space of 48 hours, Lomas progressed from a position of just securing his card for the next season to becoming an exempt player for two years, and as he set off to celebrate he observed: 'The opportunities on the European Tour are wonderful.'

Richard Dodd

You've had to change the way you maintain your fairways to reflect new, higher standards of quality. We know your equipment needs to be up to the challenge.

Ransomes®

Fairway Mowers.

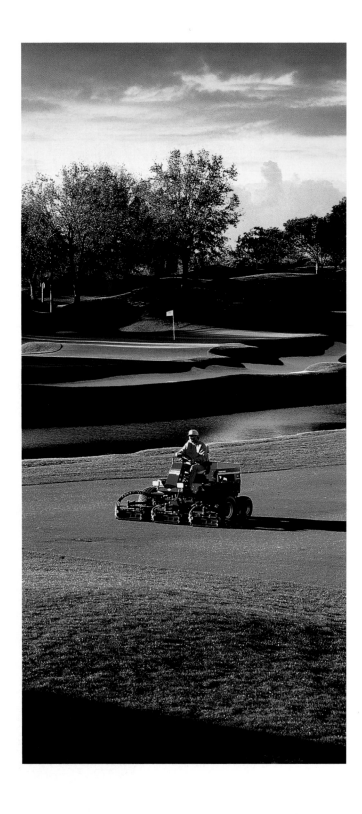

Today's fairways demand a level of quality that was formerly reserved for greens. To meet these higher standards, course managers have found a superb choice in the Ransomes® family of fairway mowers. The T-Plex 185 is perfect for highly visible tees and surrounds. The 250, 305 and 7-unit 405 are the industry's only "right" weight mowers. The 405 features a wide 156" cutting swath while the Commander 3500 is a production powerhouse. Ransomes mowers have been designed to maintain the same perfect finish from one side of the fairway to the other. When you start with Ransomes reel mowers, you finish with the best.

For a free demo or the name of your nearest dealer please call: **0500 026208**

RANSOMES
CUSHMAN
RYAN
For The Best Results

Ransomes, Ransomes Way, Ipswich, England IP3 9QG. Tel: 01473 270000. Fax: 01473 276300.
© Ransomes 1996. All rights reserved.

Woosnam is dominant

Ian Woosnam took his fourth title of the season with a compelling performance

Never in the history of the European Tour were so many records broken by one man in one tournament – nearly. Ian Woosnam was that man, and it would not be overstating the case to describe his golf in the curtailed Volvo German Open as near perfect as makes no difference.

Agreed, he was playing on a Schloss Nippenburg course that encouraged low scoring – with vestigial rough and holding greens, it was always going to favour the man bold enough to bombard the flags consistently.

Agreed, his vastly greater experience over his immediate rivals was a telling factor. Agreed, he was a man on a mission, of which more later. Agreed, he was enjoying his best season for six summers or more. But no matter what is going in your favour, there are still 156 of you at the start, and you still have to beat the lot. And that Woosnam did, in spades.

When stair-rod rain, thunder, lightning and even hailstones forced Tournament Director Andy McFee reluctantly to call off the fourth round in mid-afternoon on the Sunday, Woosnam was already so far under par – 20, to be precise – that it would have been a remarkable score over 72 holes, let alone 54.

He won with a three – round total of 193, and was six ahead of his nearest rivals. If he had done little more than remain vertical for 18 holes, he would almost certainly have won in a canter, so much had he dominated this low-scoring tournament.

Playing on one of the courses owned by PGA European Tour Courses, the joint venture between the Tour and the International Management Group, he was the undisputed star turn. And the rest? Frankly, on this week, at this venue, in this tournament, little more than spear-carriers. And they were willing to admit it, every man-jack of them.

Woosnam went into the tournament feeling good. That quick, confident, slightly defiant strut that enters his gait

when he is on top of his game was present, even in the pre-tournament pro-am. With Colin Montgomerie, his rival in a seemingly two-horse race for the coveted first place on the Volvo Ranking , absent

Paul Broadhurst, that there was more than just a bid for glory behind his obvious determination to succeed. He was as happy as Larry after his day's work, and in talking expansively about his plans for the

list in 1995 and had slumped to 56th in the world-wide Sony Ranking, and it was not good enough for a man who had been number one in the world, for goodness sake.

Andrew Coltart floats a bunker shot en route to first round 67.

tending his sick father, the £116,660 winner's prize was there for the taking. And Woosnam intended to take it.

As ever a martyr to his own honesty, Woosnam admitted after finishing the first day on 64, two shots behind the remarkable course-record round produced by

rest of the season, revealed that it was not just the simple re-discovery of his once-famed competitive juices that was driving him on.

It was, he said, that he had negotiated a five-year contract with his sponsors that would result in bonuses based on performance, on winning the Volvo Ranking and achieving a better world ranking. He had finished 65th in the European money

Whatever it was that had sparked him, it continued to do the job in the second round, and after a second 64 he led by a single stroke from a rejuvenated Robert Karlsson, with Fernando Roca and Iain Pyman a further shot back, one ahead of Carl Suneson and Stephen Field. Note the names. Worthy names, all of them. But as the halfway cut fell at five under par, equalling the European Tour record

Robert Karlsson
(above) and
Fernando Roca
(right) were among
those in second
place.

Bernhard Langer had a disappointing result on the course he designed.

set in the 1992 BMW International, it is pertinent to examine their playing records in European competition. They had won once between the five of them. Woosnam had triumphed 30 times. For once, statistics told the whole story. The man who bet against Woosnam on that Friday night was either exceptionally brave, or a dolt, with the odds heavily favouring the latter.

Herr Brave (or Herr Dolt, as the case might be) would have been sorely disappointed with his wager at the close of play on Saturday night. Woosnam was 20 under par, the best of the rest a medium-length street away. It had looked rather less than a formality that the Welshman would beat the Tour 54-hole record of 193 when he stepped onto the final tee in that

third round. So what did he do? He played the hole like a mere mortal, that's what, coming off his drive at the par-five hole and splashing into a stream, taking a penalty drop, hitting his three-wood approach shot into a bunker and taking a bogey six. So it was only a 65. Only six under par for the day, only out of sight at the top of the leaderboard.

'I could have shot anything today,' he said afterwards. He could have shot anything the next day, too, and still won. Except he didn't have to. To be honest, it didn't really matter. Woosnam had this one bang to rights. It was a fair cop, and Schloss Nippenburg gave up without a struggle.

Mel Webb

Leaderboard (right) shows Frank Nobilo's final round which he completed before play was cancelled.

Pos	Name	Country	Rnd 1	Rnd 2	Rnd 3	Rnd 4	Total	Prize Money £
1	Ian WOOSNAM	(Wal)	64	64	65		193	116660
2	Iain PYMAN	(Eng)	66	64	69		199	46557
	Thomas GÖGELE	(Ger)	67	65	67		199	46557
	Fernando ROCA	(Sp)	66	64	69		199	46557
	Robert KARLSSON	(Swe)	67	62	70		199	46557
6	Diego BORREGO	(Sp)	69	63	68		200	22750
	Miguel Angel MARTIN	(Sp)	66	66	68		200	22750
8	Stephen FIELD	(Eng)	66	65	70		201	14406
	Paul BROADHURST	(Eng)	62	70	69		201	14406
	Roger CHAPMAN	(Eng)	72	62	67		201	14406
	Stephen AMES	(T&T)	68	65	68		201	14406
	Carl SUNESON	(Sp)	65	66	70		201	14406
13	Barry LANE	(Eng)	68	67	67		202	9900
	Ronan RAFFERTY	(N.Ire)	64	72	66		202	9900
	David CARTER	(Eng)	66	69	67		202	9900
	Michael JONZON	(Swe)	67	67	68		202	9900
	Heinz P THÜL	(Ger)	70	67	65		202	9900
	Greg TURNER	(NZ)	70	67	65		202	9900
	David WILLIAMS	(Eng)	67	67	68		202	9900
20	Pedro LINHART	(Sp)	67	67	69		203	7455
	Francisco CEA	(Sp)	68	66	69		203	7455
	Gary EMERSON	(Eng)	68	69	66		203	7455
	Des SMYTH	(Ire)	66	69	68		203	7455
	Paul EALES	(Eng)	67	68	68		203	7455
	Raymond RUSSELL	(Scot)	63	69	71		203	7455
	Lee WESTWOOD	(Eng)	66	71	66		203	7455
	Jonathan LOMAS	(Eng)	67	67	69		203	7455
	Peter BAKER	(Eng)	70	66	67		203	7455
	Paul LAWRIE	(Scot)	66	69	68		203	7455
30	Michael CAMPBELL	(NZ)	64	72	68		204	5770
	Paul MCGINLEY	(Ire)	67	69	68		204	5770
	Mats LANNER	(Swe)	64	71	69		204	5770
	Steve WEBSTER	(Eng)	69	66	69		204	5770
	José Maria CAÑIZARES	(Sp)	67	68	69		204	5770
	Emanuele CANONICA	(It)	69	68	67		204	5770
	Robert COLES	(Eng)	68	66	70		204	5770
37	Daniel CHOPRA	(Swe)	70	67	68		205	4620
	Antoine LEBOUC	(Fr)	68	69	68		205	4620
	Miles TUNNICLIFF	(Eng)	66	71	68		205	4620
	Bernhard LANGER	(Ger)	64	71	70		205	4620
	Mark JAMES	(Eng)	69	67	69		205	4620
	Mark ROE	(Eng)	65	72	68		205	4620
	Wayne RILEY	(Aus)	64	71	70		205	4620
	Raymond BURNS	(N.Ire)	69	67	69		205	4620
	Thomas BJORN	(Den)	66	68	71		205	4620
46	Domingo HOSPITAL	(Sp)	70	67	69		206	3500
	Michael WELCH	(Eng)	67	69	70		206	3500
	Ignacio GARRIDO	(Sp)	71	66	69		206	3500
	Carl MASON	(Eng)	69	66	71		206	3500
	Jamie SPENCE	(Eng)	67	70	69		206	3500
	Mark MOULAND	(Wal)	67	70	69		206	3500
	Terry PRICE	(Aus)	67	68	71		206	3500
53	Fabrice TARNAUD	(Fr)	69	68	70		207	2426
	Steven BOTTOMLEY	(Eng)	68	69	70		207	2426
	Pierre FULKE	(Swe)	70	66	71		207	2426
	Frank NOBILO	(NZ)	71	66	70		207	2426
	Andrew COLTART	(Scot)	67	70	70		207	2426
	Dean ROBERTSON	(Scot)	68	69	70		207	2426
	Santiago LUNA	(Sp)	68	68	71		207	2426
	Ricky WILLISON	(Eng)	69	64	74		207	2426
	Peter FOWLER	(Aus)	68	69	70		207	2426
62	Klas ERIKSSON	(Swe)	68	69	71		208	1890
	Gary ORR	(Scot)	67	68	73		208	1890
	Juan Carlos PIÑERO	(Sp)	67	70	71		208	1890
65	Tony JOHNSTONE	(Zim)	68	69	72		209	1187
	Per NYMAN	(Swe)	65	71	73		209	1187
	Russell CLAYDON	(Eng)	65	72	72		209	1187
	Per-Ulrik JOHANSSON	(Swe)	71	66	72		209	1187
	Francis HOWLEY	(Ire)	69	67	73		209	1187
70	Eamonn DARCY	(Ire)	65	68	77		210	1042
71	André BOSSERT	(Swi)	68	69	74		211	1040
72	John HAWKSWORTH	(Eng)	67	68	79		214	1038

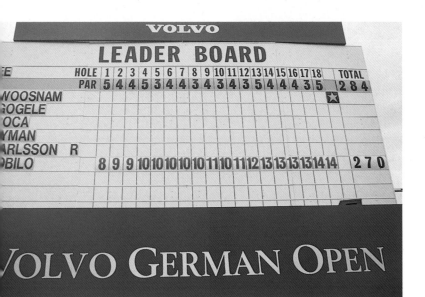

THE COURSE

Schloss Nippenburg, designed by Bernhard Langer, offered every player every chance to make birdie on every hole. As such, the course, with its light rough and holding greens, was made for the likes of winner Woosnam. But when the wee Welshman is in the sort of form he was in for this tournament, no course is immune from grievous bodily harm.

Allenby connects to third title

Robert Allenby remained upwardly mobile to capture his third victory of the season

*I*t needed a touch of sanity from Robert Allenby to put everything into perspective after a controversial week at Collingtree Park. The young Australian had just clinched his third European Tour win of the year at the first play-off hole against Spain's Miguel Angel Martin, having stayed the course while many others walked away bemoaning the condition of the greens or something else.

Allenby just wanted to thank his lucky stars he was playing golf and winning heaps of money when others were not so fortunate. To underline the point he dedicated his victory to Matthew Fleming, a young friend who had just died of Aids in Australia. 'He was 20, a haemophiliac, and he just got a wrong dose of blood,' he said. 'He was close to me because he had come to my golf day, where all the funds go to a cancer support unit in Melbourne, the previous year. He was going to come to this year's event in May but he fell into a coma. I went home for a week's break before Collingtree and while I was there I heard he had died. When I arrived at Collingtree I said to myself be patient and you will come through. You've just got to look on the bright side. We are playing for so much money and they did make the course playable. We've all got to play in the same conditions.'

The problem was that the greens, for what was the first points-counting tournament for the 1997 Ryder Cup by Johnnie Walker, had deteriorated and Tournament Director Mike Stewart apologised to the players, the fans and the sponsors, mobile telephone company One 2 One, who were making their Tour debut with

£700,000 in prize-money.

Not that South African Gavin Levenson found many problems. Having finished 135th in the Volvo Ranking in 1995, he was fifth reserve at the start of the week. A phone call to his home in Johannesburg suggested he might like to travel and by the time he stepped on to

Pedro Linhart stumbled in the final round.

Levenson had a two-shot advantage over Colin Montgomerie with a posse of ten other players on 69. At halfway, Levenson was back on the slippery slope. A 75 left him a shot behind Mark Roe and Allenby, who posted 71s for 140, four under, while Sweden's Daniel Chopra with 68 was the only man to break 70, and 32 players failed to break 80. It was a difficult day.

After round three Levenson had slipped even further back with a 76 but Allenby was firmly in control after another 71 for 211, five under, with Pedro Linhart the only serious challenger one behind after a battling 67. They were the only players under par. Roe crashed to a 78 after driving out-of-bounds at the first, while Chopra took 79 including a quintuple bogey ten at the last. Not that Linhart was all that interested in Ryder Cup points. 'It's a good event to watch on TV,' he said, 'but I'd hate to play in it. Too much pressure.'

By halfway in the final round he was marching backwards, towards a 78 for joint ninth spot. Allenby, meanwhile, was cruising. Seven under par at the turn, he led by three from Martin, who was out in 32 with three birdies and an eagle at the long ninth when he holed from a bunker.

But suddenly Allenby faltered. Three shots went in six holes from the 11th, trimming his lead to one, and when Martin birdied the 17th they were level at four under. Even then Allenby could have avoided a play-off but his putt for birdie on the par five 18th's island green, slipped by. Both finished on 284, Allenby with a

the plane he was playing in place of his good friend Mark McNulty. He certainly made the most of it, shooting a first round 66 which included eight birdies and only 23 putts. 'My caddie Mick Jones said: 'You are going to miss them today but it doesn't make any difference. You might get a few in so just keep going.'

That first day also saw two lengthy interruptions for lightning and thunderstorms and when play was eventually halted, half the field were still on the course. When they returned the following morning a stiff wind had sprung up, which was reflected in the high scoring.

When the first round was complete

Peter O'Malley (above) among the reeds. Runner-up Miguel Angel Martin (below).

It was a tale of two Spaniards. Miguel Angel Martin showed his prowess by holing a 30-yard bunker shot at the long ninth for an eagle three in the final round, but he was pipped for shot of the week by Miguel Angel Jiménez. At the 18th in the final round, he had 202 yards into a breeze and over water to the pin on the island green and he calmly drilled a three iron to 15 feet then coolly holed the eagle putt. It gave him a best-of-the-day 67 and having just birdied the par four 17th meant he picked up three shots in two holes. But it was only good enough for fourth place, two shots behind Allenby and Martin, and one adrift of Rocca.

73 to Martin's 68.

Costantino Rocca and Ian Woosnam might also have made the play-off, but Rocca couldn't find a birdie in the last four holes while Woosnam's bid for an eagle at the last ended in a miserable four-putt bogey six, although his fifth place kept him on top of the Volvo Ranking.

The play-off on the 18th was an anti-climax, Martin taking seven after a poor drive, and conceding Allenby his par putt. It was Allenby's fourth win in four play-offs and he was spot-on when he concluded: 'It's been a funny week.'

David Hamilton 195

COLLINGTREE PARK ETC, AUGUST 28-31, 1996 · PAR 72 · YARDAGE 6728

Pos	Name	Country	Rnd 1	Rnd 2	Rnd 3	Rnd 4	Total	Prize Money £
1	Robert ALLENBY	(Aus)	69	71	71	73	284	116660
2	Miguel Angel MARTIN	(Sp)	75	70	71	68	284	77770
3	Costantino ROCCA	(It)	71	73	72	69	285	43820
4	Miguel Angel JIMÉNEZ	(Sp)	74	72	73	67	286	35000
5	Ian WOOSNAM	(Wal)	70	76	71	70	287	29640
6	José COCERES	(Arg)	69	78	71	70	288	24500
7	Joakim HAEGGMAN	(Swe)	71	77	70	71	289	19250
	Antoine LEBOUC	(Fr)	74	73	70	72	289	19250
9	Pedro LINHART	(Sp)	72	73	67	78	290	12751
	Colin MONTGOMERIE	(Scot)	68	76	77	69	290	12751
	Klas ERIKSSON	(Swe)	71	75	72	72	290	12751
	Robert COLES	(Eng)	74	76	71	69	290	12751
	Peter MITCHELL	(Eng)	74	71	74	71	290	12751
	Philip WALTON	(Ire)	71	74	74	71	290	12751
15	Mike CLAYTON	(Aus)	69	76	73	73	291	9464
	Mark ROE	(Eng)	69	71	78	73	291	9464
	Phillip PRICE	(Wal)	72	76	74	69	291	9464
	Adam HUNTER	(Scot)	70	79	73	69	291	9464
	Peter O'MALLEY	(Aus)	71	73	75	72	291	9464
20	Stephen MCALLISTER	(Scot)	73	76	69	74	292	8085
	David GILFORD	(Eng)	69	74	77	72	292	8085
	Peter HEDBLOM	(Swe)	70	75	75	72	292	8085
	Iain PYMAN	(Eng)	71	75	75	71	292	8085
24	Eamonn DARCY	(Ire)	74	76	69	74	293	7140
	Domingo HOSPITAL	(Sp)	73	77	75	68	293	7140
	Roger CHAPMAN	(Eng)	71	76	74	72	293	7140
	Retief GOOSEN	(SA)	71	74	75	73	293	7140
	Bradley HUGHES	(Aus)	73	75	72	73	293	7140
29	Gavin LEVENSON	(SA)	66	75	76	77	294	6020
	Tony JOHNSTONE	(Zim)	72	77	72	73	294	6020
	David HOWELL	(Eng)	70	74	78	72	294	6020
	Wayne RILEY	(Aus)	71	78	71	74	294	6020
	Daniel CHOPRA	(Swe)	74	68	79	73	294	6020
	Bob MAY	(USA)	74	75	70	75	294	6020
35	Francisco CEA	(Sp)	70	71	76	78	295	4970
	Steven BOTTOMLEY	(Eng)	71	79	72	73	295	4970
	Jean VAN DE VELDE	(Fr)	73	76	72	74	295	4970
	Martin GATES	(Eng)	71	77	72	75	295	4970
	Paul EALES	(Eng)	75	71	72	77	295	4970
	Raymond RUSSELL	(Scot)	69	78	74	74	295	4970
	Anders HAGLUND	(Swe)	71	77	73	74	295	4970
	Mark MOULAND	(Wal)	71	77	73	74	295	4970
43	Emanuele CANONICA	(It)	69	76	76	75	296	4200
	Paul BROADHURST	(Eng)	73	75	74	74	296	4200
	Raymond BURNS	(N.Ire)	75	75	72	74	296	4200
46	Michael JONZON	(Swe)	72	76	76	73	297	3430
	Stuart CAGE	(Eng)	69	81	75	72	297	3430
	Fredrik LINDGREN	(Swe)	74	74	73	76	297	3430
	David CARTER	(Eng)	72	77	76	72	297	3430
	Thomas BJORN	(Den)	72	78	75	72	297	3430
	Gary CLARK	(Eng)	75	73	76	73	297	3430
	Barry LANE	(Eng)	73	77	70	77	297	3430
	Paul LAWRIE	(Scot)	72	75	72	78	297	3430
54	Ove SELLBERG	(Swe)	71	74	79	74	298	2660
	Andrew SHERBORNE	(Eng)	74	76	74	74	298	2660
	Rolf MUNTZ	(Hol)	69	81	74	74	298	2660
57	Seve BALLESTEROS	(Sp)	73	75	78	73	299	2380
58	George RYALL	(Eng)	74	75	73	78	300	2065
	Andrew COLTART	(Scot)	72	75	79	74	300	2065
	Paul CURRY	(Eng)	76	71	74	79	300	2065
	Eduardo ROMERO	(Arg)	70	76	76	78	300	2065
	Ross DRUMMOND	(Scot)	72	78	75	75	300	2065
	Greg CHALMERS	(Aus)	73	77	77	73	300	2065
64	Oyvind ROJAHN	(Nor)	73	76	73	79	301	1540
	Paul AFFLECK	(Wal)	74	73	76	78	301	1540
	David HIGGINS	(Ire)	72	78	76	75	301	1540
67	Eric GIRAUD	(Fr)	74	75	73	80	302	1047
	Ricky WILLISON	(Eng)	76	74	76	76	302	1047
69	Mark DAVIS	(Eng)	71	73	84	75	303	1044
70	Michael WELCH	(Eng)	76	73	77	79	305	1042

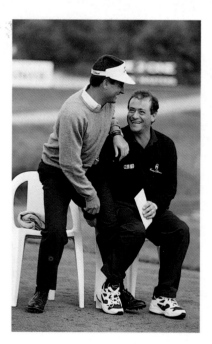

Miguel Angel Martin finds Costantino Rocca occupying his seat at the prize-giving

THE COURSE

Situated adjacent to junction 15 of the M1 motorway just outside Northampton, Collingtree Park is the work of Johnny Miller, former Open and US Open champion. It has the feel of an American resort course with several of the holes being bordered by housing. Water is also a key factor, coming into play on ten holes, most noticeably the signature 18th where the fairway is flanked down the left by a lake to the island green.

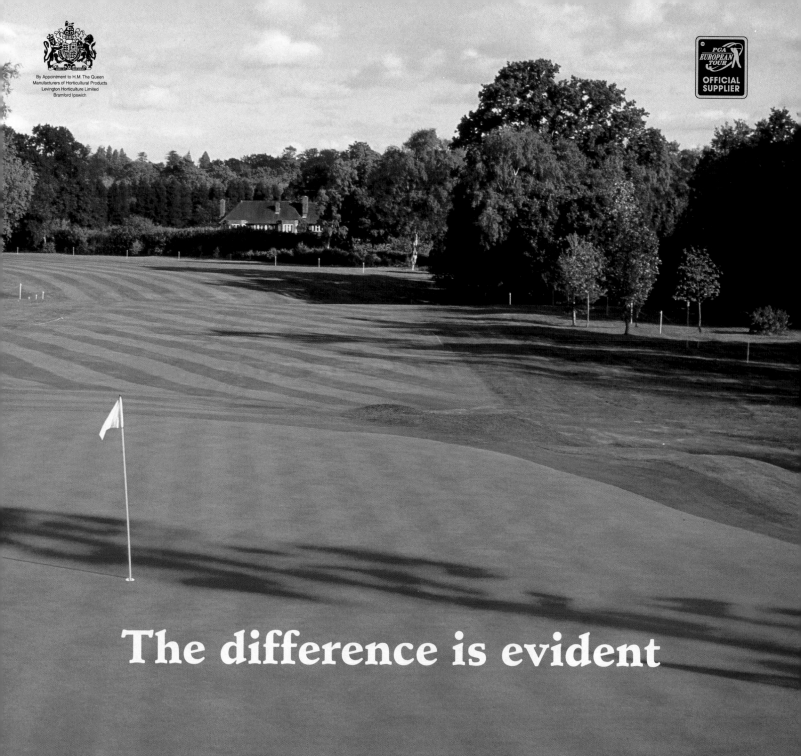

The difference is evident

The Levington DIFFERENCE™

Levington® products are chosen by professionals looking for the very best results: the PGA European Tour recommends Levington professional turfcare products such as those used at The Wentworth Club. The All England Lawn Tennis and Croquet Club, Wimbledon also uses Levington products on its famous courts and a host of professional nurseries use Levington compost, fertilizers and chemicals.

Levington is dedicated to producing the best for the gardener too. Levington Multi-Purpose Compost and Levington Lawn Food have both been judged overall best buys in independent consumer tests.

If you would like to see the difference for yourself, look out for Levington garden products at your local garden centre. We are so confident of them we will offer you your money back if you are not satisfied with our products' performance when used as recommended - subject to proof of purchase. And if you want any help or advice about any of our products just call the Levington Freecall Garden Helpline on 0500 888558.

Montgomerie scales the heights

Closing rounds of 61 and 63
sent Colin Montgomerie to the top
in Switzerland

*C*olin Montgomerie and Sam Torrance, friends and rivals both on and off the golf course, saw their Canon European Masters week go full circle on the spectacular Crans-sur-Sierre course 5,000 feet up the Swiss Alps. On the Tuesday of the tournament week, they teamed up as partners to beat a star-studded field in winning the Canon Shoot-Out Finals. And when the tournament began they became fierce rivals again as they pursued victory and also individual aims.

Montgomerie wanted the European Masters title after eight consecutive years of trying and he also wanted to overtake the absent Ian Woosnam and return to the top of the Volvo Ranking. Torrance also had twin targets: victory and elevation into the higher echelons of the Ranking in order to secure his place in the end-of-season Volvo Masters.

Each achieved his secondary aim of the week but, of course, there could be only one winner. Would it be Montgomerie, seeking his third European Tour victory of the season or would it be Torrance, whose highlight of the year to date was in winning the Andersen Consulting European Regional Championship – where he beat fellow Scot Montgomerie in the final?

When both players scored opening rounds of 65 at Crans-Sur-Sierre, just one shot behind pace-setter Paul Broadhurst,

we knew the game was on. Little did we know it at the time, though, but we were to witness some of the finest golf of the season over the next three days. Torrance continued his fine form with a second round of 63, a stunning performance which left him six strokes clear of the field and, more importantly to him, eight ahead of Montgomerie. Torrance had 15 birdies and an eagle in his first two rounds and he revealed that at the beginning of the week, he had flown his father down to the Wentworth Club from Scotland and together they had worked on his game for five hours. 'It was great and the practice paid off,' said Torrance. 'My golf the last two days has been better than I played all last year and certainly the best I have played this year and I definitely put that down to dad'. One of Torrance's playing partners was Severiano Ballesteros, the Ryder Cup by Johnnie Walker team captain, who twice expressed the opinion after the second round 63 that it was the

The Canon Business Centre
was a popular facility.

Montgomerie had scored an infuriating and frustating second round of 71 which included seven birdies, three bogeys, two double bogeys and only six pars. Was Sam now out of reach, Montgomerie, was asked? 'No, and I'm proof of that as I showed in 1992,' was the reply, a reference to when Montgomerie lost a six-stroke lead as Jamie Spence scored a last-round 60 to snatch the title.

Sam Torrance (above) focuses on a putt. Paul Curry (below) is surrounded by sand.

best he had ever seen Torrance play. 'It was a nice compliment and I asked him if that meant I was already in the Ryder Cup team', said the mischievous Torrance.

So, the scene was set for the weekend with the crowded leaderboard looking like this:

128 Sam Torrance
134 Paul Broadhurst
135 Lee Westwood, Olle Nordberg
136 Colin Montgomerie, Gary Orr, Paul Curry, Miles Tunnicliff, Darren Clarke, Ross Drummond, Robert Coles, Roger Chapman, Bradley Hughes, Eric Geraud
137 Barry Lane, Malcolm Mackenzie, Carl Suneson.

They were prophetic words because the big Scot showed what was possible with a remarkable third round of 61 which included ten birdies in the first 14 holes, at which point he began thinking seriously in terms of a 59. 'I had the opportunity to shoot 59 today and it proves that it's on and that I'm capable of doing it,' he said. Montgomerie rated his 61 as the best round of golf he'd ever played in Europe

and he ranked it alongside his final round 65 in the US PGA Championship at the Riviera Club in Los Angeles when he tied with Steve Elkington.

'Where was Sam Torrance when all this was happening? He was doing very nicely, thank you, with a third round 68 which kept him in the lead by one shot. But he must have sensed that Montgomerie was now in full flight and although Sam scored another 68 on the final day to become the only player to break 70 in all four rounds he finished runner-up by, incredibly, four shots.

Montgomerie added a 63 to set a new

tournament record of 260 and his 18 under par score for 36 holes was a European Tour record, as was his 124 total. For good measure, record crowds of 44,800 turned out to see the records tumble. It was a wonderful week of golf,

Celebrating the 50th anniversary of the event were, left to right, Christian Barras, George O'Grady, Gaston Barras, Ken Schofield, Johnny Storjohann, John Paramor and Charles Andre Bagnoud.

fittingly so because this was the 50th anniversary of the playing of the Swiss Open/Canon European Masters at Crans-sur-Sierre. And the last word went not to the new champion but to the gracious Sam Torrance, who said: 'I have nothing but admiration for Colin. He's a fabulous golfer and he deserves to be the European number one for the fourth year.'

Richard Dodd   201

CRANS-SUR-SIERRE, SWITZERLAND, SEPTEMBER 5-8, 1996 • PAR 71 • YARDAGE 6663

Pos	Name	Country	Rnd 1	Rnd 2	Rnd 3	Rnd 4	Total	Prize Money £
1	Colin MONTGOMERIE	(Scot)	65	71	61	63	260	127950
2	Sam TORRANCE	(Scot)	65	63	68	68	264	85250
3	Paul CURRY	(Eng)	66	70	65	66	267	48070
4	Peter MITCHELL	(Eng)	68	70	71	64	273	32613
	Seve BALLESTEROS	(Sp)	71	68	68	66	273	32613
	Gary ORR	(Scot)	66	70	68	69	273	32613
7	Thomas BJORN	(Den)	67	72	68	67	274	19813
	Darren CLARKE	(N.Ire)	68	68	70	68	274	19813
	Miguel Angel JIMÉNEZ	(Sp)	71	67	67	69	274	19813
10	Mats LANNER	(Swe)	72	69	69	65	275	13766
	Andrew OLDCORN	(Scot)	74	68	67	66	275	13766
	Paul BROADHURST	(Eng)	64	70	71	70	275	13766
	Lee WESTWOOD	(Eng)	65	70	68	72	275	13766
14	Fredrik LINDGREN	(Swe)	71	69	70	66	276	11060
	Stephen FIELD	(Eng)	70	68	68	70	276	11060
	Ross DRUMMOND	(Scot)	70	66	69	71	276	11060
	Carl SUNESON	(Sp)	70	67	68	71	276	11060
18	Padraig HARRINGTON	(Ire)	69	71	71	66	277	9280
	Jarmo SANDELIN	(Swe)	72	70	72	63	277	9280
	Miguel Angel MARTIN	(Sp)	69	70	70	68	277	9280
	Robert COLES	(Eng)	68	68	70	71	277	9280
	Per-Ulrik JOHANSSON	(Swe)	67	73	66	71	277	9280
23	Daniel CHOPRA	(Swe)	68	72	72	66	278	7610
	Christian CÉVAER	(Fr)	73	66	73	66	278	7610
	Angel CABRERA	(Arg)	69	73	68	68	278	7610
	Marc FARRY	(Fr)	70	72	68	68	278	7610
	Olle NORDBERG	(Swe)	66	69	74	69	278	7610
	Roger CHAPMAN	(Eng)	68	68	72	70	278	7610
	Bradley HUGHES	(Aus)	66	70	71	71	278	7610
	Per NYMAN	(Swe)	70	68	69	71	278	7610
	David HIGGINS	(Ire)	72	67	66	73	278	7610
32	Patrik SJÖLAND	(Swe)	66	74	72	67	279	6382
	Barry LANE	(Eng)	67	70	71	71	279	6382
34	Eduardo ROMERO	(Arg)	65	75	70	70	280	5762
	Pierre FULKE	(Swe)	73	69	69	69	280	5762
	Carl MASON	(Eng)	69	71	72	68	280	5762
	David WILLIAMS	(Eng)	69	71	70	70	280	5762
	Manuel PIÑERO	(Sp)	71	70	69	70	280	5762
	Domingo HOSPITAL	(Sp)	69	69	67	75	280	5762
40	Retief GOOSEN	(SA)	72	70	68	71	281	4522
	Joakim HAEGGMAN	(Swe)	70	71	67	73	281	4522
	David GILFORD	(Eng)	69	70	71	71	281	4522
	Mark ROE	(Eng)	70	72	69	70	281	4522
	David HOWELL	(Eng)	70	71	70	70	281	4522
	Silvio GRAPPASONNI	(It)	72	70	71	68	281	4522
	Stephen MCALLISTER	(Scot)	71	68	74	68	281	4522
	Derrick COOPER	(Eng)	72	69	73	67	281	4522
	Paul LAWRIE	(Scot)	70	70	70	71	281	4522
	Miles TUNNICLIFF	(Eng)	72	64	74	71	281	4522
50	Michael CAMPBELL	(NZ)	69	73	71	69	282	3592
	Fabrice TARNAUD	(Fr)	72	70	67	73	282	3592
52	David A RUSSELL	(Eng)	72	70	69	72	283	3205
	Jean VAN DE VELDE	(Fr)	71	71	69	72	283	3205
	Eric GIRAUD	(Fr)	67	69	69	78	283	3205
55	Peter FOWLER	(Aus)	72	68	72	72	284	2662
	Steen TINNING	(Den)	69	73	71	71	284	2662
	Michael WELCH	(Eng)	72	70	74	68	284	2662
	Malcolm MACKENZIE	(Eng)	65	72	71	76	284	2662
59	Sven STRÜVER	(Ger)	69	72	72	72	285	2332
	Mathias GRÖNBERG	(Swe)	69	70	74	72	285	2332
61	Howard CLARK	(Eng)	73	69	70	75	287	2115
	Gary EMERSON	(Eng)	74	67	73	73	287	2115
	Gordon SHERRY	(Scot)	72	70	73	72	287	2115
	Robert ALLENBY	(Aus)	71	71	74	71	287	2115
	Gary CLARK	(Eng)	70	72	76	69	287	2115
66	Matthew HAZELDEN	(Eng)	71	71	73	74	289	1152
67	Juan Carlos PIÑERO	(Sp)	69	71	79	71	290	1150
68	Massimo FLORIOLI	(It)	68	74	75	74	291	1146
	Stephen AMES	(T&T)	69	72	76	74	291	1146
	Marco SCOPETTA	(Swi)	73	69	79	70	291	1146

THE COURSE

Crans-sur-Sierre is world renowned for its alpine beauty, and now it has been made tougher by some course re-design by Severiano Ballesteros. The 16th hole was transformed into a 235-yard par three, which was the talking point of the week. Some liked it and some didn't but Ballesteros' verdict was: 'It's a fantastic hole, the best hole on the course.'

OUR CONFERENCE ROOM

To receive a free "Canon Story" booklet, contact: Canon Europa N.V., P.O. Box 2262, 1180 EG Amstelveen, The Netherlands. http://www.europe.canon.com

In some conference rooms, you don't have to suffer. Because Canon believes in breaking down barriers of communication. Bringing people closer together. By providing productive, friendly, flexible products. Which means you save time inside the office. So you can spend more time outside, doing what you really want to do. Such as concentrating on the real challenge, on the golf course. The drive for excellence. The thrill of the contest. The pleasure of achievement. It's a passion we all share. After all, business works better when it brings a little more leisure into your life.

Canon
A PLEASURE TO WORK WITH

So together, let's care.

Parnevik powers home

Jesper Parnevik won the third

European Tour title of his career

with a five-stroke victory in Paris

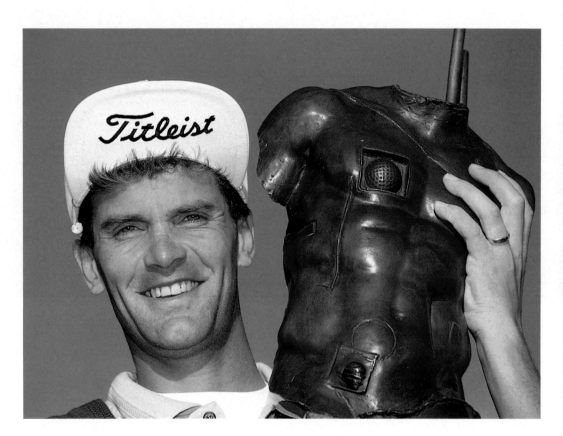

T here was a poignancy about Jesper Parnevik indelibly engraving his name on the illustrious Honours Board of the Trophée Lancôme. His victory at St. Nom la Bretèche was the third by a Swedish golfer on the 1996 European Tour, but the first since the untimely death during the week of the Open Championship of Jan Blomqvist at the age of 54.

Blomqvist is credited with masterminding the development of Swedish golf. A journalist, television reporter and former coach in top-class ice-hockey and handball, he was himself a fanatical five handicap golfer. He made a study of the psychology of golf, explained his intention and ambitions to the Swedish Golf Federation and enlisted the help of dieticians, specialists in physical and mental training, doctors, and consultants in sports medicine. His initial success in helping to guide Sweden to the silver medal in the 1982 Eisenhower Trophy launched a revolution since it was only in 1984 that a Swedish player first put together four sub-par rounds in a European Tour event.

In 1987 Blomqvist predicted that a Swedish golfer would become Open Champion by the end of the century. 'I have no doubt that it will happen during that time.' he said. 'We are getting closer and closer to the ultimate success, and it's happening much faster than I thought possible. When a Swedish golfer wins the Open Championship it will be a greater achievement than when Bjorn Borg first won Wimbledon.'

Sadly, Blomqvist, a man of vision, did not live to see his prediction become reality. Yet, coincidentally, Parnevik came within a finger-touch of winning the Open Championship at Turnberry in 1994. Parnevik claims not to have lost any sleep over the observations that on that sunlit afternoon on the Ayrshire coast he snatched defeat from the jaws of victory by pulling a blind over his eyes. He elected not to look at the leaderboard, and he played the 18th hole in the dark with-

out realising that Nick Price had eagled the 17th. Price won and Parnevik, with a bogey at the last, was left to muse over what might have been.

You learn from your mistakes. Most certainly Parnevik has and, unquestionably, he was proud to peer from under that trademark upturned peak at the final leaderboard of the 27th Trophée Lancôme. It confirmed his place in history alongside the likes of Jacklin, Palmer, Aaron, Miller, Casper, Ballesteros, Price, Langer, Woosnam and Olazábal, all major championship winners, as the victor of

what has matured into one of the most prestigious tournaments in the world.

Parnevik was not compelled to study the leaderboard one iota on that last afternoon in Paris. He had his main rival in his sights throughout a final round of fluctuating fortune. Moreover, Colin Montgomerie, the defending champion, began with such gusto that with five successive birdies from the first hole it hardly made good viewing for Parnevik. Montgomerie, however, had twisted the lion's tail 13 months earlier when Parnevik was again his rival at the Volvo Scandinavian

Masters. Parnevik prevailed, and the Scot finished second. History was to repeat itself.

Parnevik revels in being in the forefront of the action. He had the lead at the start of all four rounds when he won for the first time on the European Tour in the 1993 Scottish Open. He led after the second and third rounds in the Volvo Scandinavian Masters, and he did the same in the Trophée Lancôme. Jamie Spence set the first day pace on 65 - one ahead of Stuart Cage, Andrew Coltart, Montgomerie and Parnevik - before

Not so much the shot of the tournament – but the shots of the tournament. In the second round at the 541-yard 16th hole, Colin Montgomerie reached the green with two superbly struck drivers then holed from 20 feet for an eagle three. 'I couldn't play three shots any better at one hole,' he said. 'I hit three perfect shots.'

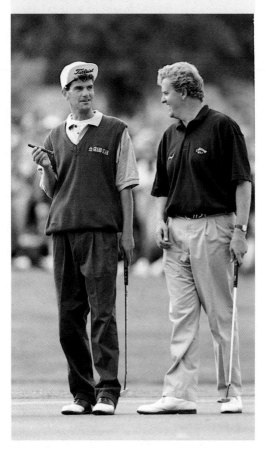

Costantino Rocca (left) in verdant surroundings.
Bernhard Langer (above) cuts loose from sand.

Parnevik captivated the elegant Parisians with rounds of 69 and 66 to move to nine under par, which was one ahead of Montgomerie and four in front of Ross Drummond, Ian Woosnam and Spence.

So to the last day. Changes had been made to the course by European Golf Design, the Tour's golf course design company: the new bunker at the first hole on the left side of the fairway at 262 yards from the tee has greatly improved the view of the hole and increased its degree of difficulty. Then at the fourth a new back tee, adding 33 yards, has placed the premium on the drive with the spinney of trees to the left and the bunker on the right providing the proper focus for the tee shot. The fifth has been transformed with the green, and its surround, having been completely redesigned with water now a feature at the front right-hand side and the rear of the green.

None of these changes, however, made any difference to Montgomerie on that final day. He threw five straight birdies at Parnevik with three putts of 20 feet, one of 12 feet and one of seven. Every man, of course, is the maker of his own fortune, and Montgomerie's honesty shone through as the tournament pendulum swung once more in Parnevik's favour. 'I dropped six shots from the sixth, I played remarkably badly for those closing holes and I never hit one golf shot.' Montgomerie said.

Parnevik, cool and composed, improved as the round unfolded. He probably secured victory as early as the 14th where he made his fifth birdie. The Swede began the hole two in front. Montgomerie missed the green then missed from seven feet for par whereas Parnevik holed from six feet for birdie. 'I knew it was mine there and then,' he said. Jan Blomqvist would have liked Jesper Parnevik's positivism.

Mitchell Platts   207

St. Nom la Bretèche, Paris, September 12-15, 1996 • Par 70 • Yards 6840

Pos	Name	Country	Rnd 1	Rnd 2	Rnd 3	Rnd 4	Total	Prize Money £
1	Jesper PARNEVIK	(Swe)	66	69	66	67	268	108330
2	Colin MONTGOMERIE	(Scot)	66	70	66	71	273	72210
3	Ross DRUMMOND	(Scot)	68	68	69	69	274	40690
4	David HOWELL	(Eng)	67	71	68	71	277	27593
	Costantino ROCCA	(It)	68	69	69	71	277	27593
	Stuart CAGE	(Eng)	66	74	70	67	277	27593
7	Paul EALES	(Eng)	71	69	68	70	278	16753
	Ian WOOSNAM	(Wal)	67	68	70	73	278	16753
	Padraig HARRINGTON	(Ire)	68	74	73	63	278	16753
10	Jamie SPENCE	(Eng)	65	73	67	74	279	11308
	Miguel Angel JIMÉNEZ	(Sp)	68	71	72	68	279	11308
	Paul BROADHURST	(Eng)	68	71	68	72	279	11308
	Rodger DAVIS	(Aus)	70	72	69	68	279	11308
	Mark ROE	(Eng)	68	73	65	73	279	11308
15	Silvio GRAPPASONNI	(It)	69	67	70	75	281	8967
	Bernhard LANGER	(Ger)	67	71	71	72	281	8967
	David GILFORD	(Eng)	75	68	68	70	281	8967
	Stephen AMES	(T&T)	75	66	71	69	281	8967
19	Peter MITCHELL	(Eng)	70	73	67	72	282	7930
	Andrew COLTART	(Scot)	66	72	74	70	282	7930
21	Per HAUGSRUD	(Nor)	71	70	72	70	283	7312
	Jonathan LOMAS	(Eng)	74	69	71	69	283	7312
	Peter BAKER	(Eng)	67	69	74	73	283	7312
	Sven STRÜVER	(Ger)	72	70	70	71	283	7312
25	Phillip PRICE	(Wal)	71	74	67	72	284	6630
	Nick FALDO	(Eng)	73	71	69	71	284	6630
	Martin GATES	(Eng)	76	67	71	70	284	6630
28	Ignacio GARRIDO	(Sp)	73	69	75	68	285	5850
	Barry LANE	(Eng)	69	73	72	71	285	5850
	Andrew SHERBORNE	(Eng)	72	71	70	72	285	5850
	Santiago LUNA	(Sp)	72	70	74	69	285	5850
	Andrew OLDCORN	(Scot)	73	69	72	71	285	5850
33	Carl MASON	(Eng)	73	68	73	72	286	5070
	Eduardo ROMERO	(Arg)	67	75	72	72	286	5070
	Howard CLARK	(Eng)	67	74	70	75	286	5070
	Greg TURNER	(NZ)	73	72	73	68	286	5070
	Patrik SJÖLAND	(Swe)	74	69	75	68	286	5070
38	Retief GOOSEN	(SA)	72	71	75	69	287	4290
	Thomas GÖGELE	(Ger)	73	71	72	71	287	4290
	Seve BALLESTEROS	(Sp)	69	75	70	73	287	4290
	Ronan RAFFERTY	(N.Ire)	70	75	67	75	287	4290
	Richard BOXALL	(Eng)	71	74	73	69	287	4290
	Chip BECK	(USA)	70	72	72	73	287	4290
	Marc FARRY	(Fr)	71	72	72	72	287	4290
45	Richard GREEN	(Aus)	70	75	71	72	288	3445
	Darren CLARKE	(N.Ire)	67	74	74	73	288	3445
	Stephen MCALLISTER	(Scot)	74	70	71	73	288	3445
	Antoine LEBOUC	(Fr)	69	70	71	78	288	3445
	Gary ORR	(Scot)	70	75	68	75	288	3445
	Rolf MUNTZ	(Hol)	74	66	73	75	288	3445
51	Tony JOHNSTONE	(Zim)	68	76	74	71	289	2795
	Sam TORRANCE	(Scot)	68	72	73	76	289	2795
	Jean VAN DE VELDE	(Fr)	74	71	71	73	289	2795
	Emanuele CANONICA	(It)	77	68	73	71	289	2795
55	Mark MOULAND	(Wal)	74	71	71	74	290	2340
	Ricky WILLISON	(Eng)	72	73	73	72	290	2340
	José RIVERO	(Sp)	72	72	68	78	290	2340
58	Michael CAMPBELL	(NZ)	72	71	74	74	291	1982
	Tim PLANCHIN	(Fr)	71	74	70	76	291	1982
	Fabrice TARNAUD	(Fr)	71	72	72	76	291	1982
	Steven RICHARDSON	(Eng)	71	74	71	75	291	1982
62	Fernando ROCA	(Sp)	71	74	69	78	292	1787
	Steven BOTTOMLEY	(Eng)	72	72	77	71	292	1787
64	Derrick COOPER	(Eng)	73	72	75	74	294	1690
65	Mark DAVIS	(Eng)	71	72	73	81	297	1625

THE COURSE

The composite course at St. Nom la Bretèche, one of several fine and exclusive clubs in the Paris area, has a par of 70. Fred Hawtree created both the Red and the Blue course in the early 1960's on lightly-wooded, undulating terrain in a part of the countryside known as La Tuilerie. For the 1996 edition of the Trophée Lancôme additional length and the re-shaping of bunkers not only increased the visual impact of the course but in some cases changed the focus of the hole.

TWO MAJOR WINNERS FROM BRIDGESTONE.

Nick Faldo is back, winning his third green jacket with a new determination and a revolutionary new ball from Bridgestone – the Precept Tour Double Cover. The world's first wound, double cover 4-piece golf ball especially engineered for the serious golfer who demands even higher performance than a 3-piece balata.

Ultrasoft spin cover
Reinforced 2nd cover
Wound layer
High repulsion inner core

This ingenious construction has given Nick Faldo added distance, superior feel and control with unprecedented durability. Making it as big a break-through in technology as Bridgestone's celebrated Precept EV Extra Spin. The incredible high spin 2-piece ball that enabled

Nick Price to sink his famous Open Championship-winning putt at Turnberry.

Deceptively simple in technology the EV gives extra yards on every drive, yet when hit with an iron the high velocity core and Super Spin cover combine to give consistent stop on the greens. (An ordinary ball would just keep on rolling).

Super Spin cover
High velocity gradational core

So now Bridgestone gives you two outstanding technologies played by two of today's greatest players. Whatever your style of play, whatever your handicap, there's a Bridgestone ball that will make your game. For details contact Bridgestone Sports Division on: 0121-511 1488.

PRECEPT TOUR DOUBLE COVER
FOUR PIECE WOUND — SUPERIOR DISTANCE
TOUR FEEL & SPIN — EXCEPTIONAL DURABILITY

PRECEPT EV EXTRA SPIN
TWO-PIECE HIGH SPIN — SUPERIOR DISTANCE
PRECISION CONTROL

BRIDGESTONE

It's the ball that makes your game

A *star is* Bjorn

Thomas Bjorn joined the ranks of

first-time winners with a consummate victory

over the scenic Loch Lomond course

*K*een students of the golfing form guide detected the tell-tale signs some weeks before Thomas Bjorn's maiden European Tour victory. The 25-year old Dane had been a winner in waiting since the previous October, when he led the European Challenge Tour Order of Merit with £46,471. In the two months preceding the inaugural Loch Lomond World Invitational, he had twice

finished seventh and, in fact, led for three rounds of the Volvo Scandinavian Masters.

So if there was an element of surprise about Bjorn's success, it was only because the pundits hadn't read the signs correctly. In his own mind, there is no doubting Thomas knew he possessed the game and the steely nerve to succeed. Certainly it was a seminal moment for Danish profes-

sional golf. Bjorn may have triumphed four times during his Challenge Tour apprenticeship, but no Dane had, until then, managed to win on the European Tour.

This modest but enormously powerful and talented young man from Silkeborg set about doing for his country's golf what the Danish football team achieved for their sport in Euro '92. 'I won

Nick Faldo (above) was fulsome in his praise of designer Tom Weiskopf's (left) masterpiece.

Tour spoke volumes for the quality of Bjorn's achievement.

Faldo came to praise the course. Bjorn had no time for such niceties and came with the sole intention of burying every one of his challengers in his quest for a debut Tour title. This was no fluke. Only Bjorn managed to shoot under par in all four rounds over the Tom Weiskopf-Jay Morrish designed course which attracted universal praise.

Faldo, seldom given to hyperbole, went as far as to describe the scenic lay-out as 'the best course in Great Britain by miles'. One could just imagine Loch Lomond owner, Lyle Anderson, purring with delight when he overheard that remark.

Sadly, the US Masters champion flattered to deceive over the four days. After opening with an encouraging three under par 68, he suffered a deterioration in fortunes, culminating in a 77 to close. His

SHOT OF THE WEEK

Without question, Peter Baker's birdie four at the 505-yard par five third. Nothing remarkable about a birdie, it might seem at first glance. But this four was achieved with the Mid-lander's second ball. Baker carved his tee shot into the woods on the right of the fairway and played a provisional. From there, his 235-yard three iron flew left to right and disappeared into the hole for a remarkable birdie.

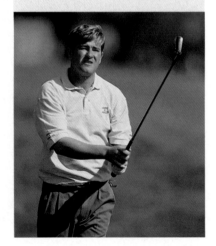

four times on the European Challenge Tour last year, so I knew I was capable of winning,' Bjorn explained matter of factly. 'I just had to lift my game to a higher level.'

That he did so in the presence of Nick Faldo, Colin Montgomerie, Ian Woosnam and the cream of the European

total of 291 was truly eclipsed by Bjorn, whose four sub-par rounds of 70,69,68,70 left him clutching the winner's cheque of £125,000.

Also left in the shade were Montgomerie and Woosnam, at the time waging a private war for the honour of finishing European number one. Montgomerie, following a 72 and three 70s, claimed a share of fourth place while Woosnam settled for a tie for 20th. However, that was merely one of the sideshows as the main event built to a gripping crescendo on Sunday afternoon.

Jamie Spence had led the way on the first day with a 67, as Faldo seemed in the right frame of mind to launch a challenge in a group of three players on 68. Enter Jean Van de Velde. The Frenchman adhered to some tentative words of advice from his lovely wife, Brigitte; altered his putting stroke and shot a course record 65. That magnificent effort, on one of the toughest and best-conditioned new

Colin Montgomerie's (above) consistency was not quite enough. Wifely advice paid off for Jean Van de Velde (below).

courses on the rota, elevated Van de Velde into a tie for second, one behind Bjorn, at halfway. The Frenchman, winner of the Roma Masters in 1993, out-scored the Dane by one (67-68) on the third day.

The two men were tied on six under, and out on their own, four ahead of Australian Robert Allenby.

The final day dawned fair, and if Bjorn needed additional inspiration, he found it on arrival at Ross Dhu House, the grand clubhouse once the home of the Colquhoun Clan. A note had been left in his locker by the Glasgow Rangers and Denmark soccer international, Brian Laudrup. It said: 'Good Luck, I hope you win.'

Bjorn, who conceded that Brian's brother Michael was his true sporting idol, admitted: 'It was a wonderful touch. It made me feel good.' Allenby and Mont-gomerie never got in a serious blow. Van de Velde led briefly in the final round but birdies at the 14th and 15th for the Dane proved decisive. His 70 edged Van de Velde by one stroke, and it was Bjorn who was accompanied by the skirl of the bagpipes onto the victory rostrum.

Gordon Simpson   213

LOCH LOMOND GOLF CLUB, GLASGOW, SEPTEMBER 19-22, 1996 • PAR 71 • YARDAGE 7005

Pos	Name	Country	Rnd 1	Rnd 2	Rnd 3	Rnd 4	Total	Prize Money £
1	Thomas BJORN	(Den)	70	69	68	70	277	125000
2	Jean VAN DE VELDE	(Fr)	75	65	67	71	278	83320
3	Robert ALLENBY	(Aus)	69	71	71	70	281	46940
4	Colin MONTGOMERIE	(Scot)	72	70	70	70	282	34635
	Jonathan LOMAS	(Eng)	71	73	70	68	282	34635
6	Richard GREEN	(Aus)	72	73	71	67	283	24375
	Darren CLARKE	(N.Ire)	68	73	73	69	283	24375
8	Miguel Angel MARTIN	(Sp)	73	73	69	69	284	16830
	Mark MCNULTY	(Zim)	73	72	70	69	284	16830
	Peter O'MALLEY	(Aus)	70	78	68	68	284	16830
11	Eamonn DARCY	(Ire)	71	76	66	72	285	12923
	Greg TURNER	(NZ)	78	70	70	67	285	12923
	Barry LANE	(Eng)	69	74	71	71	285	12923
14	David GILFORD	(Eng)	71	74	72	69	286	11245
	Stephen AMES	(T&T)	76	71	68	71	286	11245
16	Lee WESTWOOD	(Eng)	74	73	69	71	287	9917
	Glen DAY	(USA)	72	74	71	70	287	9917
	Miguel Angel JIMÉNEZ	(Sp)	77	70	72	68	287	9917
	José COCERES	(Arg)	68	77	75	67	287	9917
20	David HOWELL	(Eng)	70	73	75	70	288	8437
	Ian WOOSNAM	(Wal)	73	69	75	71	288	8437
	Per HAUGSRUD	(Nor)	77	72	71	68	288	8437
	Des SMYTH	(Ire)	75	72	70	71	288	8437
	Roger CHAPMAN	(Eng)	71	75	69	73	288	8437
	Martin GATES	(Eng)	76	70	71	71	288	8437
26	Jamie SPENCE	(Eng)	67	74	72	76	289	7425
	Andrew COLTART	(Scot)	74	71	70	74	289	7425
	Andrew SHERBORNE	(Eng)	73	72	72	72	289	7425
29	Paul MCGINLEY	(Ire)	72	74	69	75	290	6281
	Retief GOOSEN	(SA)	72	72	75	71	290	6281
	Ricky WILLISON	(Eng)	72	77	71	70	290	6281
	Peter BAKER	(Eng)	69	73	77	71	290	6281
	Costantino ROCCA	(It)	72	74	72	72	290	6281
	Eduardo ROMERO	(Arg)	77	70	73	70	290	6281
	Ross DRUMMOND	(Scot)	69	79	69	73	290	6281
	Pierre FULKE	(Swe)	71	72	73	74	290	6281
37	Marc FARRY	(Fr)	76	71	74	70	291	5475
	Nick FALDO	(Eng)	68	73	73	77	291	5475
39	Padraig HARRINGTON	(Ire)	76	74	71	71	292	5025
	Rodger DAVIS	(Aus)	76	72	68	76	292	5025
	Pedro LINHART	(Sp)	69	76	72	75	292	5025
	Gordon SHERRY	(Scot)	74	75	72	71	292	5025
43	Rolf MUNTZ	(Hol)	74	75	74	70	293	4425
	Thomas GÖGELE	(Ger)	70	75	69	79	293	4425
	Iain PYMAN	(Eng)	73	78	74	68	293	4425
	Ignacio GARRIDO	(Sp)	72	74	73	74	293	4425
47	Diego BORREGO	(Sp)	73	78	72	71	294	3600
	Andrew OLDCORN	(Scot)	75	73	76	70	294	3600
	Gary CLARK	(Eng)	75	71	76	72	294	3600
	Peter MITCHELL	(Eng)	73	77	73	71	294	3600
	Adam HUNTER	(Scot)	77	71	75	71	294	3600
	Raymond RUSSELL	(Scot)	76	74	69	75	294	3600
	Richard BOXALL	(Eng)	75	76	70	73	294	3600
54	Domingo HOSPITAL	(Sp)	72	78	73	72	295	2700
	Joakim HAEGGMAN	(Swe)	76	73	72	74	295	2700
	Paul BROADHURST	(Eng)	79	72	75	69	295	2700
	Jim PAYNE	(Eng)	73	76	73	73	295	2700
	David CARTER	(Eng)	75	75	71	74	295	2700
59	Ronan RAFFERTY	(N.Ire)	73	75	73	75	296	2212
	Fernando ROCA	(Sp)	76	72	76	72	296	2212
	Derrick COOPER	(Eng)	74	75	74	73	296	2212
	Sven STRÜVER	(Ger)	75	75	72	74	296	2212
63	Brian MARCHBANK	(Scot)	75	76	73	73	297	1987
	Peter HEDBLOM	(Swe)	75	74	74	74	297	1987
65	Michael CAMPBELL	(NZ)	69	80	77	72	298	1875
66	Tony JOHNSTONE	(Zim)	80	71	72	76	299	1124
	Juan Carlos PIÑERO	(Sp)	78	72	75	74	299	1124
68	Santiago LUNA	(Sp)	76	73	75	76	300	1120
	Gary NICKLAUS	(USA)	75	76	73	76	300	1120

THE COURSE

In the words of Nick Faldo: 'Absolutely fabulous.' Weiskopf regards Loch Lomond as his masterpiece, and it's difficult to argue. The natural beauty of the Loch and mountains create a magnificent backdrop for an immaculately prepared course. Almost every hole invites trouble, while at the same time being a joy to the eye.

*Official Suppliers of Champagne to
the PGA European Tour.*

Johansson books his ticket

Per-Ulrik Johansson made certain
he would be playing in the Volvo Masters
with victory in Ireland

A sudden burning desire to compete in the end-of-season Volvo Masters enabled Per-Ulrik Johansson to dig deep and achieve his goal with a remarkable display of will power. He was languishing in 96th place in the Volvo Ranking when it occurred to him that he was on course, a downward course, to missing his first trip to Valderrama since joining the European Tour in 1991. And he decided to do something about it.

Johansson, with £64,000 in winnings, estimated he needed a further £60,000 with three counting events left to qualify for the Volvo Masters. Armed with that knowledge, he arrived at The K Club in County Kildare, near Dublin, for the Smurfit European Open with an abundance of desire but precious little confidence. Yet, somehow he focused on his target and by Sunday evening was crowned as champion.

Sounds romantic, sounds simple. And in a way it was. The steely Swede, though, revealed that he nearly passed up the week at the magnificent K Club because his game was so bad. It had certainly been a poor year for him and apart from fourth place in the Alamo English Open in June and eighth in the US PGA Championship, Johansson had struggled all season.

'I almost didn't come here and I almost didn't go to the US PGA, either,' he said after collecting the £125,000 Smurfit European Open first prize. 'It was mid-summer in Sweden and it was so nice at home, but I went to America and by finishing eighth I qualified for next year's US Masters and the US PGA again.

'A similar thing happened to me two years ago when I won the Chemapol Trophy Czech Open. I was at my house in Marbella, I wasn't playing well and I heard it was snowing on the course in the Czech Republic. But I went, and I won. I had exactly the same feeling before the Smurfit European Open. I'd missed the cut in my last two tournaments and I was thinking maybe I should forget about the Volvo

Masters this time and spend the winter sorting out my game. But the more I thought about Valderrama, the more I wanted to be there.'

It was a surprising story, not least because Johansson has been a consistently strong performer on the European Tour. In his first year on Tour in 1991, he was a member of Sweden's winning Alfred Dunhill Cup and World Cup teams, he won the Belgian Open and ended the season by being named the Sir Henry Cotton

Rookie of the Year. He was a member of the winning 1995 Ryder Cup by Johnnie Walker side at Oak Hill and as he teed up for the first round at The K Club he had won almost £1.5million in his career.

Johansson admitted after his thrilling win that he had not expected to even make the halfway cut, though he must have been hopeful after an opening 71 which left him in joint 20th place, six strokes behind local hero Padraig Harrington. The young Dubliner had

Costantino Rocca
(above) and Miguel
Angel Martin (right)
both had designs
on the title.

WORLD'S BIGGEST GIMME

For once, Colin Montgomerie was not in at the finish.

S H O T   O F   T H E   W E E K

Michael Welch, in his first season on the European Tour, holed a seven iron at the 173-yard 17th in the third round and won a £19,000 Renault Laguna Grandtour. It was the seventh ace of the 23-year old's career, his fourth in competition but his first since turning professional in 1994.

THE COURSE

Without exception, the players declared The K Club course to be one of the finest venues on the European Tour. Designed by Arnold Palmer with rolling fairways, huge contoured greens and acres of watery graves, the course is set in peaceful County Kildare and boasts one of Ireland's finest hotels.

continued from p 217

broken The K Club course record with a seven under par 65 (later equalled by Paul Broadhurst and Australian Richard Green) and he remained in contention to the end, much to the delight of the Irish crowds.

'If somebody had said I would shoot 65 today I'd have laughed because I didn't think it was possible, ' said Harrington,

who earned a share of the weekly £3,000 Tour Course Record Award as well as two cases of Jameson Whiskey for scoring an eagle three at the 18th. 'This is a tough course and I'd never

No repeat for defending champion Bernhard Langer.

come close to breaking 70 before this week,' he added.

Harrington was joint third with Broadhurst and Miguel Angel Martin on 138 at the halfway stage, one stroke behind Costantino Rocca and the resurgent Jim Payne. Johansson was joint tenth but 24 hours later after a third round of 66

The K Club, Dublin, September 26-29, 1996 · Yardage 7159 · Par 72

Pos	Name	Country	Rnd 1	Rnd 2	Rnd 3	Rnd 4	Total	Prize Money £
1	Per-Ulrik JOHANSSON	(Swe)	71	70	66	70	277	125000
2	Costantino ROCCA	(It)	67	70	69	72	278	83320
3	Andrew COLTART	(Scot)	71	68	69	71	279	42220
	Roger CHAPMAN	(Eng)	72	69	69	69	279	42220
5	Miguel Angel MARTIN	(Sp)	69	69	71	71	280	31770
6	Paul BROADHURST	(Eng)	73	65	68	75	281	22500
	Jim PAYNE	(Eng)	68	69	72	72	281	22500
	Thomas BJORN	(Den)	74	69	70	68	281	22500
9	Eduardo ROMERO	(Arg)	73	71	70	68	282	16740
10	Per HAUGSRUD	(Nor)	71	71	73	68	283	13442
	Dean ROBERTSON	(Scot)	70	70	74	69	283	13442
	Padraig HARRINGTON	(Ire)	65	73	71	74	283	13442
	Michael JONZON	(Swe)	68	74	70	71	283	13442
14	Derrick COOPER	(Eng)	76	67	66	75	284	9681
	Niclas FASTH	(Swe)	66	76	70	72	284	9681
	Angel CABRERA	(Arg)	72	70	72	70	284	9681
	Malcolm MACKENZIE	(Eng)	71	73	70	70	284	9681
	Domingo HOSPITAL	(Sp)	72	73	70	69	284	9681
	Rodger DAVIS	(Aus)	69	70	73	72	284	9681
	Sandy LYLE	(Scot)	73	69	70	72	284	9681
	Jamie SPENCE	(Eng)	73	70	73	68	284	9681
	Paul MCGINLEY	(Ire)	70	73	71	70	284	9681
	Barry LANE	(Eng)	70	73	68	73	284	9681
24	Richard GREEN	(Aus)	72	75	65	73	285	7650
	Colin MONTGOMERIE	(Scot)	73	74	70	68	285	7650
	Lee WESTWOOD	(Eng)	70	72	73	70	285	7650
	Darren CLARKE	(N.Ire)	72	72	72	69	285	7650
	Raymond RUSSELL	(Scot)	70	70	72	73	285	7650
29	David GILFORD	(Eng)	75	71	68	72	286	6637
	Sven STRÜVER	(Ger)	73	70	72	71	286	6637
	Peter O'MALLEY	(Aus)	69	73	71	73	286	6637
	Gary NICKLAUS	(USA)	71	71	74	70	286	6637
33	Tom LEHMAN	(USA)	74	69	73	71	287	5850
	Raymond BURNS	(N.Ire)	72	69	70	76	287	5850
	Ian WOOSNAM	(Wal)	74	72	74	67	287	5850
	Stephen FIELD	(Eng)	71	75	73	68	287	5850
	Rolf MUNTZ	(Hol)	74	68	73	72	287	5850
38	Bernhard LANGER	(Ger)	71	71	71	75	288	5175
	José COCERES	(Arg)	72	71	74	71	288	5175
	David HIGGINS	(Ire)	73	70	72	73	288	5175
	Peter MITCHELL	(Eng)	73	70	71	74	288	5175
42	Paul EALES	(Eng)	72	74	69	74	289	4500
	André BOSSERT	(Swi)	71	71	75	72	289	4500
	Peter BAKER	(Eng)	74	70	75	70	289	4500
	Michel BESANCENEY	(Fr)	73	73	71	72	289	4500
	Mathias GRÖNBERG	(Swe)	73	74	70	72	289	4500
47	Gordon BRAND JNR.	(Scot)	69	76	70	75	290	3975
	Jimmy HEGGARTY	(N.Ire)	72	70	71	77	290	3975
49	Michael WELCH	(Eng)	69	72	74	76	291	3375
	Steen TINNING	(Den)	71	75	69	76	291	3375
	Miguel Angel JIMÉNEZ	(Sp)	72	70	73	76	291	3375
	Stephen MCALLISTER	(Scot)	76	71	72	72	291	3375
	Daniel CHOPRA	(Swe)	73	70	74	74	291	3375
	Emanuele CANONICA	(It)	74	72	74	71	291	3375
55	Eamonn DARCY	(Ire)	73	73	72	74	292	2418
	Anssi KANKKONEN	(Fin)	76	71	74	71	292	2418
	Ignacio GARRIDO	(Sp)	72	73	75	72	292	2418
	Patrik SJÖLAND	(Swe)	75	72	74	71	292	2418
	Mike MCLEAN	(Eng)	71	75	73	73	292	2418
	Adam HUNTER	(Scot)	72	71	74	75	292	2418
	David CARTER	(Eng)	74	69	72	77	292	2418
	Stuart CAGE	(Eng)	72	73	79	68	292	2418
63	Diego BORREGO	(Sp)	69	76	74	74	293	1743
	Richard BOXALL	(Eng)	71	73	75	74	293	1743
	Iain PYMAN	(Eng)	73	73	75	72	293	1743
	Klas ERIKSSON	(Swe)	75	72	69	77	293	1743
67	Paul CURRY	(Eng)	76	70	76	72	294	1122
	John BICKERTON	(Eng)	77	70	71	76	294	1122
69	José Maria CAÑIZARES	(Sp)	71	73	78	73	295	1118
	Miles TUNNICLIFF	(Eng)	68	73	73	81	295	1118
71	Roger WESSELS	(SA)	69	76	77	78	300	1115
72	Christian CÉVAER	(Fr)	73	74	77	80	304	1113
73	Steven BOTTOMLEY	(Eng)	77	70	76	85	308	1111

Tom Lehman came golfing in Ireland.

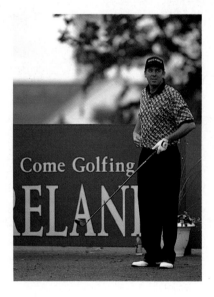

he was in third place on nine under par 207, one stroke behind leaders Rocca and Broadhurst.

There were nine players within four strokes of the lead starting the final round and with just nine holes to play there were five players separated by only one stroke. Johansson was among them and he clinched victory with birdies at the last two holes for a final round of 70 and an 11 under par winning score of 277. That put him one clear of Rocca, whose chance to tie with a last hole birdie disappeared when his tee shot ran out of fairway and into thick rough. Roger Chapman and Andrew Coltart shared third place.

It was Johansson's third victory on the European Tour, and his most important to date. The field included former Open and US Masters winner Sandy Lyle, Colin Montgomerie, Open champion Tom Lehman, Ian Woosnam, and defending champion Bernhard Langer.

'It's a great feeling to win again,' said Johansson. 'I love Ireland, the crowds are great and The K Club course is tremendous. I'm really proud of the way I won and the way I achieved my goal of earning a place in the Volvo Masters.'

Richard Dodd

A World Leader in Packaging

Workmanship from Waterford,
Ireland...

The development of global export markets has created sophisticated demands for packaging which will protect, present and promote a diverse range of products. Fruit and flowers are transported between continents, arriving as fresh as they were picked. Complex electronics need specialised protection for worldwide distribution. Delicate china and glassware must reach distant destinations in perfect condition.

Jefferson Smurfit Group plc has over sixty years' experience in meeting these demands innovatively and cost effectively. Together with its associates, Jefferson Smurfit Group has steadily grown to become the world's largest paper-based packaging organisation and largest recycler of paper, with 400 facilities in over 20 countries throughout Europe, Scandinavia, North and South America, and Asia Pacific.

Smurfit has total control of the packaging manufacturing process, starting with sourcing and sorting waste paper for its own recycling mills, or producing virgin pulp from its own forests, through to the manufacture of paper and board and the production of a broad range of packaging for

diverse markets. Throughout its operations worldwide and across its product range, Smurfit applies its commitment to consistently reliable quality and to environmentally responsible production.

From corrugated board to newsprint; sturdy cases to colourful labels; intricate cartons to specialised sacks, Smurfit is skilled in answering the world's packaging needs.

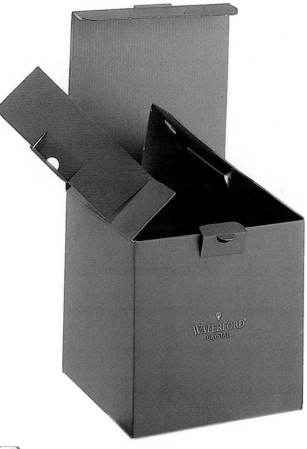

Displayed in Denver,
USA!

JEFFERSON
SMURFIT
GROUP plc

Worldwide Headquarters:
Clonskeagh, Dublin 4, Ireland.
Phone: (+353 1) 2696622 Fax: (+353 1) 2694481
World Wide Web: htttp://www.smurfit.ie

Smurfit Ireland & UK • Smurfit Continental Europe • Smurfit Latin America • Jefferson Smurfit Corporation USA

Double celebration in Berlin

Darren Clarke won the title
while Colin Montgomerie secured
his fourth consecutive Volvo Ranking

T he first Linde-sponsored German Masters at Motzener See, near Berlin, will be remembered as the 1996 tournament that had two champions. First there was Darren Clarke, a 24-under-par winner, and poised to fulfil the potential that was clearly apparent three years earlier when he beat Nick Faldo and Severiano Ballesteros to gain his maiden victory in Belgium. Then there was Colin

Montgomerie, fourth on the day, but acclaimed as Volvo Ranking winner for a record-equalling fourth successive year.

While Clarke was the toast of Ireland, and particularly Portrush, Montgomerie the marvel was the toast of Europe where, since the start of 1993, no one has come close to matching his consistent excellence. After Berlin the statistics showed he had ten victories, ten seconds, and a total

of 47 top ten placings in the 82 events since the beginning of his surge to supremacy. Only seven times had he been out of the top 20, and he had failed to make the cut on just 12 occasions. He had played 302 rounds, mostly in the pressure cooker of contention, for which he was 466 under par. Such is the growth of prize funds on the European Tour since the days when Peter Oosterhuis won the Vardon Trophy four times in a row between 1971-74, that Montgomerie has earned £3 million official money. By the end of 1996 he had joined Faldo and Bernard Langer as members of Europe's most elite club, with career earnings in excess of £5 million.

Yet for all his magnificence, Montgomerie met his match on a crisp autumn Sunday when not only the ambitious Clarke, but also Mark Davis and Paul Broadhurst finished ahead to deny him a

Colin Montgomerie clinched the Volvo Ranking.

double celebration. Two closing rounds of 65 on a weekend of flat calm were not enough to ensure a fourth 1996 victory, as Clarke produced a closing 63, and Davis a career-best 62 to be champion and runner-up.

With the Berliner Golf Club course in perfect condition, and the greens holding and true, low scoring was inevitable. Five players, Paul McGinley, Peter Baker, Marc Farry, Mark Mouland and José Coceres began with 66, and 68 of the select field of 102 bettered par in the first round.

Clarke began with a 70 as did Montgomerie, and was one behind Ian

THE COURSE

Designed by Kurt Rossknecht, the Motzener See course is the ultra-modern home of the Berliner Golf and Country Club. Wind is its principal defence, especially on the more exposed inward half where water is the chief hazard on five holes. The first nine holes skirt woodland and call for precise shot-making to well bunkered greens. Further changes to make it more challenging to the professionals are envisaged for 1997, but the signature hole remains the 449-yard 18th where a mid or long iron is normally required to find a narrow island green.

With birdies galore and eagles a'plenty there were many candidates. Padraig Harrington hit the flagstick with an eight iron at the 17th and almost won a motor car worth £60,000. Andrew Coltart sank a seven iron from 145 yards for a two at the par four tenth. But the vote goes to new Master Darren Clarke for the perfect shot with a pitching wedge from 111 yards at the fourth in the final round for the eagle two that inspired him to victory.

Four sub-70 rounds gave Ernie Els a share of fifth place.

In golf, confidence is imperative for success and Clarke's had often been at a low ebb throughout a summer in which his inability to convert the birdie chances his excellent long game had created, had him close to despair. He had sought help from many quarters, so it was ironic that he was now benefiting from words of encouragement Montgomerie had given him during the recent Canon European Masters in Switzerland. The Scot, a long-time admirer of the big Irishman's ability, had raised his spirits, and stiffened his resolve to make the most of his talent, especially as a fresh Ryder Cup campaign had just begun. The change of attitude, and a widening of his putting stance resulted in Clarke having an eagle and six birdies in sharing second place at halfway, his length enabling him to fly the ball over most of the fairway bunkers.

Montgomerie and Els, who both had 67, remained the favourites, especially after Woosnam, who was troubled by a sore back, took 75 to miss the cut by one stroke, and recognised, like Faldo, Ballesteros and Sam Torrance in the three previous seasons, that Montgomerie would be his master. 'I had been playing two tournaments every week,' said a

Woosnam, his chief money-list protagonist, and two adrift of Ernie Els, his long-time rival, who had been beaten in a play-off for the title two years earlier by Ballesteros. Defending champion Anders Forsbrand was already fading with a 74. Open champion Tom Lehman had begun with 71 and would also not qualify, while Bernhard Langer, who had created the event to commemorate his 1985 Augusta triumph would end a subdued 23rd.

Clarke's second round 64 gave the leaderboard a distinct Irish flavour — leader McGinley had added a 67, and Padraig Harrington had shot 68-67 — and convinced him he had the game to win again. A month earlier he had changed coaches for a second time in six months, and had begun consulting former Tour player Peter Cowen, who had Lee Westwood, the new Volvo Scandinavian Masters champion among his pupils.

BERLINER G & CC, MOTZENER SEE, BERLIN, OCTOBER 3-6, 1996, • YARDAGE 6848 • PAR 72

Pos	Name	Country	Rnd 1	Rnd 2	Rnd 3	Rnd 4	Total	Prize Money £
1	Darren CLARKE	(N.Ire)	70	64	67	63	264	108330
2	Mark DAVIS	(Eng)	69	67	67	62	265	72210
3	Paul BROADHURST	(Eng)	71	64	65	66	266	40690
4	Colin MONTGOMERIE	(Scot)	70	67	65	65	267	32500
5	Paul MCGINLEY	(Ire)	66	67	70	65	268	23260
	Ernie ELS	(SA)	68	67	68	65	268	23260
	Peter BAKER	(Eng)	66	70	64	68	268	23260
8	Paul EALES	(Eng)	67	67	67	68	269	13930
	Padraig HARRINGTON	(Ire)	68	67	66	68	269	13930
	Thomas BJORN	(Den)	71	66	69	63	269	13930
	Peter MITCHELL	(Eng)	71	67	64	67	269	13930
12	Thomas GÖGELE	(Ger)	67	75	64	64	270	11180
13	Michael CAMPBELL	(NZ)	67	68	69	67	271	9983
	Ronan RAFFERTY	(N.Ire)	73	68	65	65	271	9983
	Costantino ROCCA	(It)	70	71	64	66	271	9983
16	José COCERES	(Arg)	66	71	69	66	272	9160
17	Greg TURNER	(NZ)	68	68	66	71	273	8775
18	Paul LAWRIE	(Scot)	70	72	66	66	274	7852
	Jean VAN DE VELDE	(Fr)	71	67	69	67	274	7852
	Bob MAY	(USA)	73	68	67	66	274	7852
	Andrew COLTART	(Scot)	68	71	68	67	274	7852
	Mark JAMES	(Eng)	69	70	67	68	274	7852
23	Gordon BRAND JNR.	(Scot)	69	69	70	67	275	6922
	Marc FARRY	(Fr)	66	70	70	69	275	6922
	Bernhard LANGER	(Ger)	71	69	67	68	275	6922
	Mark MOULAND	(Wal)	66	69	71	69	275	6922
27	Joakim HAEGGMAN	(Swe)	69	70	67	70	276	5776
	Jay TOWNSEND	(USA)	68	70	67	71	276	5776
	Miguel Angel JIMÉNEZ	(Sp)	68	70	73	65	276	5776
	Steen TINNING	(Den)	69	68	69	70	276	5776
	Niclas FASTH	(Swe)	69	67	73	67	276	5776
	Per-Ulrik JOHANSSON	(Swe)	71	70	67	68	276	5776
	Santiago LUNA	(Sp)	72	68	67	69	276	5776
	Jamie SPENCE	(Eng)	73	69	67	67	276	5776
35	Peter O'MALLEY	(Aus)	68	72	68	69	277	5005
	David CARTER	(Eng)	69	68	74	66	277	5005
37	Jarmo SANDELIN	(Swe)	74	69	70	65	278	4485
	Richard BOXALL	(Eng)	70	71	69	68	278	4485
	Silvio GRAPPASONNI	(It)	71	71	69	67	278	4485
	Jim PAYNE	(Eng)	70	72	69	67	278	4485
	Lee WESTWOOD	(Eng)	73	70	71	64	278	4485
	Emanuele CANONICA	(It)	68	75	70	65	278	4485
43	Christian CÉVAER	(Fr)	69	71	65	74	279	3770
	Seve BALLESTEROS	(Sp)	70	72	65	72	279	3770
	Eduardo ROMERO	(Arg)	71	70	65	73	279	3770
	Mark MCNULTY	(Zim)	72	69	65	73	279	3770
	Phillip PRICE	(Wal)	70	70	69	70	279	3770
48	Mark ROE	(Eng)	70	71	72	67	280	3120
	Steve WEBSTER	(Eng)	71	72	70	67	280	3120
	Jonathan LOMAS	(Eng)	69	68	71	72	280	3120
	Tony JOHNSTONE	(Zim)	70	69	71	70	280	3120
	Paul CURRY	(Eng)	70	71	69	70	280	3120
53	Ross MCFARLANE	(Eng)	68	73	66	74	281	2730
54	Stuart CAGE	(Eng)	70	71	69	72	282	2470
	Malcolm MACKENZIE	(Eng)	77	66	67	72	282	2470
	Mats LANNER	(Swe)	70	71	66	75	282	2470
57	Michael JONZON	(Swe)	68	72	72	71	283	2210
58	David A RUSSELL	(Eng)	67	72	75	70	284	2015
	Martin GATES	(Eng)	69	67	76	72	284	2015
	Peter HEDBLOM	(Swe)	72	70	72	70	284	2015
61	Diego BORREGO	(Sp)	72	69	71	73	285	1852
	Steven BOTTOMLEY	(Eng)	72	69	70	74	285	1852
63	Steven RICHARDSON	(Eng)	71	70	73	72	286	1722
	Sven STRÜVER	(Ger)	74	68	71	73	286	1722
65	Retief GOOSEN	(SA)	71	71	74	71	287	1300
	Andrew SHERBORNE	(Eng)	69	72	76	70	287	1300
67	Fredrik LINDGREN	(Swe)	72	71	71	74	288	973
68	Heinz P THÜL	(Ger)	71	72	70	77	290	971
69	Oyvind ROJAHN	(Nor)	70	73	75	73	291	969

relieved Montgomerie, 'one against Ian and one against everyone else. Now I can relax and play with freedom, be more aggressive, and hit the putts a bit harder.' He was as good as his word in the third round and needed to be to stay in touch with Baker (64), Paul Broadhurst (65), and Harrington (66) who had 24 birdies and an eagle between them to join Clarke (67) and Paul Eales, who had a third 67, in the top five. With Costantino Rocca and Peter Mitchell also scoring 64, and Els with a second 68 among the eleven leaders covered by three strokes, the stage was set for another furious onslaught when Sunday dawned overcast and still.

Only two of the 69 qualifiers were over par and the scoreboards were crim-son with birdies and eagles long before Clarke pitched in for an eagle two at the fourth and reached the turn in 30 to sweep into a three-stroke lead at 22 under. Montgomerie, with an eagle three from 45 feet at the eighth had gone out in 32. Davis turned in 31, and Baker and Broadhurst, each with 34, all four sharing second place at 19 under. Harrington, Mitchell, Eales and Els were giving chase. Clarke was still three ahead with six holes left and put himself beyond reach with his birdies at the 13th and 15th, and another from 25 feet at the short 17th. Davis, twice a former Austrian Open champion, just won the struggle for second place when he birdied four of the last six holes to get back in 31, with Broadhurst (66) third.

Montgomerie's birdie at the 17th nudged him ahead of Els, McGinley and Baker.

For Clarke it was a victory of major significance. He had propelled himself into the top ten of the Volvo Ranking. He had also created a springboard towards his ambition of a first Ryder Cup by Johnnie Walker appearance at Valderrama. 'I have set my heart on making the European team there,' he said.

For Montgomerie there was the satisfaction of being number one again and he will not rest on his laurels. 'Winning five Volvo Rankings in a row would be a fabulous achievement in this day and age,' he said. 'I will be playing the same 18-tournament schedule next year, so it is possible.'

Mike Britten

Record third win
for the United States

The USA became the first country to win

the Alfred Dunhill Cup three times after

a memorable week at St Andrews

They had the strongest team on paper and, for once, the form book was right. On a gleaming Sunday afternoon when a quickening wind drifted over the Old Course, the United States became the first nation to win the Alfred Dunhill Cup for the third time.

The team of Mark O'Meara, Phil Mickelson and Steve Stricker took the trophy and £300,000 worth of prize money in the 12th Alfred Dunhill Cup thanks to an impressive 2-1 win over a gallant New Zealand side led by Frank Nobilo, who reached their first final in eight visits to St Andrews.

Stricker enjoyed his first trip to St Andrews so much — 'The people are very warm and their love of the game makes me appreciate just being there,' he said — that he won five ties out of five. His victory by six strokes over Grant Waite in the final secured America's victory after

O'Meara had lost to Nobilo and Mickelson defeated Greg Turner.

The quality of golf in all three matches was high and ended the tournament on the same compelling note with which play had begun on Thursday when the even-tempered O'Meara could have been forgiven an attack of road rage.

As only a mild zephyr puffed across the links from the sea, the American captain took advantage of the benign conditions to set a record score for the front nine of 28 thanks to a preposterous series of eight consecutive birdies which equalled the record on the European Tour.

When the 39-year old from North Carolina turned for home, he was dreaming of breaking 60 as well as surpassing Curtis Strange's course record of 62.

As he strode onto the 17th tee, O'Meara was ten under par. The American's tee shot landed in a favourable position and he was happy enough when

Mark O'Meara bonds with Costantino Rocca (left) and Colin Montgomerie just misses out (right).

was good enough to wallop Costantino Rocca but left Strange's record intact.

With Stricker beating Silvo Grappasoni by seven shots, America defeated Italy 2-1 and were immediately in command of Group One.

In Group Two, the holders, Scotland, fell at the first hurdle against unseeded Sweden in spite of the fact that Colin Montgomerie, Raymond Russell and Andrew Coltart all broke 70.

Worse was to come for the Scots on Friday when they produced their poorest performance at the Home of Golf since their infamous defeat at the hands of Paraguay in 1993. The odds against India beating Scotland in St Andrews should be broadly similar to the chances of a Scottish chef winning a cookery competition in Calcutta for the best curry.

Nevertheless, India, who were making their debut in the Alfred Dunhill Cup, won 2-1 as Gaurev Ghei, ranked 696th in the world, managed to defeat Montgomerie, the world number two and Coltart, who is in the top 70, lost at the first extra hole to Jeeve Singh, who was nowhere to be found in the rankings.

The USA, meantime, were made to

his second shot flew off the face of his five iron. Unluckily, the ball trickled over the green and landed on the road.

O'Meara chose to putt the ball back up the bank where it became entangled in the long grass. His next putt rolled six feet past the hole and he missed the one back for a double-bogey six. O'Meara's 63

jump through hoops by England as Mickelson came back from behind to birdie two of the last three holes against Lee Westwood and secure a 2-1 win after O'Meara followed up his 63 with a 75 against Barry Lane, whose round of 18 consecutive pars was reminiscent of Nick Faldo's consistency.

THE COURSE

The Old Course was in condition worthy of the Open Championship itself. The historic links brought out the best in a strong field and even on an opening day without wind, when the course seemed at its most vulnerable, Mark O'Meara was denied a shore of Curtis Strange's record 62 by a double-bogey six at the 17th. With memorable shots to follow later in the week here from Wayne Westner and Grant Waite, the Road Hole confirmed its status as one of the most thrilling in all of championship golf.

Jarmo Sandelin of Sweden thought his second at the par five 14th was about to swoop out-of-bounds on Thursday in his match against Colin Montgomerie of Scotland. He even shouted 'fore' to warn the galleries. Luck was on his side when he found the ball nestling a few feet inside the fence. The Swede, who still had 110 feet left to the hole, took out his putter and secured victory against the Scot by nailing the longest putt of his life. 'It broke', explained Sandelin later, 'from left-to-right.'

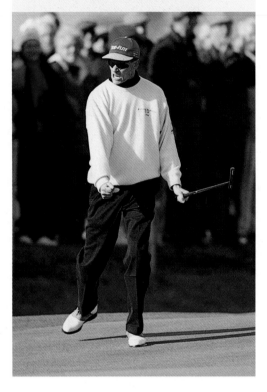

New Zealand joy (above) and the Indians on the Swilcan bridge (below).

On Saturday, there was a shoot-out in Group Three between South Africa and Ireland as both sides went into the last day with wins over Wales and Canada. The Road Hole again played a decisive part in the proceedings. After Ernie Els had lost and Retief Goosen won, Wayne Westner struck a memorable five iron out of the rough which flew 192 yards to the green before landing three feet from the hole. It was enough for Westner to edge out Padraig Harrington.

As America and Sweden made expected progress to the semi-finals, it was left to New Zealand to add colour to a grey, rainy day with a 3-0 win over Australia which turned Group Four on its head. Even then, Frank Nobilo's side needed Germany to beat Japan to be sure of a place in Sunday's knock-out matches. The smiles on the faces of New Zealand's players explained the outcome better than any prose.

Having tugged on their waterproofs on Saturday, the semi-finalists peeled down to sweaters on Sunday as the Old Course was bathed in sparkling sunshine. The Americans felt at home and out-gunned the Swedes even though Jarmo Sandelin added Mickelson's scalp to his earlier conquests of Montgomerie and Nick Price of Zimbabwe.

While their captain, Nobilo, lost out to Els, New Zealand took their place in the final after Turner beat Goosen and Waite's glorious wedge shot to inside a foot of the 17th flag at the third extra hole settled his match against Westner.

So the stage was set for a final which added to the wins of 1989 and 1993 for the Americans. There was also a promise afterwards that the championship will remain in St Andrews for at least the next three years. The USA have already booked their flights for 1997.

Mike Aitken   233

OLD COURSE, ST. ANDREWS, 10TH-13TH OCTOBER, 1996 • YARDAGE 6,933 • PAR 72

Final

USA	2	1	NEW ZEALAND
Mark O'Meara	72	69	Frank Nobilo
Phil Mickelson	69	72	Greg Turner
Steve Stricker	67	73	Grant Waite

Semi-Final

USA	2	1	SWEDEN
Mark O'Meara	68	74	Peter Hedblom
Steve Stricker	70	73	Patrick Sjoland
Phil Mickelson	71	68	Jarmo Sandelin

Semi-Final

NEW ZEALAND	2	1	SOUTH AFRICA
Grant Waite	74	74	Wayne Westner
Greg Turner	71	72	Retief Goosen
Frank Nobilo	72	69	Ernie Els

Group One

Country	Matches Played	Matches Won	Ind. Games Won
USA	3	3	7
ENGLAND	3	1	5
ITALY	3	1	4
SPAIN	3	1	2

DAY 1

USA beat ITALY 2-1
Mark O'Meara (63) beat Costantino Rocca(70)
Phil Mickelson (72) lost to Emanuele Canonica (72)*
2nd extra hole
Steve Stricker (68) beat Silvio Grappasonni (75)

SPAIN lost to ENGLAND 0-3
Ignacio Garrido (77) lost to Lee Westwood (69)
Miguel A Jiménez (71) lost to Jonathan Lomas (70)
Diego Borrego (76) lost to Barry Lane(69)

DAY 2

USA beat ENGLAND 2-1
Mark O'Meara (75) lost to Barry Lane (72)
Steve Stricker (75) beat Jonathan Lomas (79)
Phil Mickelson (72) beat Lee Westwood (73)

SPAIN beat ITALY 2-1
Miguel A Jiménez (69) beat Silvio Grappasonni (79)
Ignacio Garrido (74) beat Emanuele Canonica (79)
Diego Borrego (76) lost to Costantino Rocca (73)

DAY 3

USA beat SPAIN 3-0
Mark O'Meara (67) beat Miguel A Jiménez (68)
Steve Stricker (70) beat Diego Borrego (74)
Phil Mickelson (66) beat Ignacio Garrido (77)

ITALY beat ENGLAND 2-1
Costantino Rocca (72) beat Lee Westwood (74)
Silvio Grappasonni (68) beat Jonathan Lomas (69)
Emanuele Canonica (76) lost to Barry Lane (74)

Group Two

Country	Matches Played	Matches Won	Ind. Games Won
SWEDEN	3	3	8
ZIMBABWE	3	2	4
INDIA	3	1	3
SCOTLAND	3	0	3

DAY 1

ZIMBABWE beat INDIA 2-1
Tony Johnstone (73) lost to Ali Sher (72)
Mark McNulty (70) beat Gaurav Ghei (73)
Nick Price (70) best Jeev Milka Singh (71)

SCOTLAND LOST TO SWEDEN 1-2
Andrew Coltart (67) beat Peter Hedblom (70)
Raymond Russell (69) lost to Patrik Sjoland (68)
Colin Montgomerie (69) lost to Jarmo Sandelin (68)

DAY 2

ZIMBABWE lost to SWEDEN 0-3
Tony Johnstone (76) lost to Patrik Sjoland (73)
Nick Price (75) lost to Jarmo Sandelin (75)
Mark McNulty (73) lost to Peter Hedblom (72)

SCOTLAND lost to INDIA 1-2
Andrew Coltart (74) lost to Jeev Milka Singh (74)
Colin Montgomerie (79) lost to Gaurav Ghei (78)
Raymond Russell (71) beat Ali Sher (84)

DAY 3

ZIMBABWE beat SCOTLAND 2-1
Tony Johnstone (70) beat Andrew Coltart (72)
Mark McNulty (69) beat Colin Montgomerie (70)
Nick Price (76) lost to Raymond Russell (72)

INDIA lost to SWEDEN 0-3
Jeev Milka Singh (74) lost to Patrik Sjoland (68)
Gaurav Ghei (72) lost to Peter Hedblom (69)
Ali Sher (73) lost to Jarmo Sandelin (72)

Group Three

Country	Matches Played	Matches Won	Ind. Games Won
SOUTH AFRICA	3	3	6
IRELAND	3	2	6
WALES	3	1	4
CANADA	3	0	2

DAY 1

SOUTH AFRICA beat CANADA 2-1
Wayne Westner (68) beat Rick Todd (77)
Ernie Els (65) beat Rick Gibson (73)
Retief Goosen (76) lost to Jim Rutledge (69)

IRELAND beat WALES 2-1
Darren Clarke (71) lost to Mark Mouland (70)
Paul McGinley (68) beat Paul Affleck (70)
Padraig Harrington (70) beat Phillip Price (74)

DAY 2

IRELAND beat CANADA 3-0
Darren Clarke (76) beat Rick Gibson (80)
Padraig Harrington (73) beat Rick Todd (73)
Paul McGinley (71) beat Jim Rutledge (77)

SOUTH AFRICA beat WALES 2-1
Retief Goosen (78) lost to Phillip Price (73)
Ernie Els (70) beat Mark Mouland DISQ
Wayne Westner (72) beat Paul Affleck (76)

DAY 3

CANADA lost to WALES 1-2
Rick Gibson (71) beat Mark Mouland (75)
Jim Rutledge (72) lost to Phillip Price (71)
Rick Todd (72) lost to Paul Affleck (70)

SOUTH AFRICA beat IRELAND 2-1
Retief Goosen (70) beat Darren Clarke (70)
Ernie Els (71) lost to Paul McGinley (69)
Wayne Westner (69) beat Padraig Harrington (70)

Group Four

Country	Matches Played	Matches Won	Ind. Games Won
NEW ZEALAND	3	2	6
AUSTRALIA	3	2	5
JAPAN	3	1	4
GERMANY	3	1	3

DAY 1

NEW ZEALAND beat GERMANY 2-1
Grant Waite (69) beat Heinz-Peter Thul (69)
Greg Turner (74) lost to Thomas Gogele (71)
Frank Nobilo (66) beat Sven Strüver (71)

AUSTRALIA beat JAPAN 2-1
Wayne Riley (71) lost to Naomichi Ozaki (67)
Steve Elkington (68) beat Kazuhiro Takami (74)
Greg Norman (72) beat Hajime Meshiai (74)

DAY 2

NEW ZEALAND lost to JAPAN 1-2
Frank Nobilo (73) lost to Naomichi Ozaki (69)
Grant Waite (72) beat Hajime Meshiai (73)
Greg Turner (73) lost to Kazuhiro Takami (70)

AUSTRALIA beat GERMANY 3-0
Wayne Riley (74) beat Heinz-Peter Thul (76)
Greg Norman (71) beat Sven Strüver (73)
Steve Elkington (71) beat Thomas Gogele (80)

DAY 3

AUSTRALIA lost to NEW ZEALAND 0-3
Wayne Riley (76) lost to Grant Waite (69)
Steve Elkington (73) lost to Greg Turner (69)
Greg Norman (68) lost to Frank Nobilo (66)

JAPAN lost to GERMANY 1-2
Naomichi Ozaki (72) lost to Sven Strüver (70)
Hajime Meshiai (77) lost to Thomas Gogele (71)
Kazuhiro Takami (73) beat Heinz-Peter Thul (74)

Prize Money

Winners

Country	Team £	Player £	Total £
USA	300,000	100,000	300,000

Runners-Up

Country	Team £	Player £	Total £
NEW ZEALAND	150,000	50,000	150,000

Losing Semi-Finalists

Country	Team £	Player £	Total £
SWEDEN	95,000	31,666	
SOUTH AFRICA	95,000	31,666	190,000

Group One

Country	Team £	Player £	Total £
USA (1)			
ENGLAND	45,000	15,000	
ITALY	25,500	8,500	
SPAIN (8)	19,500	6,500	90,000

Group Two

Country	Team £	Player £	Total £
SWEDEN			
ZIMBABWE (4)	45,000	15,000	
INDIA	25,500	8,500	
SCOTLAND (5)	19,500	6,500	90,000

Group Three

Country	Team £	Player £	Total £
SOUTH AFRICA (3)			
IRELAND (6)	45,000	15,000	
WALES	25,500	8,500	
CANADA	19,500	6,500	90,000

Group Four

Country	Team £	Player £	Total £
NEW ZEALAND (7)			
AUSTRALIA (2)	45,000	15,000	
JAPAN	25,500	8,500	
GERMANY	19,500	6,500	90,000

* Number in parentheses indicates seeds

dunhill

The Alfred Dunhill Centenary Watch.
Indispensable whatever the angle.

Kite wins on flying visit

US Ryder Cup captain Tom Kite
combined a trip to Valderrama with
his first victory for over three years

For US Ryder Cup team captain Tom Kite, La Moraleja II will be remembered as the course where the 1992 US Open champion learned to win again. But the Oki Pro-Am also saw a little-known Argentinian step into the limelight.

With the opposing Ryder Cup by Johnnie Walker captains in Madrid, both looking to get in an early psychological blow, the stage was set for a dramatic weekend, when on Friday night, European skipper Severiano Ballesteros led the field, with his counterpart Kite just a stroke behind.

The plot could not have been better produced, so far as golfing drama was concerned, by any impresario.

But somebody forgot to show the script to 27-year old Argentinian rookie Angel Cabrera. His was supposed to be only a bit-part. He ended up hogging the stage.

Cabrera, a protege of his fellow Cordoban, Eduardo Romero, came to the inaugural event, played over La Moraleja I and II over the first two rounds with amateur team members, one of the half-dozen or so players knowing the tournament was make or break for next year's card.

By the time Cabrera left he had taken Kite to the limits before America's captain prevailed for his first victory for over three and a half years. Cabrera won his 1997 Tour card in some style, second to one Ryder Cup captain and in front of the other, shattering La Moraleja II's course record on the way.

Round one saw Spain dominate. Pedro Linhart took full advantage of his local caddie's course knowledge to glide to within a stroke of Rodger Davis' 1986 La Moraleja I record, a seven under par 65 earning the Las Palmas man a two-shot lead over both courses' fields.

Two late bogeys pegged Linhart back on Friday night, to leave him alongside Ballesteros, England's Stuart Cage and the former Ryder Cup Swede Joakim Haeggman, all six under par. Ballesteros was six under par for the round, too, his 66 setting the Johnnie Walker Tour course record at La Moraleja II, as the presence of Kite proved a spur.

If the plot was thickening through Kite tracking Ballesteros, then Saturday's third round saw the production reach dizzy heights of intrigue and spectacular

237

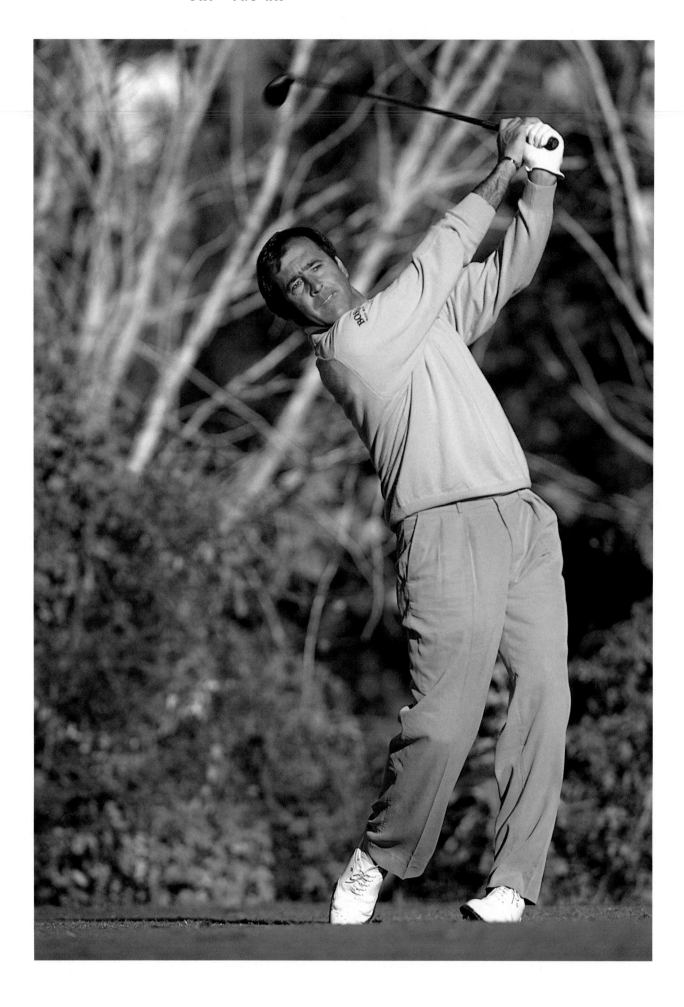

SHOT OF THE WEEK

In the third round, either of Severiano Ballesteros' eagle twos, holing out with a sand-iron from 90 yards and a wedge from 135 yards, might qualify. Angel Cabrera's chip-in from 60 feet for an eagle, and any one of Tom Kite's chips and pitches-in, would be worthy. When the chips were down though, Kite produced the tournament-winner, his sand-iron to a foot over the bunker on the last. 'I had 110 yards to the flag, if it wasn't perfect I was under the lip of the bunker like the day before. I hit it right on the money.'

repertoire by the chief players — and the scene-stealer from Cordoba.

Kite pitched in no less than five times during the third round, once for eagle, the rest for birdies, as he shot 64. Never did he dream, he said, that he could throw in a Saturday 64 after going out only a stroke behind, and still not lead.

It was Cabrera who held sway, his 62, also with a chip-in eagle, breaking

Seve Ballesteros (left)
and Angel Cabrera (right)
pressed for the title.

David Gilford (left) wrapped up fourth place behind a revitalised Tom Kite (right).

David Gilford was four off the lead. Ballesteros arguably, provided the most spectacular round of a memorable day, twice holing out with second shots on par fours, but also driving out-of-bounds and hitting into water on his way to a swash-buckling 69, to be five adrift of leader Cabrera.

In a final round of high winds and eventually rain, an exhilarating start by Ballesteros and two early three putts by Cabrera, left four players in the piece. But as Gilford and Ballesteros faded, the final two holes decided it.

On the 17th, Cabrera, who had regained the lead on the previous hole crucially three-putted again to put himself back into a tie with Kite.

Then the 46-year old Texan brought to bear all his 24 years' experience on the US Tour, sliding in a sand-iron approach to a foot for birdie. A miss from six feet by Cabrera ended his chance of a play-off.

'When you haven't won for so long, you wonder if your last win was your last', said Kite. 'This is a great boost to my hopes of making the US team as a playing captain. I'm sure Seve thinks the same about his chances now, too.'

Norman Dabell

Ballesteros' previous record by four, earning him a one-stroke lead on 14 under par, over Kite.

THE COURSE

Jack Nicklaus designed La Moraleja I and his company, Golden Bear Design Associates, La Moraleja II, and the latter was chosen for the weekend's finale. The courses are like chalk and cheese, with I the tree-lined tight layout providing little room for error and II, the venue for the 1992 World Cup of Golf, wide-open but long and exposed. Strong final-day winds complemented slick greens to inhibit the scoring.

LA MORALEJA G.C. (I & II), OCTOBER 10-13, 1996 · YARDAGE 7054 · PAR 72

Pos	Name	Country	Rnd 1	Rnd 2	Rnd 3	Rnd 4	Total	Prize Money £
1	Tom KITE	(USA)	71	68	64	70	273	74500
2	Angel CABRERA	(Arg)	71	69	62	72	274	49662
3	Seve BALLESTEROS	(Sp)	72	66	69	69	276	27977
4	David GILFORD	(Eng)	69	71	66	71	277	22350
5	Klas ERIKSSON	(Swe)	71	68	72	69	280	18943
6	Miles TUNNICLIFF	(Eng)	74	69	69	69	281	15645
7	Malcolm MACKENZIE	(Eng)	69	71	72	70	282	12292
	Pedro LINHART	(Sp)	65	73	70	74	282	12292
9	David HIGGINS	(Ire)	69	70	75	69	283	9454
	Gary EMERSON	(Eng)	72	71	70	70	283	9454
11	David CARTER	(Eng)	72	72	71	69	284	6551
	Niclas FASTH	(Swe)	72	71	70	71	284	6551
	Fredrik LARSSON	(Swe)	74	72	67	71	284	6551
	Anders HANSEN	(Den)	73	72	68	71	284	6551
	Juan QUIROS	(Sp)	68	71	73	72	284	6551
	Joakim HAEGGMAN	(Swe)	69	69	73	73	284	6551
	Steve WEBSTER	(Eng)	70	71	70	73	284	6551
	Mats LANNER	(Swe)	75	67	68	74	284	6551
	Greg CHALMERS	(Aus)	72	70	68	74	284	6551
	Gary ORR	(Scot)	72	67	69	76	284	6551
21	Stuart CAGE	(Eng)	69	69	76	71	285	5095
	José Maria CAÑIZARES	(Sp)	69	70	76	70	285	5095
	Juan Carlos PIÑERO	(Sp)	75	69	68	73	285	5095
24	Thomas BJORN	(Den)	69	73	72	72	286	4693
	John MCHENRY	(Ire)	71	70	70	75	286	4693
	Andrew SHERBORNE	(Eng)	67	72	71	76	286	4693
27	Robert COLES	(Eng)	75	67	72	73	287	4157
	Per HAUGSRUD	(Nor)	73	69	72	73	287	4157
	Anders FORSBRAND	(Swe)	74	72	68	73	287	4157
	Mathias GRÖNBERG	(Swe)	68	76	70	73	287	4157
	Adam HUNTER	(Scot)	70	73	69	75	287	4157
32	Manuel PIÑERO	(Sp)	75	69	72	72	288	3665
	Jon ROBSON	(Eng)	70	73	70	75	288	3665
	Steven BOTTOMLEY	(Eng)	75	69	69	75	288	3665
35	Scott HENDERSON	(Scot)	72	71	72	74	289	3218
	Peter MITCHELL	(Eng)	70	70	75	74	289	3218
	Brian MARCHBANK	(Scot)	72	72	72	73	289	3218
	Ross DRUMMOND	(Scot)	70	75	72	72	289	3218
	Richard BOXALL	(Eng)	70	76	71	72	289	3218
	Santiago LUNA	(Sp)	68	74	72	75	289	3218
	Michael CAMPBELL	(NZ)	74	71	68	76	289	3218
42	Michael JONZON	(Swe)	70	75	70	75	290	2726
	Gordon BRAND JNR.	(Scot)	71	73	72	74	290	2726
	José RIVERO	(Sp)	68	75	73	74	290	2726
	John HAWKSWORTH	(Eng)	72	70	70	78	290	2726
46	David LYNN	(Eng)	72	71	72	76	291	2369
	Carl SUNESON	(Sp)	73	70	74	74	291	2369
	David J RUSSELL	(Eng)	72	72	74	73	291	2369
	Roger WESSELS	(SA)	75	71	72	73	291	2369
50	Neal BRIGGS	(Eng)	73	71	73	75	292	2011
	Miguel Angel MARTIN	(Sp)	67	76	76	73	292	2011
	Ricky WILLISON	(Eng)	75	71	74	72	292	2011
	Iain PYMAN	(Eng)	69	73	78	72	292	2011
54	Fabrice TARNAUD	(Fr)	72	74	70	77	293	1653
	David A RUSSELL	(Eng)	70	74	74	75	293	1653
	Jose ROZADILLA	(Sp)	72	73	73	75	293	1653
	Alvaro PRAT	(Sp)	73	73	75	72	293	1653
58	Mark DAVIS	(Eng)	76	70	73	76	295	1430
59	Steen TINNING	(Den)	74	72	77	73	296	1385
60	Jesus Maria ARRUTI	(Sp)	73	73	73	78	297	1318
	Mats HALLBERG	(Swe)	75	71	76	75	297	1318
62	Manuel MONTES	(Sp)	74	71	75	78	298	1251
63	Timothy SPENCE	(Eng)	77	68	76	78	299	1184
	David R JONES	(Eng)	71	75	77	76	299	1184
65	José SOTA	(Sp)	72	74	77	77	300	1117
66	Dean ROBERTSON	(Scot)	74	72	75	82	303	670

Tom Kite is hoping to wrest the Ryder Cup from Seve Ballesteros in 1997.

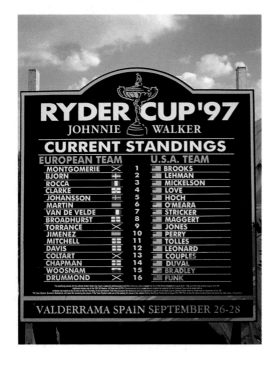

Els is unstoppable

Ernie Els became the first man to win three consecutive
Toyota World Match-Play Championships with a
sparkling display round Wentworth

They wheeled them in to take away Ernie's crown – and they wheeled them out again. Three of the four major winners of 1996, the top five players on the American money list, and Colin Montgomerie and Ian Woosnam, the top two on the European Tour. And that's not counting the previous year's beaten finalist, the Japanese match-play champion or the awesome wild card from Fiji, Vijay Singh.

Wheeled out? More like stretchered out for poor Steve Stricker who looked like he'd gone 36 rounds with Mike Tyson wearing golf gloves instead of boxing gloves after his second-round confrontation with Ernie, the greatest brinkman on the West.

All the talk beforehand had been on Els' bid to become the first player in 33 years to win the Toyota World Match-Play Championship three times in a row. The bookies made him 3-1 favourite to carve his own niche in match-play history despite the claims of one of the finest fields of recent times. Only Nick Faldo and Greg Norman, of the players entitled to be there, were missing. Yet when Els stood six down having played the first 18 holes, that 3-1 had suddenly switched to

25-1, with no takers.

There had been only one greater comeback in the event's glorious history, by a man Els idolised, Gary Player, in that still-talked-about match with Tony Lema in 1965. Six down, like Els, at lunch, Player had slumped to seven after the first after-noon hole, only to pull it all out of the bag at the 37th.

Taking inspiration from the South African hero of his youth, Els clawed his way back as the birdies dried up for Stricker. At the third in the afternoon, Els chipped-in (just as he had done two years earlier to swing a tense match with Jose-Maria Olazábal). He birdied the next and the seventh – then chipped-in again at the eighth. A drive deep into the woods at the ninth appeared to signal the end of the comeback, but an outrageous par putt from 40 feet saved the day. Stricker won

THE COURSE

The West Course 'has never been better' declared Colin Montgomerie at the start. Lush, verdant, and with greens which some of the Americans claimed were not far short of Augusta speed on the stimpmeter. It played its full 6,957 yards, hence some quite moderate scoring: Els only 13 under for his three matches as against 25 under the previous year.

his only hole of the afternoon when Els missed the short tenth, but from then on it was simply a question of whether the winning post would come in time for the American, who had won all five matches in the Alfred Dunhill Cup the previous weekend and extended his own run to six with a come-from-behind victory on day one, over Steve Elkington.

A majestic six iron to four feet levelled the match at the 15th and, still all square at the last, Stricker finally gave in to nerves when he drove into the fairway bunker on the left and barely got the ball out. Yet the match amazingly had one more enthralling chapter to unfold. From a stance in which he had his back leg buckled and almost back in the bunker, Stricker produced the shot of the week, a three wood from 238 yards that rolled

18 feet past the stick. If Els was shaken, he barely showed it, although he kept the drama going to the end, leaving himself a testing 40-inch putt in gathering gloom to secure a one up victory that no one who witnessed it will ever forget.

After that, it had to be a bit of an anti-climax. Mark Brooks, the USPGA champion, never won a hole against Els in a one-sided semi-final that ended 10 & 8, a sort of de-luxe dog licence and the second widest margin in Wentworth history. The guests were only halfway through their sushi in the Toyota marquee when they shook hands, and it had been almost the same story the day before when Steve Jones, the US Open champion, caught a

Phil Mickelson bowed out to Vijay Singh.

tartar in Singh, to the tune of 9 & 8.

Asked why he had conceded the 17th hole on the tee after driving-out-of bounds, rather than playing a second ball, Jones responded: 'The match in front was more interesting. I wanted to watch that!'

The match in question was Colin Montgomerie versus Brooks which had a curiosity of its own when the seventh was halved in six, one of the rare occasions when a double bogey has been good enough to share a hole. This was one that Brooks managed to four putt after Montgomerie had been unplayable against the face of the bunker in two and not even on the green in four. The American's fist putt from the lower level trickled all the way back, he putted back up two feet past the hole – and missed. But Brooks made amends by chipping and putting Europe's only remaining hope off the course, getting

it up and down at the last three holes in the morning and last two in the afternoon. Seven birdies in the last 11 holes gave Brooks a 67 that felt like 80.

Montgomerie had won the Battle of Britain on a stunning opening day, the finest October morning anyone could remember on a West Course so green it looked like it had been painted. It had been a cruel stroke of fate to find Montgomerie and Ian Woosnam, the only

Ernie Els (above) was bathed in sunshine against Mark Brooks (below).

members of the winning Ryder Cup team, trying to blast each other into oblivion so early in the week: 'It would have been nice if they'd given us the chance of meeting in the final,' said Woosnam, twice a winner of this event and the first British winner. Two up after eight, the Welshman had to bow the knee 4 & 2 as Montgomerie played the back nine in the morning and the front nine in the afternoon in 65, some of the best golf of a week when the scoring rarely caught fire.

As Els disposed of the top half of the draw, the spotlight in the bottom half fell on the tall, elegant Singh, who became the first unseeded player to reach the final since Bill Rogers in 1979.

On the first afternoon, Singh had to withstand a spirited fightback by Phil Mickelson, who had made a dreadful start, gifting a few holes to the Fijian with

One hand for Colin Montgomerie (left), one leg for Tom Lehman (right).

bogeys to slide five down after seven. That was not the true form of the American and he went a long way towards restoring his reputation by squaring the match after 20, then, after getting a reprieve when Singh put his second shot out of bounds at the 35th, almost taking the match into extra-time with a bunker shot at the last that hopped into the hole and out again.

After putting Jones into an early bath, Singh had his second close encounter of the American kind when taking out Tom Lehman, the Open champion, with a birdie at the first extra hole after Lehman had handed him a lifeline by triple-putting the 36th.

On Sunday morning Els and Singh went out to do battle. It wasn't an epic final but driving rain through the afternoon did not help, the only adverse

SHOT OF THE WEEK

Nothing to beat Seve Stricker's astonishing three wood shot on the 36th hole against Ernie Els. Unable to stand properly at the ball, which he had bumbled out of a fairway trap, he essayed dozens of practice swings with one leg hunched up behind him before propelling the ball, dead straight, 238 yards. It rolled 18 feet past the hole and two putts were not quite enough to stop Els going through – but what a fright the champion must have had.

WENTWORTH CLUB (WEST COURSE), SURREY, OCTOBER 17-20, 1996 · YARDAGE 6957 · PAR 72

First Round

		Prize money
Steve Stricker (USA) beat Steve Elkington (Aus)	3 & 2	£30,000
Colin Montgomerie (Scot) beat Ian Woosnam (Wal)	4 & 2	£30,000
Mark O'Meara (USA) beat Nobuo Serizawa (Jap)	7 & 5	£30,000
Vijay Singh (Fij) beat Phil Mickelson (USA)	1 hole	£30,000

Second Round

		Prize money
*Ernie Els (SA) beat Steve Stricker	1 hole	£40,000
*Mark Brooks (USA) beat Colin Montgomerie	1 hole	£40,000
Vijay Singh beat *Steve Jones (USA)	9 & 8	£40,000
*Tom Lehman (USA) beat Mark O'Meara	6 & 5	£40,000

Semi-Finals

Ernie Els beat Mark Brooks	10 & 8	—
Vijay Singh beat Tom Lehman	at 37th hole	—

Play-Off for Third & Fourth Places

		Prize money
Mark Brooks beat	1 hole	£ 60,000
Tom Lehman		£ 50,000

Final

		Prize money
Ernie Els beat	3 & 2	£170,000
Vijay Singh		£ 90,000

*seeded into the second round

Unseeded finalist Vijay Singh.

weather of a glorious week apart from a two-hour hold-up on the Friday because of flooded greens.

Singh, despite superior medal scores for the first three days, had to be the underdog against a man conducting an enduring love affair with the Burma Road. He bounded out of the stalls to go two up after three but Els responded with four quick birdies, and though Singh levelled with two imperious shots at the 18th and a cast-iron four to Els' five at the first hole after lunch, the match got away beyond recall when the South African captured four out of five holes from the 22nd. The long ninth in the afternoon was halved in gimme threes, a rare double-birdie if ever there was one, but Singh could only snatch back the 29th before Els closed him out 3 & 2 after a series of halved holes.

So Els, just 27 in Toyota week, was champion for the third consecutive time, something that neither Player nor Severiano Ballesteros, for all their five titles, could match. And in three short years, he had won exactly half a million pounds of Toyota cash: 'Hey, multiply that by seven and it would a helluva lot of rand,' said a tickled-pink winner afterwards. 'Nobody has done it three times in a row before and this is something I will really enjoy.'

Who wouldn't? To claim the scalps of golf's mighty men, Ballesteros, Olazábal, Montgomerie, Janzen, Langer, Elkington – and now Stricker, Brooks and Singh.

El of a feat, El of a match-player.

Jeremy Chapman   247

Lomas and Bottomley are perfect blend

Jonathan Lomas and Steven Bottomley combined brilliantly for victory in Bordeaux

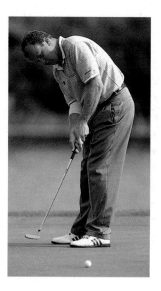

Jonathan Lomas and Steven Bottomley played one of the finest foursomes rounds ever seen in Europe when they shot an incredible 62, nine under par, on the second day to set themselves up for victory in the Open Novotel Perrier pairs event at the Medoc Golf Club in Bordeaux.

It gave this Cheshire-Yorkshire combination a four-shot lead at the end of the second round in this unique tournament and, though Richard Boxall and Derrick Cooper drew level with them on the final day, Lomas and Bottomley were never headed and finally took the £70,000 first prize by one shot.

They finished on 332, 23 under par, in a tournament that began with a four-ball, was followed by a foursomes, then greensomes and on the last day a singles aggregate in which each pairing added their two scores together.

Boxall and Cooper might have forced a play-off but Cooper had the misfortune to three-putt on the final green when he sent a putt from 30 feet six feet past and missed the return.

It meant that Bottomley had gained his first victory on Tour while it was a second success for Lomas, who had won the Chemapol Trophy Czech Open just two months before.

The tournament also saw a welcome reappearance for Michael King, the former Ryder Cup player who was forced to leave the European Tour in 1989 because of crippling spondylitis but played in this event with close friend Sam Torrance.

Torrance and King finished last of the 30 pairs, but King, now a PGA European Tour Enterprises Director, was by no means disgraced despite having acute leg, back and neck problems which considerably restricted his swing.

Apart from a slight hold-up because of mist on the third day, the event was blessed with superb weather and Frenchmen Christian Cevaer and Antoine Lebouc made the running in the first day four-ball, shooting an 11 under par 60, one shot ahead of the Irishmen Philip Walton and Raymond Burns and England's Paul Eales and Russell Claydon.

Cevaer was the strong man of his team, having eight birdies and an eagle three at the 536-yard 14th for an individual 61 but as he said: 'Antoine gave me the chances to go for my putts.'

Lomas and Bottomley were lying fourth after the four-ball on 63 but then to score 62 in the foursomes on the following day was a truly remarkable performance. Burns, who was playing in the same group, described it as: 'The finest golf round I have ever seen.'

The singles course record on this 6,909 yards course was only 65 at the time and Lomas and Bottomley went from three off the lead to four ahead. They had ten birdies with no putt longer than 15 feet as they went out and back in 31 and this great round included a bogey five at the ninth where Lomas bunkered their

THE COURSE

Medoc Golf Club, one of the finest in France, is a heath-land type course, measuring 6,909 yards, and visually like Walton Heath. There are wide fairways but with strategically-placed bunkers, bracken and heather for wayward shots, and undulating greens. Water comes into play at the short fifth and eighth holes and a stream runs through the middle of the 11th fairway.

second shot.

At this point Walton and Burns were four shots behind and Jamie Spence and Mark Mouland six back. But on day three it was Boxall and Cooper who came to the fore with a greensomes 63 to close to within two shots of Lomas and Bottomley, who shot 68.

On the final day both Boxall and Cooper three-putted the first green to fall four shots behind the leaders and Lomas and Bottomley went five clear at the second hole.

But Boxall and Cooper, twice winners of the Sunningdale foursomes and hoping for a third triumph together, clawed back the lead, drew level at the 12th, went one behind at the 13th and drew level again at the 14th.

Boxall birdied the 15th but so did Bottomley and all four men parred the

GOLF DU MÉDOC, BORDEAUX, FRANCE, OCTOBER 17-20, 1996 · YARDAGE 6316 · PAR 71

Pos	Name	Rnd 1	Rnd 2	Rnd 3	Rnd 4	Total	Prize Money £ each	Pos	Name						
1	J. Lomas/S. Bottomley	63	62	68	139	332	£35,000	16	P. Walton/R. Burns	61	68	69	145	343	£2,900
2	R. Boxall/D. Cooper	65	67	63	138	333	£25,000	17	A. Hunter/G. Orr	66	71	70	137	344	£2,750
3	W. Westner/M. Mackenzie	64	68	65	138	335	£17,500		P. Lawrie/S. McAllister	65	68	72	139	344	£2,750
4	P. Broadhurst/R. McFarlane	65	68	65	138	336	£10,750	19	D.J. Russell/R. Drummond	66	71	67	141	345	£2,600
	F. Lindgren/J. Haeggman	68	70	64	134	336	£10,750	20	M. Farry/T. Levet	70	67	66	143	346	£2,500
6	S. Richardson/A. Oldcorn	66	68	64	139	337	£6,500	21	C. Pottier/M Pendaries	65	69	71	142	347	£2,350
7	R. Davis/P. O'Malley	65	67	68	138	338	£5,125		S. Luna/J. M Canizares	64	71	69	143	347	£2,350
	J. Spence/M. Mouland	64	67	70	137	338	£5,125	23	C. Cevaer/A. Lebouc	60	74	68	146	348	£2,200
9	J. Sandelin/F. Tarnaud	66	69	70	135	339	£4,375	24	O. Rojahn/N. Fasth	65	72	73	139	349	£2,100
	P. Curry/ A. Sherborne	65	73	68	133	339	£4,375	25	J.C. Cambon/N. Kalouguine	64	71	68	148	351	£2,000
11	W. Riley/ C. Mason	65	69	66	140	340	£3,750	26	M. Lanner/M. Jonzon	65	73	75	140	353	£1,900
	P. Eales/R. Claydon	61	72	68	139	340	£3,750	27	M. McLean/N. Briggs	66	76	68	144	354	£1,800
	Q. Nobilo/D. Frost	64	72	69	135	340	£3,750	28	A. Forsbrand/J. van de Velde	71	72	72	143	358	£1,700
14	B. Lane/M. Roe	65	70	69	137	341	£3,125	29	E. Giraud/T. Planchin	69	73	73	144	359	£1,600
	R. Russell/D. Robertson	65	75	65	136	341	£3,125	30	S. Torrance/M. King	69	73	72	150	364	£1,500

16th. Then came real drama when Bottomley went into a greenside bunker at the short 17th only to play a superb recovery to save his par.

So it was level with one to play and Bottomley, Lomas and Cooper all hit the green in two but Boxall, after bunkering his tee shot, was still 67 yards from the pin after his second shot. He then hit a magnificent third to eight feet, Cooper putted six feet past and both Bottomley and Lomas two putted for pars. Boxall bravely holed his putt for par but Cooper's second putt missed by an inch and the contest was over.

Lomas and Bottomley were all smiles but so, too, was Sweden's Freddie Lindgren, who smashed the course record with 62 and finished joint fourth with Joakim Haeggman.

John Oakley

Richard Boxall (far left) in explosive mode. Mark Mouland (left) pitches and Derrick Cooper (right) lines up vital putt to tie.

SHOT OF THE WEEK

Joakim Haeggman played the shot of the week at the 355-yard seventh hole when he struck a lob wedge from 50 yards and the ball landed ten feet past the pin, spun back and hit partner Freddie Lindgren's ball four feet from the hole before going in-off for an eagle two. 'Not many people can do that', said Haeggman with a broad smile

McNulty the Master

Mark McNulty took his
third title of the year with a
comfortable victory at Valderrama

nd so to Valderrama. The next
time we say that it will be for
the 1997 Ryder Cup by Johnnie Walker
next September, the realisation of a dream
for Club President Jaime Patiño, for
Severiano Ballesteros, and for Spain.

The 1996 Volvo Masters, though, was
no mere dress rehearsal. It is far too

important in its own right for that. It is
the last – and often in the past the most
gripping – act in a year-long drama which
on this occasion had visited no fewer than
18 countries.

No course on the whole European
Tour demands a player's attention like
this wondrous Robert Trent Jones cre-

ation. Allow your mind to wander, even
to thoughts of representing Europe
against the Americans in 1997, and the
penalty will surely be paid. Such an exact-
ing test is not everybody's cup of tea. But
Mark McNulty loves it. That was the case
before the week of the tournament. By
the end of it the love was sealed with the

THE COURSE

American Ryder Cup captain Tom Kite inspected Valderrama the week before the Volvo Masters and summed up the course in two words – spectacular and tough. Robert Trent Jones designed the layout trying to disturb as few of the existing cork oak trees, some dating back to when Columbus set sail, as possible. Hundreds more were then saved from the axe elsewhere and planted along with olive trees, mature pines, flowers and shrubs. Always in superb condition, the course, located between mountains and the Mediterranean with the Rock of Gibraltar visible in the distance, has been voted the best in continental Europe. The only place Kite thought he might find better fairways was in heaven.

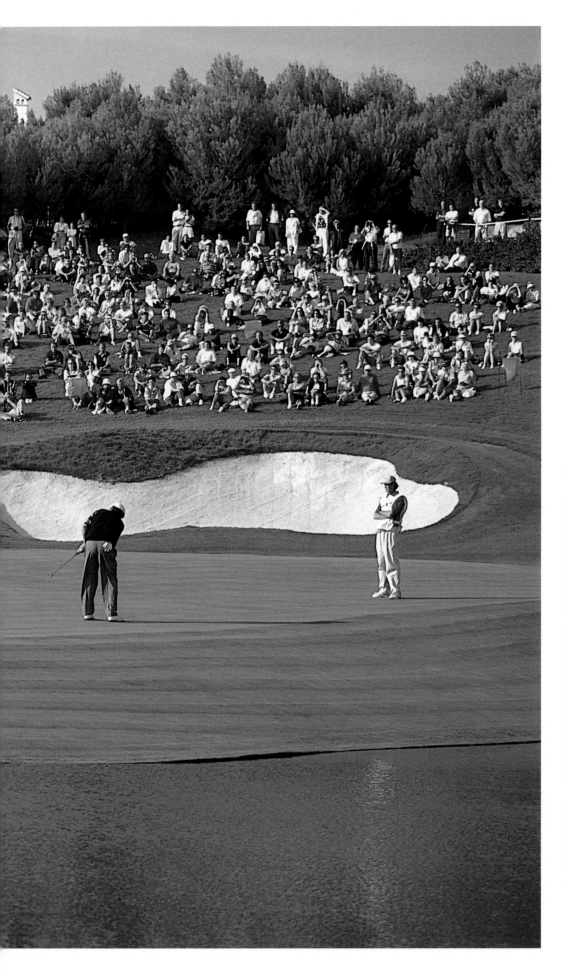

kiss of the trophy.

'We all know Valderrama is very tough,' said the experienced Zimbabwean. 'But in all my years of coming here I have always felt that maybe I would be able to sneak a win.' It was to be some sneak. 'During my practice round on Tuesday I said to my caddie that this might be my best chance. (And also his last, at least for the time being, because the staging of the Ryder Cup means a change of home for the Volvo Masters from 1997.) I was in a good frame of mind for what is a very, very stern examination paper. This course makes me want to play well and I've always tried not to moan and cry.

Mark McNulty was totally focused at Valderrama.

But I understand those who do. You can get great players complaining here because it's so frustrating when you get out of position.'

The 66 players in the field quickly became 65. Very quickly, in fact. Australian Robert Allenby had fractured his sternum in a car crash a month before, but to meet the conditions of the Volvo Bonus Pool he had travelled from Melbourne to hit the one shot which he hoped would maintain his third position on the Volvo Ranking. There was, naturally, huge media interest in Allenby teeing off and then withdrawing, but the winner of the Alamo English and

Colin Montgomerie (left)
digs deep while
Bernhard Langer (right)
fades a tee shot.

All season long Denmark's Thomas Bjorn, Ireland's Padraig Harrington and Scotland's Raymond Russell were involved in a thrilling battle to be the leading rookie on the European Tour's Volvo Ranking. They each captured a title, between them had no fewer than 21 top ten finishes and earned a combined £846,332. Bjorn prevailed in the end, his tenth place leaving him one ahead of Harrington and four in front of Russell, but Harrington's attempt to overhaul him at the Volvo Masters included the Shot of the Week. The 25-year old's seven iron to the 173-yard third in the first round of his first appearance in the event gave him the first hole-in-one of his professional career.

Peugeot French Opens and also the One 2 One British Masters emphasised it was not a mercenary trip and that the £73,000 it proved to be worth would be donated to two charities, the Challenge Cancer Support Network and the Teenage Cancer Trust.

Colin Montgomerie's opening drive – something a little more impressive than Allenby's 39-yard tap – earned him £150,000 from the Bonus Pool, reward for

259

his fabulous achievement of four successive Volvo Ranking titles. Unlike the previous season, when the issue went to the last putt of the last round, the big Scot could afford to relax, sure in the knowledge that he could not be caught by his principal adversary Ian Woosnam. Professional pride still meant that Montgomerie wanted to

John Paramor (above) rides to a ruling. Halfway leader Paul Curry (right)

match Woosnam's four victories during the year, but it was not to be. For once, his name did not appear on the leaderboard all week.

First day honours went to Trinidad's Stephen Ames with a four under par 67, but England's Paul Curry was only one behind, and when he added a second round 68 the halfway lead was his. 'I've just concentrated on keeping the ball in play.' said the 35-year old. 'This is not a course to take by the scruff of the neck, but then I cannot do that anyway.'

Valderrama, as is its habit, bit back at the two early leaders on the Saturday. Curry slumping to an 81 (including an eight on the treacherous 17th), and Ames to a 77. But McNulty,

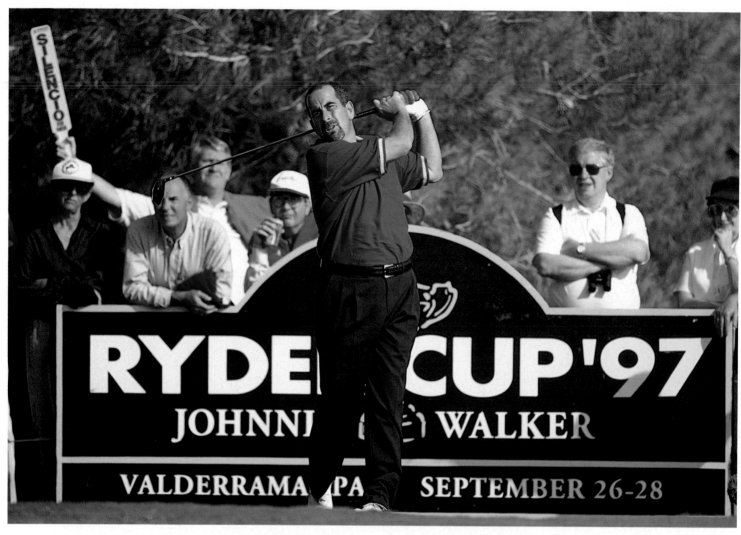

Brave finish from Sam Torrance (above). Hugo Boss blousons were presented to all 1996 Tour Winners.

fortified he reckoned, by some Rjoja to celebrate his 43rd birthday the night before, kept a bogey off his card and with birdies on the first, fourth, tenth, and 11th returned a 67 to leap into a four-stroke advantage.

In the eight previous runnings of the Volvo Masters nobody had won the title by more than two strokes. Here was a chance, though, for the European Tour's most successful non-European — 14 wins and approaching £3 million in prize-money – to end the season on the highest note.

It was a chance McNulty did not miss. Although the gap closed to two during the front nine, he again started the inward half with two birdies (thanks to a wedge to ten feet and sand-wedge to five), and thereafter he was pretty much on cruise control. By the time he reached the final hole he was six clear and by the time he finished it he had won by seven, a drive, four iron and a birdie putt adding the icing to the cake.

In the distant battle for second place, Wayne Westner fired a closing 67, and Sam Torrance his second successive 68 to join Lee Westwood and José Coceres on the one under par mark of 283.

But this was one man's week. McNulty had played just 13 of the 37 Volvo Ranking tournaments, but had won three of them and the third, which lifted him to fifth in the final money list, was the biggest and the best. While his £463,847 earnings may still have been dwarfed by Montgomerie's record £875,146, McNulty could not have been happier as he closed this particular chapter in the life of the Volvo Masters and of Valderrama. Bring on the Ryder Cup.

Mark Garrod

VALDERRAMA, SOTOGRANDE, SPAIN, OCTOBER 24-27, 1996 · YARDAGE 6819 · PAR 71

Pos	Name	Country	Rnd 1	Rnd 2	Rnd 3	Rnd 4	Total	Prize Money £
1	Mark MCNULTY	(Zim)	72	69	67	68	276	150000
2	José COCERES	(Arg)	71	70	71	71	283	59902
	Sam TORRANCE	(Scot)	73	74	68	68	283	59902
	Wayne WESTNER	(SA)	70	74	72	67	283	59902
	Lee WESTWOOD	(Eng)	71	71	70	71	283	59902
6	Andrew OLDCORN	(Scot)	74	66	72	72	284	31950
7	Stephen AMES	(T&T)	67	71	77	70	285	24750
	David CARTER	(Eng)	70	75	72	68	285	24750
9	Richard GREEN	(Aus)	72	74	70	70	286	17437
	Frank NOBILO	(NZ)	71	71	70	74	286	17437
	Peter MITCHELL	(Eng)	74	71	71	70	286	17437
	David FROST	(SA)	73	75	70	68	286	17437
13	Carl SUNESON	(Sp)	71	69	76	71	287	13620
	Gary ORR	(Scot)	72	70	70	75	287	13620
	Paul BROADHURST	(Eng)	73	73	70	71	287	13620
16	Greg TURNER	(NZ)	72	70	71	75	288	11843
	Paul CURRY	(Eng)	68	69	81	70	288	11843
	Bernhard LANGER	(Ger)	73	69	74	72	288	11843
19	Wayne RILEY	(Aus)	73	70	69	77	289	11000
20	Raymond RUSSELL	(Scot)	72	72	73	73	290	10250
	Diego BORREGO	(Sp)	74	71	73	72	290	10250
	Roger CHAPMAN	(Eng)	71	74	75	70	290	10250
	Jonathan LOMAS	(Eng)	70	77	73	70	290	10250
	Thomas BJORN	(Den)	71	74	73	72	290	10250
25	Paul LAWRIE	(Scot)	69	74	73	75	291	9125
	Darren CLARKE	(N.Ire)	72	71	76	72	291	9125
	Andrew SHERBORNE	(Eng)	74	72	75	70	291	9125
	Ian WOOSNAM	(Wal)	76	69	72	74	291	9125
29	Tony JOHNSTONE	(Zim)	73	77	72	70	292	8000
	Padraig HARRINGTON	(Ire)	69	73	77	73	292	8000
	Colin MONTGOMERIE	(Scot)	71	75	71	75	292	8000
	Russell CLAYDON	(Eng)	71	70	81	70	292	8000
	Ross MCFARLANE	(Eng)	76	73	76	67	292	8000
34	Eduardo ROMERO	(Arg)	76	72	74	71	293	6366
	Gordon BRAND JNR.	(Scot)	68	78	75	72	293	6366
	Peter BAKER	(Eng)	75	73	74	71	293	6366
	Paul EALES	(Eng)	74	74	74	71	293	6366
	Miguel Angel MARTIN	(Sp)	73	75	74	71	293	6366
	Miguel Angel JIMÉNEZ	(Sp)	73	74	73	73	293	6366
	Andrew COLTART	(Scot)	73	76	70	74	293	6366
	David HOWELL	(Eng)	72	73	75	73	293	6366
	Rodger DAVIS	(Aus)	75	70	77	71	293	6366
43	Costantino ROCCA	(It)	69	74	76	75	294	5250
	ZHANG LIAN-WEI	(Chi)	75	73	74	72	294	5250
45	Per-Ulrik JOHANSSON	(Swe)	71	77	74	73	295	4766
	Paul MCGINLEY	(Ire)	78	72	72	73	295	4766
	Mark DAVIS	(Eng)	77	71	74	73	295	4766
48	David GILFORD	(Eng)	73	72	75	76	296	4300
	Marc FARRY	(Fr)	75	77	71	73	296	4300
	Patrik SJÖLAND	(Swe)	77	77	74	68	296	4300
51	Iain PYMAN	(Eng)	71	76	76	74	297	3750
	Ross DRUMMOND	(Scot)	76	74	74	73	297	3750
	Peter HEDBLOM	(Swe)	74	76	75	72	297	3750
	Retief GOOSEN	(SA)	75	78	73	71	297	3750
55	Jean VAN DE VELDE	(Fr)	80	70	75	74	299	3250
	Jamie SPENCE	(Eng)	76	71	74	78	299	3250
	Ronan RAFFERTY	(N.Ire)	74	72	80	73	299	3250
58	Domingo HOSPITAL	(Sp)	76	72	77	75	300	3060
59	Jim PAYNE	(Eng)	69	76	80	76	301	2970
60	Ignacio GARRIDO	(Sp)	81	72	75	74	302	2835
	Alexander CEJKA	(Ger)	78	73	74	77	302	2835
62	Seve BALLESTEROS	(Sp)	74	76	76	78	304	2700
63	Joakim HAEGGMAN	(Swe)	76	74	79	76	305	2610
64	Jarmo SANDELIN	(Swe)	73	83	79	71	306	2520
65	Daniel CHOPRA	(Swe)	81	79	78	73	311	2430
66	Robert ALLENBY	(Aus)	RETD					2340

Valderrama
Club President
Jaime Patiño.

IS IT THE POWER?

IS IT THE INTELLIGENCE?

IS IT THE INNER QUALITIES?

VOLVO

...OR IS IT SIMPLY THE INDIVIDUALITY?

Easy to handle and sophisticated, submissive and powerful. Safe, yet exciting. Here, designers and engineers have been given free rein to create the car of their dreams. With five cylinders producing 240 bhp and capable of 0-100 kph in 7 seconds, the Volvo C70 has the most powerful and advanced engine in any Volvo car to date. It has been designed around the same safety features as the Volvo 850. And, as you can see, the designers have clearly reached new heights. Now it's your turn.

VOLVO C70, FREE FOR A DATE FROM APRIL 1997

VOLVO

Nobilo strikes gold in Atlanta

Frank Nobilo overcame a four-stroke deficit in the final round to retain his Sarazen World Open title

Frank Nobilo's repeat victory in the $1.9 million Sarazen World Open Championship at majestic Chateau Elan near Atlanta, and the impressive performance of Challenge Tour campaigner Gary Marks in finishing top European in joint fifth place, spoke volumes for the strength in depth of golf on this side of the Atlantic as well as epitomising the spirit of global opportunity.

Gene Sarazen pioneered the have-clubs-will-travel concept, journeying by sea, (in the 1920s and 1930s), road, rail and air to Europe, Africa, Asia and South America to compete. In the 1960s and 1970s he made his Shell Wonderful World of Golf films, and just three months short of his 95th birthday 'The Squire' was back in Georgia, where his famed double-eagle at the 15th at Augusta National clinched victory in the 1935 Masters, swapping stories with his modern day successors.

He co-designed The Legends course for Chateau Elan owner Donald Panoz, and his life-sized bronze effigy, complete with jauntily tilted hat and shooting-stick, gazes benignly upon all-comers from behind the 18th green.

Frank Nobilo, who calculated he would have competed in 18 countries by the end of the year, symbolises the global golfer of the 1990s and it could not have been more fitting that, having come from four behind Spain's Miguel Angel Jiménez to win last year, he sprang from four behind American Scott Hoch to triumph again – by an emphatic four strokes after a closing 66 to Hoch's 74 with a 16 under par 272 tally which clipped a shot off Ernie Els' 1994 aggregate.

It was a delicious climax to a year in which his fortunes fluctuated dramatically between the joy of victory in the Deutsche Bank Open – TPC of Europe in Hamburg, the deep satisfaction of

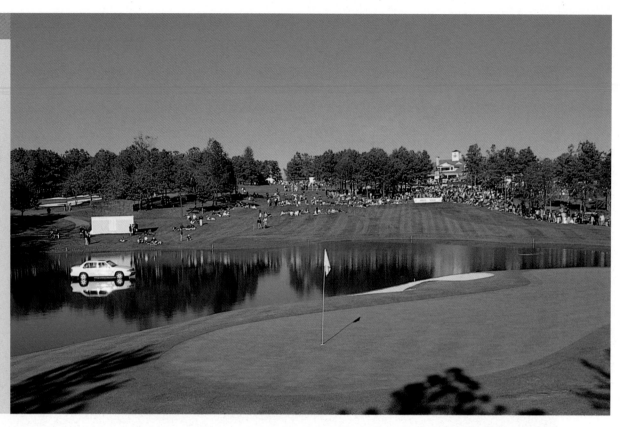

THE COURSE

Gene Sarazen, Sam Snead and Kathy Whitworth co-designed The Legends course in rolling parkland with local architect Denis Griffiths, who created the adjacent Chateau and Woodlands layouts. The three golfing greats each selected six favourite holes and key characteristics of their choices were carefully reproduced – Augusta's par three 12th inspired the 15th and its par five 13th The Legends' fifth – and you can't see the joins.

finishing fourth in the US Masters, eighth in the US PGA Championship and 13th in the US Open, and the frustrations of illness and injury – particularly the shoulder problems he endured for three months, which forced him to undergo daily treatment and ice his arms every night before going to bed during his Atlanta stay.

Local orthopaedic surgeon Chris Edwards, a specialist in baseball injuries, pinpointed the cause to 'the seventh nerve', which runs from the neck to the fingertips, and Nobilo left America not only a richer man (by $342,000) but a much more optimistic one, reassured that the condition was treatable and that he would soon be able to return to the programme of punishing physical exercise he believes he must follow to progress to majors glory.

Nobilo's opening 66 left him a stroke behind little known American Todd Barranger from Knoxville, Tennessee, the Thailand Open Champion, who ended the week a creditable joint ninth with young compatriot Stephen Fresch, the Malaysian Open titleholder (the past two winners of all national opens – currently 66 – earned invites), while another young

American, Bahamas Open champion P. J. Cowan, finished alongside Volvo Masters champion Mark McNulty, 1990 US Open runner-up Mike Donald the Bermuda Open winner and Britain's Gary Marks in 11th place. Offered the opportunity to make their mark by the event's unique format, the quartet gleefully grabbed it.

Marks, 32, a studious Londoner who spent ten years as an assistant at Betchworth Park, Surrey, and three as a teaching professional at the Jack Nicklaus Golf Centre in Malden before opting for a tournament playing career, earned his Sarazen spurs by winning the 1994 Polish Open and he was a European Challenge Tour winner again in Portugal in 1996. At Chateau Elan he shot 69, 72, 71, 73 to finish three under par and win $35,356 and he admitted: 'Standing on the range beside Jack Nicklaus, Fred Couples, Nick Price, Ben Crenshaw and John Daly was a dream come true.'

Continuing the domination of the event by European Tour campaigners was also a dream come true for Nobilo. 'It's the first time in my career I've successfully

Scott Hoch (right) had a troubled final round.

defended a title and for it to happen in Mr Sarazen's tournament, which offers every player in the world the chance to play against the very best, was very special. He has given his whole life to golf and being able to spend time with him is a rare privilege. I hope he lives to be 100.'

A second day 68 left Nobilo two behind Hoch, who earned his Georgia start with last year's Dutch Open success in Hilversum, and fired a course record 64 on day two. A Saturday 70 to Nobilo's 72 edged him four strokes clear and a winning follow-up to his Michelob Championship triumph looked likely for the man who had already banked $1million prize-money in 1996

It did not happen. Nobilo's 33 to the turn in round four cut the margin back to two and he then birdied the tenth, 13th and 14th to jump two ahead of Hoch, who bogeyed the short 12th, then wrecked his slim chance of forcing a play-off by taking two in a bunker for a six at the 17th.

Nobilo has birdied all 18 holes on the course in his three Sarazen outings, which have yielded a princely $718,600 prize-money — it works out at $938 and 20

The Legends, Chateau Elan, Atlanta, Georgia, October 31-November 3, 1996 • Yardage 7159 • Par 72

Pos	Name	Country	Rnd 1	Rnd 2	Rnd 3		Total	Prize Money $
1	Frank Nobilo		66	68	72	66	272	342,000
2	Scott Hoch		68	64	70	74	276	205,000
3	Craig Stadler		68	69	70	71	278	99,000
	Payne Stewart		69	68	71	70	278	99,000
5	Nick Price		68	72	70	69	279	69,000
6	Mark Calcavecchia		70	70	72	70	282	60,125
	Davis Love III		70	67	73	72	282	60,125
8	Angel Cabrera		72	70	73	68	283	53,000
9	Stephen Flesch		73	68	73	70	284	47,000
	Todd Barranger		65	70	76	73	284	47,000
11	Mark McNulty		69	70	77	69	285	35,356
	Mike Donald		74	73	68	70	285	35,356
	P J Cowan		71	70	72	72	285	35,356
	Gary Marks		69	72	71	73	285	35,356
15	Mathias Gronberg		73	69	71	73	286	26,550
	Daniel Chopra		69	70	70	77	286	26,550
17	Miguel Angel Jimenez		72	70	74	71	287	22,750
	Paul Broadhurst		69	73	72	73	287	22,750
19	Eduardo Romero		71	73	73	71	288	19,450
	Padraig Harrington		70	72	73	73	288	19,450
21	Edward Fryatt		72	73	77	67	289	17,575
	Philip Walton		73	71	75	70	289	17,575
23	Andrew Oldcorn		73	70	73	74	290	16,150
24	Paul McGinley		71	70	74	76	291	14,725
	Anders Forsbrand		73	74	72	72	291	14,725
26	John Cook		68	72	77	75	292	12,206
	Christopher Williams		71	67	76	78	292	12,206
	Fred Couples		68	79	73	72	292	12,206
	Mark James		73	73	73	73	292	12,206
30	Barry Lane		71	72	75	75	293	10,450
	Fuzzy Zoeller		72	75	72	74	293	10,450
	Lucas Parsons		70	75	73	75	293	10,450
	Steve Y S Kwon		70	75	73	75	293	10,450
34	Clay Devers		78	67	73	76	294	8,930
	Raul Fretes		75	72	75	72	294	8,930
	Chad Magee		70	73	78	73	294	8,930
	Jon Robson		71	73	76	74	294	8,930
38	Steve Schroeder		72	75	75	73	295	7,980
39	Jack Nicklaus		71	75	79	71	296	7,426
	John Wade		77	68	77	74	296	7,426
	Alexander Cejka		74	72	75	75	296	7,426
42	Jaime Gomez		73	74	79	71	297	6,745
	Stephen Field		72	73	79	73	297	6,745
	John Daly		72	74	71	80	297	6,745
	Adam Hunter		75	71	77	74	297	6,745
46	Ian Hutchings		75	71	77	75	298	6,270
47	Steve Alker		71	72	80	76	299	5,985
	Elliott Boult		70	76	74	79	299	5,985
49	Ben Crenshaw		73	71	79	77	300	5,625
	Jim Payne		77	69	73	81	300	5,625
51	Marcelo Santi		76	69	76	82	303	5,500
	Retief Goosen		73	71	76	83	303	5,500

cents a shot for his 11 rounds, last year's event having been shrunk to 54 holes by torrential rain.

'Squire's Selections' Payne Stewart and Craig Stadler shared third place on 278 with Nick Price finishing on 279 and Mark

SHOT OF THE WEEK

Shot of the week was the hole-in-one by 27-year old Italian Marcello Santi with a pitching-wedge at the 124-yard seventh in round two. A Volvo car on offer for an ace at the lake-fronted 15th went unclaimed. So did three $1million jackpots and a road-ster car for aces at specified holes in the eve of championship par three tournament. Sadly there was no jack-pot on offer for Signor Santi's feat.

Calcavecchia and Davis Love tieing sixth on 282. Swedes Mathias Gronbert and Daniel Chopra tied 15th on 286, one ahead of Jiménez and Paul Broadhurst, with Ireland's Padraig Harrington continu-ing to impress in his rookie year with a level par 288 for joint 19th pace. Fred Couples (292) never recovered from a sec-

ond day 79, Jack Nicklaus ended on 296 and John Daly, after a closing 80, on 297 – an erratic mixed bag of one eagle, 16 birdies, 33 pars, 17 bogeys and five double bogeys.

Gordon Richardson

Payne Stewart (left) and Craig Stadler (right) shared third place.

Can't get away to the golf course?

Let us bring <u>Golf</u> to you!

www.golfweb.co.uk

The ultimate cyber-golf experience!

Top equipment at great prices • Over 20,000 golf courses, online
All the action from 23 tours • Over 40 top golf writers
The largest golf classifieds • Consult a pro about your swing

**You don't have to daydream about golf, let GolfWeb
bring it right to your computer!**

●GolfWeb™
Everything Golf on the World Wide Web!

10 Lexham Gardens., London, W8 5JH, England
send email to golfweb@golfweb.co.uk

Faldo is the standard-bearer

Nick Faldo's victory in the US Masters was the highlight of the year but other European Tour players made their presence felt

Nick Faldo's success at the US Masters was one of those unforgettable events that will remain at the forefront of the mind's eye, no matter how much time passes. Sensational is one of those words that has become tired through ill-use but how else could one describe his triumph and the impact that it had upon the game? Certainly it was a victory that had everything: it hallmarked all Faldo's virtues but also something else as well, portraying him in a softer light, his embrace of Greg Norman at the finish being right up there with the great sporting gestures of all time.

Some weeks later the duel between Norman and Faldo was still the talk of the clubhouse. The theme that kept returning to conversations time and again was this: the pride that everyone felt at being associated with a sport where the two leading competitors could take defeat and victory with such equal dignity and grace.

The trickle-down effect was obvious

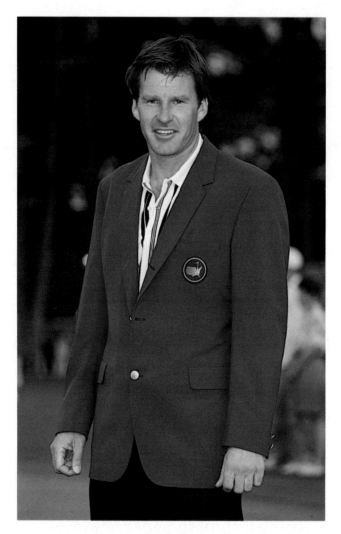

when Faldo returned to the European Tour the following month for the Benson and Hedges International Open and, particularly, for the Open Championship at Lytham. He was overwhelmed by the support he received from a public only too willing to salute a player who had shown an assassin's touch during play but true compassion for the vanquished at the finish. In the aftermath of Augusta, Faldo said that he thought it would be remembered more for Norman's loss than his victory but the months that followed demonstrated perhaps that both will be afforded equal billing.

Certainly a player of Norman's noble standing should not spill a six shot lead with 18 holes to play. But such a fact simply underlines the depth of Faldo's achievement. On a day when the pressure was intense and the pins in all the most difficult positions, Faldo shot 67, the best round of the day.

Two moments stand out as choice lessons for anyone who seeks to follow his path to greatness. The first came at the par three 12th. By this stage Faldo was level and had found the treacherous sliver of green with his tee shot. What would Norman do? Faldo did not even watch. As Norman's ball plummeted in

Sympathy for
Greg Norman
as Nick Faldo
wins his third
US Masters title.

First major
championship
victories for Tom
Lehman (above),
Mark Brooks (right)
and Steve Jones
(far right).
Frank Nobilo
(opposite) had a
chance in the
US Open.

the water Faldo was searching in a drinks cabinet for refreshment. He did not even look up to see what all the commotion was about, why the audience was emanating a chorus of oohs and aahs. The first rule of major championship golf is always: concentrate on your own game. And then at the next hole, two shots ahead, Faldo was undecided as to what to play for his long approach to the green. If he had put it in the creek that lies short of the putting surface, the advantage would have been back with Norman. Faldo took an age, putting clubs back into his bag and picking them out again. Eventually he made the choice, and found the green. Lesson number two: never play until you're absolutely sure of what you're trying to achieve.

So Europe's run of success at the Masters continued, Faldo's win making it nine green jackets out of the last 14 to have been awarded. Naturally, his achievement gets the gold medal as far as the feats of European Tour golfers in this year's major championships is concerned,

but there was plenty of competition for silver and bronze.

Alexander Cejka, a rookie at all three events, nevertheless was one of only 16 players to make the cut at each; Frank Nobilo demonstrated his remorseless consistency in finishing fourth at the Masters, 13th at the US Open and 8th at the USPGA; Colin Montgomerie came within a rub of the green of perhaps collecting his first major at the US Open; and Per-Ulrik Johansson and Jesper Parnevik both finished in the top ten at the USPGA.

If Nobilo was never likely to win at Augusta that was far from the case at Oakland Hills, the scene of the United States Open, where the talented Kiwi's unerring driving and iron play placed him in the thick of things. However, Nobilo's putting touch deserted him during the final round and so it was left to Montgomerie to challenge for the title.

The Scot was eventually undone by an unfortunate double bogey five at the 13th and anyone who followed his progress on the final day must have felt at least a

smidgeon of sympathy for him at the finish. For 18 holes he totally outplayed his partner, Davis Love, and yet it was the American who came to the final hole needing a par to force a play-off. In the end, a three-putt bogey undid Love as well, allowing Steve Jones, a qualifier for the event, to record the most improbable win of the year.

For much of the USPGA Championship youth had its fling and in this respect Parnevik and Johansson represented Europe well. After all their achievements in recent seasons only a first win in a major championship now lies beyond a player from Sweden. Parnevik, who eventually finished fifth, was bitterly disappointed at the close. Rather like Montgomerie, no one played better golf than he from tee to green on the final day but once more the putts shaved the hole rather than dropping.

Tied for 52nd place at Valhalla was Cejka. It was always going to be difficult for the young German to try to emulate his remarkable achievements of 1995,

when he won three tourna-
ments. In a way he did not
try, saying that his goal for
the year was to consolidate
his progress by gaining experience at the
three major championships in America.
To make the cut at each suggests the 25-
year old did just that and he earned
plaudits as well, most notably from Jack
Nicklaus, with whom he was partnered in
the third round at Augusta.

After eleven holes the great man

**Alexander Cejka (top) made the cut in all four majors.
Jesper Parnevik (above left) and Per-Ulrik Johansson (above right)
led the Swedish challenge at the USPGA.**

stood six over par for the day and Cejka
was level. Yet Nicklaus finished in 76 and
Cejka on 78. 'Thanks for the lesson,' Cejka
said at the close. Both had known what
had gone on. 'Unless you've played this
course you can never know just how
quickly it can all slip away and what happened to Alex today was all about

experience,' Nicklaus said.
And when asked if he
thought Cejka had the mak-
ings of becoming a second
Bernhard Langer, Nicklaus added: 'I think
he would rather remain the first
Alexander Cejka and if we leave him alone
and he works hard on his game I think he
will do very well for himself. He has a
presence, and that's something you do not
see very often.'

Derek Lawrenson

The most important thing that goes into our golf shoes is what doesn't go into them.

adidas®

Water, water everywhere and not a drop inside your shoes. The adi-Dry and Bernhard Langer Dry golf shoes both contain a special membrane that prevents water from getting in, while allowing perspiration to get out. Because the most important thing you can have in a golf shoe is dry feet.

Charity is the winner

The Canon Shoot-Out series
provided entertaining competition
and benefited many deserving causes

Canon Shoot-Out Grand Final
winners Colin Montgomerie
and Sam Torrance with
Mr Jajime Katayama,
President of Canon Europa.

pened to the children in Dunblane, and we were delighted to nominate the Dunblane Appeal Fund as our charity,' said an emotional Montgomerie. 'It came home even more when I learned that one spectator in the gallery at Wentworth had lost a grandchild in the tragedy.' And Sandy added: 'When Colin, Sam and I were approached to nominate a charity, we didn't even have to give it a second thought.'

Canon, official camera, binoculars, copier and facsimile suppliers to the Tour, who also introduced a travelling Business Service at 15 events, gave their Shoot-Outs programme a new charity element right at the start of the year. It was announced that Canon would donate £50 for every birdie and £100 for every eagle scored throughout the series to the PGA European Tour Benevolent Trust which offers financial help to current and past Tour members, their dependants and others in need whose livelihoods have been earned in connection with professional golf.

As an exciting, extra incentive, it

*B*elieve it or not, there can be three winners of a foursomes tournament. The Canon Shoot-Out series, an increasingly popular feature of the European Tour, proved so when Colin Montgomerie and Sam Torrance emerged from the grand final at Crans-sur-Sierre proudly sharing their success as 1996 champions with charity.

By the time the sixth successive season of Canon Shoot-Out action completed a ten-match schedule covering Italy, France, England, Ireland, Holland, Sweden and Switzerland, another £43,000

had been raised for deserving, seriously heart-touching causes.

The most spectacular fund-raising of all was achieved at the Canon Champions Challenge Shoot-Out at Wentworh on the eve of the Volvo PGA Championship. All ten players involved donated their prize money to charity and there weren't many dry eyes to be seen around the 18th green when a cheque for £12,500, the combined winnings of Colin Montgomerie, Sandy Lyle and Sam Torrance, was immediately handed over to the Dunblane Appeal.

'It is still hard to believe what hap-

stirred many of Europe's finest players to outstanding feats during the series which carried increased prize-money of £10,500 at each event and a record £57,000 for the final. The first Shoot-Out was staged at the Bergamo Golf Club prior to the Conte of Florence Italian Open after the originally scheduled opening event at the Alfred Dunhill South African PGA Championship had to be abandoned because of relentless rain. Barry Lane and Andrew Coltart – a draw on the first tee decided all partnerships for the series – combined superbly to win.

Local favourites Costantino Rocca and Bergamo professional Silvano Locatelli dropped out with the highest score among the five pairs after four holes of stroke-play as the rules demanded. Then David Gilford and Anders Forsbrand lost a shoot-out from a greenside bunker. The Argentinian formation of Eduardo Romero and José Coceres were next to bow out, and that left David Feherty and Sam Torrance in a final-hole duel with Lane and Coltart who survived with a solid par four. They each earned £2,000

Seve Ballesteros (above) and Bernhard Langer (below) were in Canon action throughout the season.

while Rocca won the 'nearest the pin' competition for a set of Canon Image Stabiliser Binoculars. He also claimed £50

for charity with a birdie putt from 25 feet and Romero earmarked £100 for the Tour Benevolent Trust by holing a pitch from 40 yards for an eagle two.

Similar dramas were enacted at each shoot-out as the Canon series continued. Scotland's Andrew Coltart won again in the Peugeot Open de España week at Club de Campo, Madrid, this time in company with Irishman Darren Clark. Next on the victory rostrum were Severiano Ballesteros and Nick Faldo, a combination boasting 102 tournament wins, including 11 major championships. They won the Canon Champions Challenge Shoot-Out at Wentworth and £16,000 went to their respective Charitable Trusts. Colin Montgomerie and Sandy Lyle were runners-up to earn £10,000 for the Dunblane Appeal.

Shoot-Out winners Colin Montgomerie and Ian Woosnam gave the Murphy's Irish Open at The Druid's Glen a memorable curtain-raising performance heightened by the five partnerships scoring ten birdies to raise another £500 for charity. When the series moved on to the

Sun Dutch Open at Hilversumsche, America's Scott Hoch and local favourite Rolf Muntz emerged as winners. On to the Volvo Scandinavian Masters at Forsgardens Golf Club and there Bernhard Langer and Sam Torrance survived a best-of-three shoot-out finale to win. Once again. however, charitable actions dominated. Langer and Torrance, along with Peter Hedblom and Jarmo Sandelin, the runners-up, donated the whole of their prize money to the dependants of Jan Blomqvist, an exceptional figure in Swedish golf who had recently died at a cruelly young age.

Irishmen Darren Clarke and Padraig Harrington were four under par for seven holes when they won the Canon Shoot-Out at the Volvo German Open on the Schloss Nippenburg course. The field turned ten birdies into another £500 for the Tour Benevolent Trust.

And so to the grand final before the Canon European Masters on the marvellously scenic Crans-sur-Sierre course at the foot of the Swiss Alps. Sam Torrance and Colin Montgomerie played the front nine holes in four under par to win from Severiano Ballesteros and Eduardo Romero. Huge crowds watched as the two Scots each earned £9,000, a Canon prize, and a Tiffany's crystal trophy. In return, they gave Mr Jajime Katayama, President of Canon Europa, a 1996 Tour Yearbook signed by all ten Canon

Nick Faldo, Pat Guerin, Director of Communication Products, Canon, and Seve Ballesteros at Wentworth (top). Ian Woosnam flies the flag (centre), and Rolf Muntz and Scott Hoch focus on their prizes (below).

finalists as a token of their appreciation for a series thoroughly enjoyed by competitors and spectators alike.

Said Sam: 'Colin and I were fourball partners when Europe won the Ryder Cup at Oak Hill last year. We lost our match and were a bit peeved because we both played fantastically. So being put together again by the draw on the first tee gave us something to prove. It was great.'

For an encore, another shoot-out was staged on the eve of the Trophée Lancôme at St. Nom la Bretèche, Paris. Severiano Ballesteros, second in the previous two Canon events, enjoyed a deserved win in partnership with Jean Van de Velde. The day's action saw four birdies and that was another £200 towards a grand total of £3,000 for the European Tour Benevolent Trust.

Top of the Birdies and Eagles Table for the Canon Shoot-Out series was Colin Montgomerie, followed by Padraig Harrington, Sam Torrance and Severiano Ballesteros. But it was Torrance who headed the final 1996 Canon Shoot-Out Order of Merit with Harrington and Ballesteros sharing second place.

Unless, of course, you count the season's real winner – charity.

Mark Wilson

Canon Shot of the Year

Colin Montgomerie,

18th hole, Emirates Golf Club,

Dubai Desert Classic

When Colin Montgomerie arrived at the Emirates Golf Club in March for the Dubai Desert Classic he had not played a tournament round for three months. He emerged some 30lbs lighter having spent the winter working on his fitness while awaiting the birth of his second daughter.

Naturally, he was a little apprehensive as to how he would perform on his 1996 debut but two driver shots to the first hole restored his confidence.

As the tournament progressed, Montgomerie drew ever closer to the lead which was held by Miguel Angel Jiménez. In the final round, in which the two were paired together, Montgomerie took a one-stroke advantage to the 18th tee. After a good drive on this 547-yard, par five, the Scot was faced with a 215-yard carry into the wind over water to find the green.

He knew that Jiménez was likely to make a birdie and, using his driver off the fairway, sent the ball climbing over the hazard to land safely on the green and secure the title.

The shot was a worthy winner of the Canon Shot of the Year as the victory gave Montgomerie the impetus to go on and capture his fourth consecutive Volvo Ranking title as Europe's number one.

Canon

281

Champions in the making

The European Challenge Tour continued

to provide an ideal training ground`

for future champions

Thomas Bjorn and Diego Borrego provided further evidence in 1996 of how the developing European Challenge Tour is continuing to breed true champions.

Both Bjorn and Borrego emerged from the 1995 Challenge Tour. Borrego was in seventh heaven by April of 1996 when, in only his seventh European Tour event, he won the Turespaña Masters Open Comunitat Valenciana Paradores de Turismo at El Saler, Valencia, in his native Spain. Then in September, Bjorn demonstrated his huge potential by capturing the Loch Lomond World Invitational on the bonnie bonnie banks north of Glasgow.

These were notable performances not only because Bjorn and Borrego achieved their first European Tour victories, but also because they were gained on courses held in the highest esteem. El Saler, where the links holes bear comparison with the best courses in the United Kingdom, is the work of Javier Arana, and it has long been regarded as one of the supreme tests of golf on the Continent. The course at

UAP Grand Final Winner Ian Garbutt finished top of the rankings.

Loch Lomond Golf Club was designed by Tom Weiskopf and Jay Morrish and opened only in 1993. It has already been acclaimed in its brief existence and Bjorn was one of only seven players to better par over the four days of the inaugural Loch Lomond World Invitational. Indeed, Bjorn shot four successive sub-par rounds.

Then Bjorn explained the background, and maybe the secret to him becoming the first Danish player to win

on the European Tour. 'I won four times on the European Challenge Tour in 1995 so I knew I was capable of winning,' he said. 'The Challenge Tour is a great opportunity for young players, and it helps them improve so much. I believe it is better to play the Challenge Tour for at least a year rather than go straight on the European Tour. For me if the Challenge Tour keeps on improving it's going to be a great breeding ground for young players of the future. We would then have two strong Tours. It was certainly a wonderful way for me to make a dream come true by qualifying to play in 1996 on the European Tour. I knew when I moved over that I would have to lift my game to a new level, but I had been prepared for that by the Challenge Tour.'

Borrego also pointed to the Challenge Tour for sharpening his game in 1995 when he finished third in the Rankings behind Bjorn. 'After I lost my card in 1994 following one year on the European Tour, I decided to go on the Challenge Tour. My ambitions had not been dampened by

nation and move onto the 1996 European Tour. Then, at Royal Mougins in April, his graduation through the Challenge Tour, Qualifying School and Apollo Week — the European Tour Training School — was complete as he won the Air France Cannes Open.

All of which further supports the founding of the European Challenge Tour in 1989 when it was created with the full backing of the European Golf Federations. Its primary goal was to provide playing opportunities for every talented and ambitious golf professional. This exciting proving ground has already produced players such as Italy's Costantino Rocca, Germany's Alexander Cejka, England's Paul Eales, Sweden's Jarmo Sandelin and New Zealand's Michael Campbell. Each

Vanslow Phillips (left) and Joakim Rask (right) and Dennis Edlund (below) booked their places on the European Tour.

losing my card, but I could not join the Challenge Tour until June of 1995 because I was giving lessons at my club. I wanted to get back on the European Tour and the Challenge Tour offered that chance. the competition is very good, and I was delighted to win the Perrier Open Pro-Am although I had to shoot the round of my life — a 63 — on the last day to do so. The victory at El Saler was the reward of hard work, and a few soothing words from Manuel Pinero before the last round, but behind it was the experience gained by playing on the Challenge Tour.'

To further illustrate the importance of the Challenge Tour it is imperative to look further down the 1995 rankings list. Raymond Russell is a case in point. Russell, the 1992 Scottish Youths' champion and a Walker cup player in 1993, failed to win his card at the 1994 European Tour Qualifying School Finals. So he turned to the Challenge Tour. In 1995 he played in 21 events and finished 41st in the Rankings with £11,862, but the experience he gleaned was invaluable. He was able to return to the Qualifying School in the right frame of mind to pass the exami-

year brings a new challenge with a developing circuit that thrives on opportunity and incentive which was again fully evident right to the last putt during a 1996 season of 44 events played in 18 countries, and offering prize money in excess of £2 million.

Rocca, looking back on a career in which he has so far helped Europe regain

the Ryder Cup by Johnnie Walker on American soil and captured the Volvo PGA Championship at Wentworth, said: 'I think it is important for every young player to play the Challenge Tour. It is tough, but it is good for you because it fully prepares you for the European Tour.' The comments of such players as Rocca outline the need to offer the Challenge Tour Members — 340 were eligible in 1996 — an even more attractive goal so that from 1996 the number of playing graduates from the Challenge Tour to the European Tour from the rankings was increased from ten to 15. Moreover, those who finished between 16th and 35th benefited from exemption to the European Tour Qualifying School Finals.

All who started out on the 1996 European Challenge Tour at the Kenya Open, won by Scotland's Mike Miller at Muthaiga, had good reason to acknowledge that, for them, eight months of honing their skills in such a competitive arena would not only provide the ultimate examination to proving their readiness to play weekly alongside world-class champions, but also that their prospects of

283

Former European Tour winner Robert Lee.

elevation to the European Tour had been increased.

Such was the intensity of competition that not until the UAP Grand Final on the beautiful Quinta do Peru course in Lisbon in October were the 15 graduates from the 1996 European Challenge Tour confirmed. Moreover, England's Ian Garbutt leapt, with his success in the UAP Grand Final, from 12th place to number one in the rankings with winnings of £37,661 to finish ahead of Sweden's Dennis Edlund (£34,286) and England's Robert Lee (£33,990). Moreover, New Zealand's Stephen Scahill, who won the Open dei Tessali in Italy in June, produced a strong finish in Portugal with which he moved to 13th in the rankings with Finland's Kalle Vainola, winner of the Le Pavoniere Superal Challenge 1996 and the Siab Open in the space of six tournament weeks, eventually securing the 15th and final place to the European Tour.

The story of the 1996 European Challenge Tour began with Miller's fairy-tale win in Kenya — his first success since being named the 1979 Sir Henry Cotton Rookie of the Year. Italy's Massimo

Florioli then won the Open de Cote D'Ivorie in the Ivory Coast, finished joint runner-up to Simon Burnell in the Is Molas Challenge and fourth in the La Pavoniere Superal Challenge to lead the rankings. Robert Lee moved to number one after his win in the Canarias-Challenge tour, but Florioli was back on top by the end of May after finishing runner-up to Spain's Francisco Cea in the Open de Dijon.

Florioli stayed ahead moving into July, but by then England's Andrew Sandywell with a victory in the Open des Volcans had advanced into seventh place. England's Vanslow Phillips captured the Interlaken Open in Switzerland at the end of July, prior to Sweden's Dennis Edlund momentarily dominating. He won the English Challenge Tour Championship at East Sussex National and the Rolex Trophy Pro-Am at the beautiful Golf Club de Geneve in Switzerland in successive weeks, then finished runner-up in the Kentab/RGB Open in September to go fourth in the rankings. By then Sweden's

Jaokim Rask, following a succession of strong finishes, had dislodged Florioli at the top of the rankings.

Lee, winner of two European Tour events in the 1980s, moved back to the top when he was joint runner-up behind José Sota, a cousin of Severiano Ballesteros, in the Eulen Open Galea III in Bilbao, but Edlund, by finishing joint runner-up to Germany's Erol Simsek in The Bank Pekao Polish Open, assured himself of being number one entering the season-ending UAP Grand Final.

Garbutt joined a cast of 50 at Quinta do Peru for the showpiece tournament and stated before teeing off: 'It would be nice to say goodbye to the Challenge Tour with a big win.' He achieved exactly that with a superb five-birdie, no-bogey last round of 67 for a 16 under par total of 272. 'I've enjoyed two years on the Challenge Tour,' he declared. 'It's a thrill to win such a big tournament and finish number one in the rankings. Now I'm looking forward to playing on the European Tour.'

Mitchell Platts

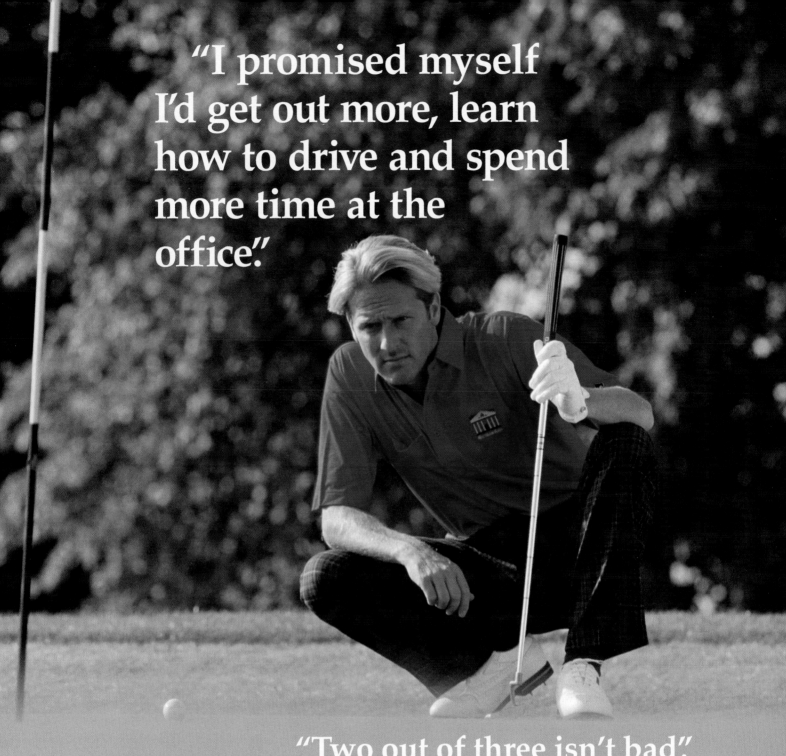

"I promised myself I'd get out more, learn how to drive and spend more time at the office."

"Two out of three isn't bad."

THE BELTON WOODS HOTEL, LINCOLNSHIRE. TELEPHONE: 01476 593200.

THE BELFRY, WISHAW, NORTH WARWICKSHIRE. TELEPHONE: 01625 470301.

DE VERE HOTEL, BLACKPOOL, LANCASHIRE. TELEPHONE: 01253 838866.

MOTTRAM HALL, PRESTBURY, CHESHIRE. TELEPHONE: 01625 828135.

Whether you're looking to improve your handicap, win your society's competition or just simply enjoy a relaxing round, De Vere golf resorts offer you the choice of champions. Set in superb locations, all of our challenging courses cater for all levels of ability. And because we are totally committed to each and every golfers needs, there is tuition and advice on hand from our team of professionals whenever you need it. Then off course you can relaxand enjoy the first class facilities, unrivalled service and hospitality we're famous for. So if your passion in life is golf, promise yourself De Vere.

For reservations please telephone the hotel of your choice.

DE VERE HOTELS

DE VERE HOUSE, CHESTER ROAD, DARESBURY, WARRINGTON, CHESHIRE WA4 4BN.

Horton hits the heights

With four victories, Tommy Horton became the first man to top £100,000 on the burgeoning European Seniors Tour

Leading money-winner Tommy Horton receives the John Jacobs Trophy from John Jacobs.

Tommy Horton's year. That's how 1996 will always be known in the growing arena of seniors' golf. The year in which the Royal Jersey professional climbed to new dizzy levels of personal achievement within the European Seniors Tour.

Four victories from 13 starts, five second places and a record £133,195 in prize-money are the headline statistics behind the most successful campaign in Horton's illustrious career. 'It's all just like a dream,' he declared after he had holed a birdie putt on the final green of the final tournament – The Player Championship – to clinch his fourth title.

The reality, though, is that the 55-year old former Ryder Cup player drove the ball longer and straighter, struck his irons consistently closer and swept in more putts with his new long-shafted Odyssey putter than ever before. That's not dreaming. That's the result of a lot of work in a long career dedicated to the search for perfection in everything this immaculate, pencil-slim professional has undertaken.

After warming up with a couple of second places – behind winners South

African Bobby Verwey in the Turkey Seniors Open and Italian Renato Campagnoli at the De Vere Hotels Classic – Horton was desperately keen to win the Hippo Jersey Open at La Moye, next door to his own Royal Jersey Club. But despite a big following he had to settle for 13th place behind runaway winner Maurice Bembridge who produced superb back-to-back closing 67s for a seven-shot victory – his first as a senior.

Horton struck his first winning blow at the new Castle Royal Seniors Classic. He celebrated his 55th birthday by beating

former Ryder Cup colleague Brian Huggett with a birdie four at the first extra hole of a sudden-death play-off. It was to be the closest Huggett, now 60, would get to win in what was for him an indifferent season following a winter almost devoid of golf due to health problems. The little Welshman battled on to ninth in the Order of Merit, his lowest in five years' of Tour play.

The Ryder Collingtree Classic was tough on everyone. A stiff, gusting north-westerly wind over the demanding parkland layout on the final day didn't help the scoring, the best of which came from Scotland's David Huish, former Ryder Cup man Malcolm Gregson and Australian Noel Ratcliffe. They each posted three over par 219 to tie before Huish, the North Berwick club professional, clinched his first Tour win with a solid par five on the island green of the tricky 18th. Gregson suffered the biggest disappointment on his journey home to Formby after missing from three feet for an outright win before the extra time.

In the following Stella German Open in Frankfurt, Horton reckoned he played

286

his best golf of this year to finish 15 under par over three rounds on a tough Idstein course. It resulted in a two-shot victory over Australian Ratcliffe, who was to prove the year's best nearly man.

Brian Barnes took a break from earning big dollars on the US Seniors Tour to successfully defend his Senior British Open title at Royal Portrush. His win was built on two middle rounds of 65 (a Championship record), and 66 which gave him a three-shot lead over former champion, New Zealand southpaw Bob Charles after three rounds. That's how it stayed to the end, although American

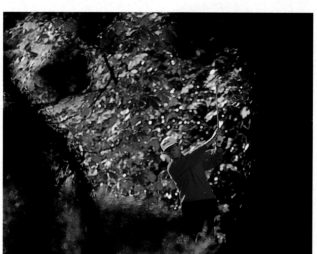

cheque for £17,500 and a new target for the rest of the season – topping the rankings with £100,000 prize money.

Malcolm Gregson's consistency was finally rewarded in the Lawrence Batley

ranked second once more and he consolidated that position with another success at the inaugural Motor City Classic at The Warwickshire where he got home by two from a trio including – would you believe, Tommy Horton.

Gary Player himself couldn't stop the Channel Islander's closing victory in the South African legend's own Player Championship at The Buckinghamshire. Beaten into second place alongside Malcolm Gregson, he saw Horton take centre stage in a fitting climax to a campaign during which he had averaged more than £10,000 for each of his 13 starts. In other words, a stag-

Malcolm Gregson (above), Brian Barnes (left) and John Morgan (right) all made their mark in 1996.

Seniors at Fixby. He registered his first win in two years, closing with a superb 65 to be four under par and two better than defending champion Italian Alberto Croce and Neil Coles.

But it was Horton again in the Northern Electric Slaley Hall, a four-shot success taking him to within £21,000 of his target. Noel Ratcliffe was runner-up alongside Spaniard Antonio Garrido.

Seniors rookie Terry Gale, another Australian, stole the show at the PGA Seniors Championship at The Belfry, using only 24 putts in a final round of 70 to beat second placed Horton by a shot.

Then followed two victories by the irrepressible John Morgan. The West Kirby professional, top of the Order of Merit in 1994 and second the following year, had chugged through the season with six top ten finishes but without the boost of a winning cheque. It finally arrived at the Scottish Seniors Open. At Aberdeen's tricky Newmacher course, Morgan took his fifth seniors title, winning by four shots from – yes Horton, whose £11,100 cheque moved him past the £100,000 milestone. Morgan was now

newcomer David Oakley gave everyone a talking point when he closed to within a shot of Barnes with five to go, before dropping back to share second place with Charles. Winning the British title remains Horton's last big ambition. It eluded him once more despite another late challenge of three under par 33 over the final nine holes which gave him fourth place, a

gering ten per cent of the Tour's total pool of £1.38 million.

No wonder he claims that the European Seniors Tour has grown to the point where more professionals can now play full time in the autumn of their careers without having to depend on selling too many tee pegs back at the shop.

Bryan Potter

"With all the suspension and safety improvements underway, you know what the new Rover 800 Series could do with now?" we asked our designers. "A new interior. Adding more burr walnut to the doors and consoles would be a start. Make the carpets even thicker cut pile while you're about it. That way drivers will feel more at home at the wheel. Speaking of which, that's where you could mount the hi-fi controls for extra convenience. Leather would be good there, too. Maybe even around the gearstick and handbrake. And how about colour coordinating the new carpet and mats range with the piping on our luxury seats? It might just be the perfect finishing touch."

Who says there's no place like home?

To fully appreciate the new decor, simply call us for a test drive on 0345 186 186.

WE'VE REDECORATED THE SITTING ROOM.

Golfer of the Month Awards 1996

The winners of the Johnnie Walker Golfer
of the Month Award receive a trophy designed
by Tiffany & Co. of London and earn £1,000
for the PGA European Tour Benevolent Trust
and £1,000 for the Golf Foundation

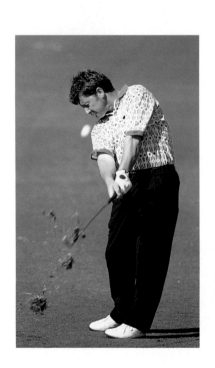

Ian Woosnam, (above) January
Sven Strüver, (far right) February
Colin Montgomerie, (right) March

There is also a Johnnie Walker
Golfer of the Year Award.
The winner in 1995
was Colin Montgomerie.

Nick Faldo,
(left) April;
Lee Westwood,
(right) August

Robert Allenby, (above left) June; Mark McNulty, (above right) July and October

Thomas Bjorn, (below) September

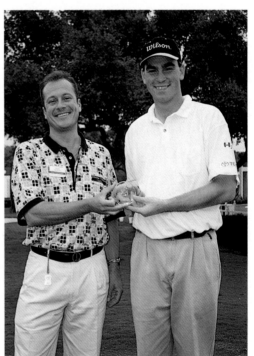

Jim Payne, (left) May

Volvo Ranking 1996

Colin Montgomerie

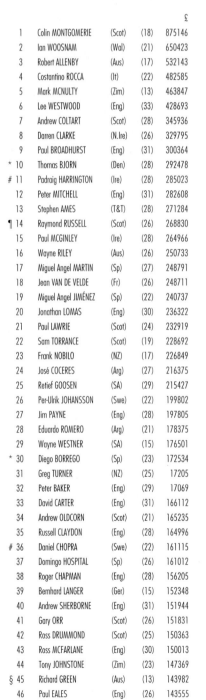

				£
1	Colin MONTGOMERIE	(Scot)	(18)	875146
2	Ian WOOSNAM	(Wal)	(21)	650423
3	Robert ALLENBY	(Aus)	(17)	532143
4	Costantino ROCCA	(It)	(22)	482585
5	Mark MCNULTY	(Zim)	(13)	463847
6	Lee WESTWOOD	(Eng)	(33)	428693
7	Andrew COLTART	(Scot)	(28)	345936
8	Darren CLARKE	(N.Ire)	(26)	329795
9	Paul BROADHURST	(Eng)	(31)	300364
* 10	Thomas BJORN	(Den)	(28)	292478
# 11	Padraig HARRINGTON	(Ire)	(28)	285023
12	Peter MITCHELL	(Eng)	(31)	282608
13	Stephen AMES	(T&T)	(28)	271284
¶ 14	Raymond RUSSELL	(Scot)	(26)	268830
15	Paul MCGINLEY	(Ire)	(28)	264966
16	Wayne RILEY	(Aus)	(26)	250733
17	Miguel Angel MARTIN	(Sp)	(27)	248791
18	Jean VAN DE VELDE	(Fr)	(26)	248711
19	Miguel Angel JIMÉNEZ	(Sp)	(22)	240737
20	Jonathan LOMAS	(Eng)	(30)	236322
21	Paul LAWRIE	(Scot)	(24)	232919
22	Sam TORRANCE	(Scot)	(19)	228692
23	Frank NOBILO	(NZ)	(17)	226849
24	José COCERES	(Arg)	(27)	216375
25	Retief GOOSEN	(SA)	(29)	215427
26	Per-Ulrik JOHANSSON	(Swe)	(22)	199802
27	Jim PAYNE	(Eng)	(28)	197805
28	Eduardo ROMERO	(Arg)	(21)	178375
29	Wayne WESTNER	(SA)	(15)	176501
* 30	Diego BORREGO	(Sp)	(23)	172534
31	Greg TURNER	(NZ)	(25)	17205
32	Peter BAKER	(Eng)	(29)	17069
33	David CARTER	(Eng)	(31)	166112
34	Andrew OLDCORN	(Scot)	(21)	165235
35	Russell CLAYDON	(Eng)	(28)	164996
# 36	Daniel CHOPRA	(Swe)	(22)	161115
37	Domingo HOSPITAL	(Sp)	(26)	161012
38	Roger CHAPMAN	(Eng)	(28)	156205
39	Bernhard LANGER	(Ger)	(15)	152348
40	Andrew SHERBORNE	(Eng)	(31)	151944
41	Gary ORR	(Scot)	(26)	151831
42	Ross DRUMMOND	(Scot)	(25)	150363
43	Ross MCFARLANE	(Eng)	(30)	150013
44	Tony JOHNSTONE	(Zim)	(23)	147369
§ 45	Richard GREEN	(Aus)	(13)	143982
46	Paul EALES	(Eng)	(26)	143555

47	Ignacio GARRIDO	(Sp)	(26)	140377
¶ 48	Carl SUNESON	(Sp)	(28)	140011
49	Jamie SPENCE	(Eng)	(25)	139506
50	Peter HEDBLOM	(Swe)	(27)	137143
51	Mark DAVIS	(Eng)	(30)	136604
52	Paul CURRY	(Eng)	(23)	135642
53	Marc FARRY	(Fr)	(28)	134110
# 54	David HOWELL	(Eng)	(27)	132527
55	Jarmo SANDELIN	(Swe)	(16)	131650
56	Iain PYMAN	(Eng)	(28)	131165
57	Gordon BRAND JNR.	(Scot)	(27)	129763
¶ 58	Patrik SJÖLAND	(Swe)	(24)	127513
59	David GILFORD	(Eng)	(23)	119565
60	Joakim HAEGGMAN	(Swe)	(24)	115490
61	Stuart CAGE	(Eng)	(31)	111921
¶ 62	Miles TUNNICLIFF	(Eng)	(24)	111140
¶ 63	Rolf MUNTZ	(Hol)	(28)	110981
64	Santiago LUNA	(Sp)	(26)	110583
¶ 65	Fernando ROCA	(Sp)	(21)	109612
66	Jon ROBSON	(Eng)	(24)	105232
67	Richard BOXALL	(Eng)	(30)	103299
68	Pedro LINHART	(Sp)	(24)	100924
69	Seve BALLESTEROS	(Sp)	(18)	100903
70	Sven STRÜVER	(Ger)	(25)	100233
71	Mathias GRÖNBERG	(Swe)	(29)	99441
# 72	Angel CABRERA	(Arg)	(19)	99073
73	Phillip PRICE	(Wal)	(28)	97781
74	Mark MOULAND	(Wal)	(28)	97383
¶ 75	Thomas GÖGELE	(Ger)	(24)	92738
76	Barry LANE	(Eng)	(19)	91783
* 77	Ricky WILLISON	(Eng)	(29)	91697
78	Malcolm MACKENZIE	(Eng)	(28)	91228

79	Mark ROE	(Eng)	(27)	88329
# 80	Per HAUGSRUD	(Nor)	(26)	82399
81	Raymond BURNS	(N.Ire)	(27)	81919
82	Peter O'MALLEY	(Aus)	(18)	80242
83	Martin GATES	(Eng)	(24)	79885
84	Fabrice TARNAUD	(Fr)	(28)	79714
85	Ronan RAFFERTY	(N.Ire)	(28)	78803
86	Derrick COOPER	(Eng)	(26)	76644
87	Carl MASON	(Eng)	(20)	72954
88	Olle KARLSSON	(Swe)	(23)	72754
89	Dean ROBERTSON	(Scot)	(29)	72409
90	Alexander CEJKA	(Ger)	(12)	72146
91	David FEHERTY	(N.Ire)	(17)	71912
92	Philip WALTON	(Ire)	(23)	71565
93	Pierre FULKE	(Swe)	(24)	70817
94	Paul AFFLECK	(Wal)	(25)	69858
95	Gary EVANS	(Eng)	(26)	69680
¶ 96	Juan Carlos PIÑERO	(Sp)	(25)	69630
97	Eamonn DARCY	(Ire)	(21)	69177
98	Steven BOTTOMLEY	(Eng)	(32)	67724
# 99	David HIGGINS	(Ire)	(23)	67513
100	Des SMYTH	(Ire)	(26)	66041
101	Adam HUNTER	(Scot)	(30)	64945
102	Robert KARLSSON	(Swe)	(19)	64456
# 103	Gary CLARK	(Eng)	(23)	64178
104	Mats HALLBERG	(Swe)	(26)	64056
105	Silvio GRAPPASONNI	(It)	(23)	61883
§ 106	Bradley HUGHES	(Aus)	(12)	61621
107	Michael JONZON	(Swe)	(30)	60835
108	José RIVERO	(Sp)	(19)	56867
109	Roger WESSELS	(SA)	(29)	56020
110	Klas ERIKSSON	(Swe)	(26)	55904
¶ 111	Robert COLES	(Eng)	(23)	55878
112	Steven RICHARDSON	(Eng)	(30)	54321
113	Gary EMERSON	(Eng)	(25)	52625
* 114	Stephen FIELD	(Eng)	(25)	51958
115	Jay TOWNSEND	(USA)	(25)	51558
116	Mark JAMES	(Eng)	(18)	51279
117	Emanuele CANONICA	(It)	(22)	51046
118	Niclas FASTH	(Swe)	(22)	50246
119	Stephen MCALLISTER	(Scot)	(27)	46780
120	Michael CAMPBELL	(NZ)	(17)	44284
121	Mats LANNER	(Swe)	(24)	43706
* 122	Per NYMAN	(Swe)	(26)	43490
123	Howard CLARK	(Eng)	(18)	42958
124	Francisco CEA	(Sp)	(11)	42492

Ian Woosnam

Robert Allenby

Costantino Rocca

168	Manuel PIÑERO	(Sp)	(16)	18914
§ 169	André CRUSE	(SA)	(3)	18841
# 170	Hendrik BUHRMANN	(SA)	(14)	18836
§ 171	Gary NICKLAUS	(USA)	(6)	18347
¶ 172	Andrew COLLISON	(Eng)	(23)	17849
¶ 173	Anders HAGLUND	(Swe)	(18)	17568
¶ 174	Max ANGLERT	(Swe)	(16)	17314
175	John HAWKSWORTH	(Eng)	(12)	16777
§ 176	Trevor DODDS	(Nam)	(3)	16736
177	Glenn RALPH	(Eng)	(10)	16100
178	André BOSSERT	(Swi)	(22)	15044
¶ 179	Anders HANSEN	(Den)	(12)	13099
# 180	Stephen GALLACHER	(Scot)	(13)	13019
181	Paul MOLONEY	(Aus)	(22)	12771
182	John MELLOR	(Eng)	(6)	12568
183	Ian PALMER	(SA)	(4)	12073
§ 184	Gordon SHERRY	(Scot)	(7)	11512

125	David A RUSSELL	(Eng)	(22)	42434
126	Fredrik LINDGREN	(Swe)	(25)	42334
§ 127	Brenden PAPPAS	(SA)	(12)	41302
128	Sandy LYLE	(Scot)	(10)	41244
# 129	Steve WEBSTER	(Eng)	(28)	40800
130	Rodger DAVIS	(Aus)	(14)	40785
¶ 131	Antoine LEBOUC	(Fr)	(23)	39903
132	Christian CÉVAER	(Fr)	(29)	39499
# 133	Bob MAY	(USA)	(16)	39409
# 134	Michael WELCH	(Eng)	(25)	39151
135	John BICKERTON	(Eng)	(28)	38133
# 136	Greg CHALMERS	(Aus)	(22)	37957
137	Mike MCLEAN	(Eng)	(29)	37715
138	Phil GOLDING	(Eng)	(27)	36395
139	David WILLIAMS	(Eng)	(26)	35856
# 140	Marcus WILLS	(Wal)	(26)	35150
§ 141	Anthony PAINTER	(Aus)	(5)	34854
* 142	Eric GIRAUD	(Fr)	(22)	34670
* 143	Francisco VALERA	(Sp)	(15)	34654
144	Mike HARWOOD	(Aus)	(13)	33533
145	José Maria CAÑIZARES	(Sp)	(17)	32189
146	Steen TINNING	(Den)	(29)	32095
# 147	Chris HALL	(Eng)	(22)	31424
* 148	Tim PLANCHIN	(Fr)	(29)	31367
149	Mark LITTON	(Wal)	(30)	30160
150	David J RUSSELL	(Eng)	(19)	29654
# 151	Francis HOWLEY	(Ire)	(26)	28865
152	Heinz P THÜL	(Ger)	(13)	27845
153	David LYNN	(Eng)	(5)	25759
154	Neal BRIGGS	(Eng)	(30)	25400
155	Peter TERAVAINEN	(USA)	(11)	24817
* 156	Emanuele BOLOGNESI	(It)	(15)	24518
¶ 157	Anssi KANKKONEN	(Fin)	(20)	24497
158	Paul WAY	(Eng)	(26)	24363
159	Peter FOWLER	(Aus)	(15)	23877
160	Terry PRICE	(Aus)	(17)	23655
161	Anders FORSBRAND	(Swe)	(14)	21835
162	Mike CLAYTON	(Aus)	(24)	21347
163	Michel BESANCENEY	(Fr)	(29)	20244
# 164	Richard DINSDALE	(Wal)	(22)	19996
¶ 165	John MCHENRY	(Ire)	(12)	19782
166	Gavin LEVENSON	(SA)	(10)	19733
167	Brian MARCHBANK	(Scot)	(15)	19225

185	Oyvind ROJAHN	(Nor)	(28)	10916
¶ 186	Ignacio FELIU	(Sp)	(12)	10414
187	Scott WATSON	(Eng)	(10)	10098
188	Ben CRENSHAW	(USA)	(1)	9525
189	Fredrik LARSSON	(Swe)	(5)	9043
190	Stephen DODD	(Wal)	(5)	7975
191	Thomas LEVET	(Fr)	(30)	7800
§ 192	Warren SCHUTTE	(SA)	(3)	7614
193	Juan QUIROS	(Sp)	(5)	7491
194	Alberto BINAGHI	(It)	(6)	7205
195	Nic HENNING	(SA)	(7)	7192
196	Paolo QUIRICI	(Swi)	(9)	7055
197	Gordon J BRAND	(Eng)	(15)	6893
198	Andrew BARNETT	(Wal)	(4)	6767
199	Jean Louis GUEPY	(Fr)	(11)	5857

§ Denotes Affiliate Member

* Denotes 1995 Challenge Tour Graduate

# Denotes 1995 Qualifying School Graduate

¶ Denotes Challenge Tour Member/Qualifying School Graduate

* Figures in parentheses indicate number of tournaments played

200	Michael ARCHER	(Eng)	(8)	5609
201	Raphaël JACQUELIN	(Fr)	(4)	5545
202	Brian BARNES	(Scot)	(1)	5475
203	René BUDDE	(Den)	(3)	5409
¶ 204	Christian POST	(Den)	(14)	5311
# 205	Mark PLUMMER	(Eng)	(8)	5085
206	Bob CHARLES	(NZ)	(1)	5000
207	Jeremy ROBINSON	(Eng)	(6)	4999
# 208	Ove SELLBERG	(Swe)	(14)	4610
209	David R JONES	(Eng)	(3)	4489
210	Vanslow PHILLIPS	(Eng)	(5)	4351
# 211	Jimmy HEGGARTY	(N.Ire)	(8)	3975
212	Gabriel HJERTSTEDT	(Swe)	(8)	3844
213	Christy O'CONNOR JNR	(Ire)	(11)	3800
214	Jeff HAWKES	(SA)	(4)	3543
215	Adam MEDNICK	(Swe)	(9)	3503
216	Jose ROZADILLA	(Sp)	(4)	3273
217	Timothy SPENCE	(Eng)	(6)	3249
218	Scott HENDERSON	(Scot)	(3)	3218
219	Anders SORENSEN	(Den)	(7)	2973
# 220	George RYALL	(Eng)	(10)	2905
# 221	Greg OWEN	(Eng)	(9)	2750
222	Andrew BEAL	(Eng)	(3)	2655
* 223	Simon HURLEY	(Eng)	(3)	2592
# 224	Jason WIDENER	(USA)	(14)	2387
225	Mikael PILTZ	(Fin)	(1)	2365
226	Liam WHITE	(Eng)	(4)	1925
227	Daniel SILVA	(Port)	(3)	1695
228	David RAY	(Eng)	(2)	1680
§ 229	Stephen SCAHILL	(NZ)	(3)	1451
230	Johan RYSTRÖM	(Swe)	(1)	1375
231	Paul LYONS	(Eng)	(4)	1260
232	Manuel MONTES	(Sp)	(1)	1251
233	David CURRY	(Eng)	(5)	1225
234	Paul R SIMPSON	(Eng)	(3)	1141
235	Stephen PULLAN	(Eng)	(3)	1125
236	Joost STEENKAMER	(Hol)	(1)	975
237	António SOBRINHO	(Port)	(3)	885
238	Bill LONGMUIR	(Scot)	(2)	700
239	Gary PLAYER	(SA)	(1)	650
240	Joakim GRÖNHAGEN	(Swe)	(4)	645
241	De Wet BASSON	(SA)	(3)	444
242	Philip TALBOT	(Eng)	(5)	442

The PGA European Tour

(A COMPANY LIMITED BY GUARANTEE)

BOARDS OF DIRECTORS
N C Coles MBE - Group Chairman
A Gallardo (Tour, Enterprises, Properties)
B Gallacher OBE (Tour, Enterprises,
                            Properties)
T A Horton (Properties)
D Jones (Tour)
M G King (Enterprises, Properties)
B Langer (Enterprises)
C Moody (Tour)
J E O'Leary (Tour, Enterprises, Properties)
R Rafferty (Tour)
D Talbot (Tour)
P M P Townsend (Enterprises, Properties)

EXECUTIVE DIRECTOR
K D Schofield CBE

DEPUTY EXECUTIVE DIRECTOR
G C O'Grady

ASSISTANT EXECUTIVE DIRECTOR
R G Hills

GENERAL COUNSEL
M D Friend

GROUP COMPANY SECRETARY
M Bray

**PGA EUROPEAN TOUR
TOURNAMENT COMMITTEE**
M James - Chairman
M Lanner - Vice Chairman
A Binaghi
R Chapman
I Gervas
B Langer
C Mason

C Montgomerie
R Rafferty
D J Russell
O Sellberg
J Spence
S Torrance MBE
D Williams

PGA EUROPEAN SENIORS TOUR
A Stubbs - Managing Director
K Waters - Deputy Managing Director
G Ralph - Tournament Director

**DIRECTOR OF TOUR OPERATIONS
AND CHIEF REFEREE**
J N Paramor

**SENIOR TOURNAMENT
DIRECTORS**
A N McFee (Director of Tour Qualifying
                        School Programme)
M R Stewart

TOURNAMENT DIRECTORS
D Garland
D Probyn

**PGA EUROPEAN CHALLENGE
TOUR**
A de Soultrait - Director

TOURNAMENT ADMINISTRATORS
M Eriksson
M Haarer
K Williams
G Hunt (Referee)
M Vidaor
J M Zamora

**PGA EUROPEAN TOUR
ENTERPRISES LTD**
G C O'Grady - Managing Director
S Kelly - Marketing Director
G Oosterhuis - Corporate Sponsorship
                        Director
I Barker - Account Director
A Crichton - Account Manager
J Birkmyre - General Manager European &
                        English Opens
E Kitson - Event Staging Manager and
                        Executive - Ryder Cup Ltd

RYDER CUP LTD
R G Hills - Ryder Cup Director

PGA EUROPEAN TOUR (SOUTH)
A Gallardo - President

COMMUNICATIONS DIVISION
M Platts - Director of Communications
                        and Public Relations
M Wilson - Consultant to
                        Executive Director
R Dodd - Press Officer

GROUP FINANCE CONTROLLER
C Allamand

GROUP FINANCIAL PLANNER
J Orr

**CORPORATE RELATIONS
CONSULTANT**
H Wickham

The Contributors

Mike Aitken *(The Scotsman)*
Alfred Dunhill Cup

Mike Britten
Dubai Desert Classic
Madeira Island Open
Conte of Florence Italian Open
Volvo Scandinavian Masters
Linde German Masters

Colin Callander *(Golf Monthly)*
The Scottish Open

Jeremy Chapman *(The Sporting Life)*
Portuguese Open
Toyota World Match-Play Championship

Norman Dabell
Sun Dutch Open
Oki Pro-Am

Richard Dodd *(PGA European Tour)*
Moroccan Open
Chemapol Trophy Czech Open
Canon European Masters
Smurfit European Open

Bill Elliott
Benson and Hedges International Open
Alamo English Open

Andrew Farrell *(The Independent)*
Apollo Week
Dimension Data Pro-Am
Alfred Dunhill South African PGA
Championship

Mark Garrod *(Press Association)*
Johnnie Walker Classic
Peugeot Open de France
Volvo Masters

David Hamilton
One 2 One British Masters

Alan Hedley *(The Journal)*
Slaley Hall Northumberland Challenge

John Hopkins *(The Times)*
Volvo Ranking Winner*
*(courtesy of *The Times*)

Jeff Kelly *(Andalucia Golf)*
Turespaña Masters Open Comunitat
Valencia Paradores de Turismo
Peugeot Open de España

Renton Laidlaw *(The Evening Standard)*
BMW International Open

Derek Lawrenson *(The Sunday Telegraph)*
The Major Championships

Michael McDonnell *(The Daily Mail)*
The Year in Retrospect

John Oakley
Hohe Brücke Open
Open Novotel Perrier

Mitchell Platts *(PGA European Tour)*
Heineken Classic
Trophée Lancôme
European Challenge Tour

Chris Plumridge *(The Sunday Telegraph)*
Andersen Consulting European Regional
Championship
Volvo PGA Championship
125th Open Championship

Bryan Potter
European Seniors Tour

Gordon Richardson
FNB Players Championship
Sarazen World Open Championship

Gordon Simpson *(The Daily Record)*
Loch Lomond World Invitational

Colm Smith *(Independent Newspapers)*
Murphy's Irish Open

Mel Webb *(The Times)*
Open Catalonia
Air France Cannes Open
Deutsche Bank Open – TPC of Europe
Volvo German Open

Mark Wilson *(PGA European Tour)*
The Canon Shoot-Out

The Photographers